Man and Beast

MAN &BEAST

The Natural & Unnatural History of British Mammals

RON FREETHY

BLANDFORD PRESS
POOLE · DORSET

First published in the U.K. 1983 by Blandford Press,
Link House, West Street, Poole, Dorset, BH15 1LL

Copyright © 1983 Blandford Books Ltd.

Distributed in the United States by
Sterling Publishing Co., Inc.,
2 Park Avenue, New York, N.Y. 10016

British Library Cataloguing in Publication Data

Freethy, Ron
  Man and beast: the natural and unnatural history
  of British mammals.
  1. Mammals—Great Britain
  I. Title
  599.0941   QL727

ISBN 0 7137 1323 2

Typeset by Asco Trade Typesetting Ltd., Hong Kong
Printed in Italy by New Interlitho S.p.A. - Milan

Contents

To ARTER

Author's Preface

Within this brief history of the mammals of Britain, I have tried to achieve a marriage between the folklore of the species and the recent discoveries of a more scientific nature. Readers may take some exception to the fact that I have omitted to mention both the horse, which now lives a feral existence in several parts of these islands, and the golden hamster, which has made a break for freedom in some areas. I have, however, merely followed the official list of British mammals and included only those which are at present included as wild animals of this country, or were at some time native to these shores, but are now extinct.

The production of a book such as this must rely heavily on the published works of others and readers wishing to enjoy a deeper look into the subject will find the bibliography useful. I am also grateful to Carol Pugh, who produced the artwork without complaint at my frequent changes of mind, and to several photographic friends who allowed me free access to their prints. Practical naturalists such as Trevor Smith, Linda Hudson, Kenneth Spencer, Brian and Bernard Lee all played a greater part than they know. The manuscript was typed by my wife Marlene from my notorious handwriting, and to her and to the editorial staff at Blandford Press, especially Beth Young and Maggie O'Hanlon, I extend my thanks.

Ron Freethy
Thorneyholme Hall
Roughlee
March 1983

Introduction

Animal life may be classified into those creatures which possess a backbone (the vertebrates) and those which do not (the invertebrates). The vertebrates in turn can be divided into five classes: fish, amphibians, reptiles, birds and mammals.

The mammals have so far proved the most adaptable of all these classes and their great evolutionary plasticity has enabled them to make the fullest use of the earth's resources—from pole to pole, from the depths of the sea and the earth to the summits of all but the highest mountains and, in the case of the bats, into the air. The remote ancestors of the mammals were the reptiles of the Triassic period (see Table 1) and it is probable that, as these creatures were so dominant at that time in the earth's history, the newcomers had to seek out a niche where reptiles were at something of a disadvantage. Reptiles are in the main diurnal and thus, from their earliest origins, mammals tended to be nocturnal.

Table 1 GEOLOGICAL TIME CHART

Millions of Years Ago	Era	Period	First Appearance
1	Cenozoic	Pleistocene	Man
10		Pliocene	
30		Miocene	
40		Oligocene	
60		Eocene	Horses, whales, carnivores
75		Palaeocene	Primates
135	Mesozoic	Cretaceous	Mammals, flowering plants
165		Jurassic	Birds
205		Triassic	Dinosaurs, turtles
230	Palaeozoic	Permian	Conifers
250		Carboniferous	Reptiles
325		Devonian	Amphibians, ferns, horsetails
360		Silurian	Fish, insects, early land plants
425		Ordovician	Vertebrates
500		Cambrian	All major invertebrate groups
3,000	Proterozoic	Pre-Cambrian	Worms, sponges, primitive invertebrates
10,000	Archaeozoic	—	Protozoans, algae
	Azoic	—	No life

One very special problem confronts creatures of the night—low temperature. Only birds and mammals, the so-called 'warm-blooded' animals (homeotherms), have the ability to keep their body temperature constant whatever the external conditions (with the exception of a recently discovered family of sharks). Thus the body temperature of a reptile during the daytime might well be higher than that of a mammal, allowing the creature to move quickly, but at night, when the body heat radiates into the cold starry sky, the reptile's temperature may fall so low that its essential bodily functions cease. At these times, the initially smaller and weaker mammal can emerge from its daytime retreat and forage with little or no opposition. Thus a high and regulated body temperature is a distinct evolutionary advantage. This maintenance of a regular temperature is by no means as simple as it appears and it has affected the development of all the body systems, none more than the skin where hair has evolved as an insulating layer (a function which has been taken over in some species by a thick layer of subcutaneous fat called *blubber*).

Living mammals are divisible into three *taxa* (sing. *taxon*, a taxonomic grouping): the monotremes (or Prototheria), the marsupials (or Metatheria) and the now dominant placentals (or Eutheria). It is all too easy to fall into the trap of thinking that evolution follows a linear path and that all we have to do to discover the origins of mammals is to search for the fossilised missing link separating them from their reptilian ancestors. Recent work, however, points to at least two separate mammalian ancestors, both of which were reptiles found during the Triassic period: the ictidosaurs and the cynodonts.

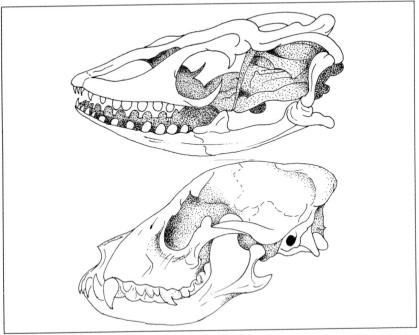

Figure 1. Skull and jawbone of a reptile (above) and a mammal (below). Note the simple teeth of the reptile and the single lower jawbone of the mammal.

Mammals are nowadays defined as warm-blooded creatures which produce milk for their young, have a diaphragm to assist in ventilating the lungs and have a four-chambered not a three-chambered heart (see Chapter 2) but none of these structures fossilise. Therefore we must look for a typically mammalian structure which does fossilise—bone! One essential difference between mammals and reptiles is that the lower jaw of mammals consists of only one bone, called the *dentary*, while that of reptiles consists of several bones (see Fig. 1). There are also significant differences in the structure of reptilian and mammalian teeth. Those of reptiles usually have only one cusp and are continually replaced throughout life, in contrast to the many-cusped teeth of mammals, which are described as *diphyodont*, meaning that only two sets of teeth—a milk dentition and a permanent dentition—are provided during the lifetime of the individual. Obviously this account is much simplified, but the fact remains that it *has* been possible to define a new species of extinct mammal on the basis of a single tooth.

The net result of much painstaking research suggests that it was during the Cretaceous period that the ancestral mammals began to diversify, giving rise to the mammals we know today. These creatures were small and nocturnal in habit, the latter feature demanding the evolution of efficient hearing. The three separate ear bones (the hammer, the anvil and the stirrup) have been discovered as fossils. It is probable that the acute sense of smell typical of many mammals also evolved at this time, but there is obviously no direct fossil evidence to back up this statement. Some workers have suggested that the evolution of flowering plants and the insects which feed on and pollinate them may have indirectly assisted the evolution of mammals. Those insects visiting flowers during the night may have provided the essential energy-rich food supply to keep the mammals active.

Creatures with a high metabolic rate are very reliant on a regular food supply and it is therefore no accident that the modern classification of the placental mammals into the various orders is based very largely upon the methods of feeding, as is the case with the insectivores, the gnawing rodents, the herbivorous beasts of the field and the often fearsome carnivores.

THE CLASSIFICATION OF MODERN MAMMALS

The Monotremes (Prototheria)

The monotremes are now reduced to six species, each obviously very primitive, and they can be considered more or less as evolutionary backwaters. They resemble reptiles in that they lay eggs, but they do have warm blood and a lower jaw made up of only one bone. They also feed their young on milk and so there is no doubt that they are mammals. They are divided into two sub-orders—the duck-billed platypuses and the spiny ant-eaters—restricted to Australia, Tasmania and New Guinea. No fossils have so far been discovered, but it is thought that the monotremes evolved in the Mesozoic era from a group of reptiles separate from that which gave rise to the other two much more closely related groups, the marsupials and the placentals. These probably had a common ancestor, but they have been on separate evolutionary paths since the early Cretaceous period; moreover, the tremendous geological changes during the Cenozoic era greatly added to their diversity.

The duck-billed platypus (*Ornithorhynchus anatinus*).

The Marsupials (Metatheria)

The marsupials derive their name from the fact that they give birth to poorly developed young which find their way into the pouch or *marsupium*. Altogether there are about 250 species naturally restricted to Australia and the Americas (mainly South America), but one species, the red-necked wallaby, is now living ferally in Britain. Most, including the best-known members—the kangaroos—are vegetarians but there are a few carnivores, including the American opossums and the Tasmanian devil.

In all marsupials, the developing embryo is never connected to its mother by means of an umbilical cord and associated placenta. The nipples, which can vary in number from two to around thirty, are enclosed within the pouch of skin. Birth occurs very early in development, the female taking up a position on her back. A female kangaroo, standing perhaps 2 m high (just over 6 ft), gives birth to a youngster only some 25 mm (1 in) in length. The mother constantly licks the area between her vagina and the pouch. The youngster follows this track of saliva, almost certainly by scent, until it is snugly in the warmth of the pouch, which is well supplied with a network of warming blood vessels. It then clings so firmly to the nipple that, should it be removed by force, the damage done to its mouth is so great that the poor creature bleeds to death.

There is no doubt that marsupials have been, and to some extent still are, a successful taxon, but the dominant form of animal life at present is, without doubt, the placental mammals, to which group we ourselves belong.

The red-necked wallaby (*Macropus rufogriseus*)—Britain's newest mammal?

The Placentals (Eutheria)

These are what we recognise as typical mammals and they each possess most of the following characteristics: giving birth to live young which have been retained within the female's body and connected to her blood stream by means of a placenta; feeding the young on milk from mammary glands; possession of hair; substantial control over body temperature; paired efficient kidneys; a four-chambered heart providing separate blood supplies for the lungs and the body. Table 2 shows that there are sixteen or perhaps seventeen living orders of placental mammals, only seven of which are represented in Britain. Altogether there are something like 3770 species (compared with about 8600 species of birds) of which we find sixty-seven (sixty-eight if we include ourselves) in Britain. Thus only about 1.9% of the world's mammals occur in these islands and some of these have been introduced whilst others are very rare vagrants.

Another important question concerns why the mammals of Britain are often slightly different from those of the same species found in other lands, even close continental neighbours. In order to understand this fully, we need to consider how the various species are named. In the eighteenth century, Linnaeus devised the Binomial System which is still the basis of modern classification. In this, he gave each species two names; the first, the generic name, has an initial capital and the second, the specific name, has no capital and is an adjective. These names are Latinised and appear in italics. No species may be given the same combination of names. Thus the red squirrel has the Latin name of *Sciurus vulgaris* and this is used by scientists all over the world when referring to this species. The binomial system is vital to the proper documentation of living organisms since common names often vary from country to country, district to district and even from one village to the next; finding up to a hundred different common names for the same species can be most confusing.

Table 2 CLASSIFICATION OF PLACENTAL MAMMALS

Order	Total Number of Species	Number of Species Occurring in Britain
1. Insectivora (hedgehogs, moles, shrews, etc)	406	7
2. Chiroptera (bats)	853	18
3. Dermoptera (flying lemurs)	2	0
4. Primates (lemurs, tree shrews, apes, monkeys, Man)	166	Man only
5. Edentata (anteaters, sloths, armadillos)	31	0
6. Pholidota (pangolins)	8	0
7. Lagomorpha (pikas, rabbits, hares)	63	3
8. Rodentia (rats, mice, voles)	1,687	15
9. Cetacea (whales, dolphins, porpoises)	84	several as vagrants
*10. Carnivora (flesh-eaters)	284	17 (including some vagrant seals)
11. Tubulidentata (aardvark)	1	0
12. Proboscidea (elephants)	2	0
13. Hyracoidea (hyraxes)	11	0
14. Sirenia (sea-cows)	5	0
15. Perissodactyla (horses, tapirs, rhinoceroses)	16	0
16. Artiodactyla (pigs, sheep, goats, antelopes, deer, camels, giraffes, hippopotami)	171	7
TOTAL	3,770	68 (including Man)

*In recent times, the seals, sea-lions and walruses have been reclassified and placed in their own order—the Pinnipedia.

Linnaeus proposed that the basic unit of life should be the species and he was of the opinion that each of these units was absolutely discrete and that it could not be altered. The combined work of Charles Darwin and Alfred Russel Wallace in the middle years of the nineteenth century changed this fundamental concept. Variations do exist and, if a species is split by an expanse of sea or the throwing up of a mountain range, then interbreeding within the separated populations may well produce a different variation (or race) in the two regions and eventually a new species may result. The work of Mendel and other later geneticists has shown that a sudden change in gene structure (*mutation*) can occasionally alter a species. Britain has been isolated by the Channel since the end of the last Ice Age some 8000 years ago and the separation has already produced isolated populations leading to a few minor variations, although not yet to a new species. These inbreedings have resulted in the formation of what have been termed *subspecies*; the British red squirrel is now called *Sciurus vulgaris leucourus* because its tail is slightly lighter than the European red squirrel, which is now given the trinomial *Sciurus vulgaris vulgaris*.

Similar species are grouped into a genus, then into a family and then into orders. The orders make up the class Mammalia. Thus the breakdown of our own red squirrel is:

Class: Mammalia (placental)
Order: Rodentia
Family: Sciuridae
Genus: *Sciurus*
Species: *Sciurus vulgaris*
Subspecies: *Sciurus vulgaris leucourus*

The red squirrel (*Sciurus vulgaris leucourus*).

It is my purpose in this book to consider in turn each of the British species, with the exception of some of the marine vagrants, such as the whales, the ringed, harp, bearded and hooded seals and the walrus. The essential features of each animal are summarised and the history and natural history are described. Also covered is the present distribution and any particular factors which may be affecting this. Finally, I have considered those mammals which were unsuccessful in competition with others and became extinct in Britain. Part of the final chapter is devoted to those animals which probably never existed but which played a very important part in European folklore and figure prominently in the Bestiaries.

As a knowledge of mammalian biology is essential to a full understanding of each species, a general account is given in the following chapter.

1 The Characteristics of Mammals

Living organisms, however simple, all have nine characteristics in common; all require *food* and must *respire*, be *irritable* to their surroundings and *excrete* waste products. Eventually they will all *die*, but many will have *grown* and been able to *reproduce* their kind, and have made some effort to *adapt* to their environment, usually by *moving* a part or the whole of their body. A good way to remember these characteristics is to use the mnemonic 'FRIED GRAM' which gives the first letter of each (feeding, respiration, irritability, excretion, death, growth, reproduction and movement.) While these functions are found in all life forms, the precise means by which they are carried out differs according to the type of organism under consideration. It is the purpose of this chapter to give a brief account of how these basic functions are carried out in placental mammals.

FEEDING

The various food items are broken down for absorption first physically (mainly by means of the teeth) and then by chemical enzymes produced in association with the digestive tract (alimentary canal or gut).

The structure of a tooth is shown in Fig. 2. This basic shape has evolved into four types, suited to different functions. The sharp *incisors* cut the food, the *canines* tear flesh and the *premolars* and *molars*, which usually have two and three roots respectively, together constitute the *cheek teeth*, which have a grinding function (Fig. 3). The number and distribution of these teeth is the most vital feature in the classification of placental mammals.

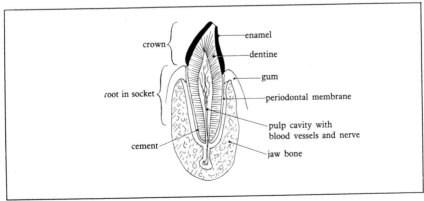

Figure 2. Cross-section of a typical mammalian tooth.

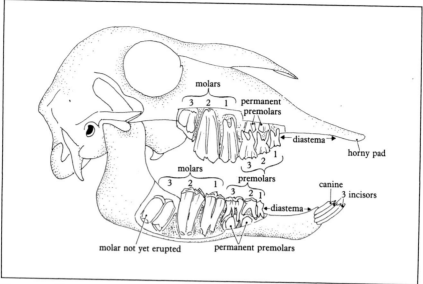

Figure 3.   Skull and jawbone of the sheep.

The insectivores and bats have a dentition ideally suited for capturing, holding and chewing invertebrates, especially worms and insects. On the upper surface of the cheek teeth, there are many small cusps which have evolved to fit this requirement. Usually the canine teeth are single-rooted with the notable exception of those of the mole, which are double-rooted.

Rodents are able to gnaw through the toughest materials, making short work of any vegetation, and can even chew into metals, including lead piping. Rats and mice destroy or damage electrical wiring, often with disastrous results to themselves and the human owners of the property. The incisors in rodents, although few in number, are large, powerful, chisel-shaped and grow continually (*open-rooted*) but are worn away at the same

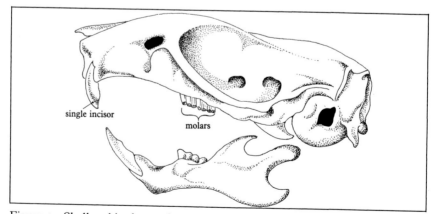

Figure 4.   Skull and jawbone of a rodent. Note the single incisor.

rate by constant use. Rodents do not have canines, but in their place is an obvious gap, called the *diastema*, between the incisors and the cheek teeth (Fig. 4). The lips can be drawn back over the cheek teeth to seal off the rest of the mouth from the incisors which can thus chip away at material which it would not be advisable for the beast to swallow.

The carnivores are characterised by their huge canines (the fangs), but even more typical are the flesh-shearing teeth called the *carnassials*. The last upper premolar and the first lower molar each have a sharp cusp which acts against the other and literally shears off lumps of flesh from the prey.

The seals are often listed in the Carnivora (see Table 2) within their own sub-order, the Pinnipedia. The fact that their cheek teeth are all similar in shape and have recurved points ideal for gripping fish, has persuaded some influential taxonomists to promote the Pinnipedia and give them their own order. A similar reclassification some years ago separated the rabbits and hares from the rodents (see Chapter 5).

Whatever the dental arrangement, the food, once it has been broken down into pieces small enough to be swallowed, enters the alimentary canal (Fig. 5). This begins at the mouth and ends at the anus and is simply a food-processing tube. The lips guard the entrace to the mouth and are sensitive in all species, especially in the young which suck milk. In herbivores, the lips are especially well developed and, in most rodents and lagomorphs, the lips are divided by a groove which allows even greater mobility—the hare-lip condition. The inside of the lower lip of ruminants is covered with rough papillae which roll the food into a ball, or *bolus*, prior to swallowing. The tongue also plays its part in this action and the food is moistened by secretions from three or four pairs of salivary glands. As a general rule, these are very important in herbivores, such as rabbits, hares, voles and ruminants, where a great deal of mastication is needed to break down tough vegetation. The carnivores, in complete contrast, tend to bolt their food and huge lumps disappear down the oesophagus at a phenomenal rate. Flesh is always easier to digest than grass.

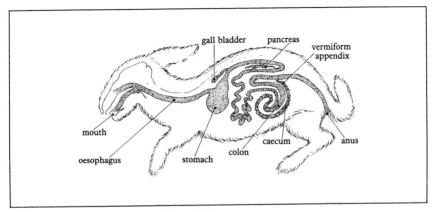

Figure 5. Alimentary canal of the rabbit.

The mammalian oesophagus is really nothing more than a simple tube connecting the mouth to the stomach and never forms a storage organ equivalent to the crop found in birds (Freethy, 1982). In the ruminants, the first part of the stomach stores vegetation and is called the paunch or *rumen* (Fig. 6) and, from this, material can be regurgitated and chewed at leisure. This is a very useful device for herbivores, which are vulnerable to predators, as it enables them to feed quickly and chew slowly in a safer spot.

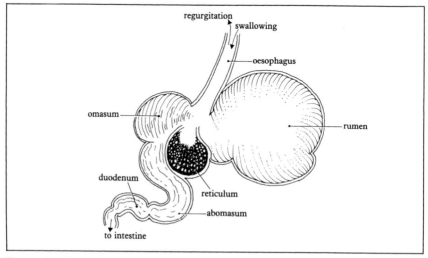

Figure 6. The stomach of a ruminant.

In carnivores, the stomach is a simple bag with openings to the oesophagus and duodenum, both possessing a circular muscle (called a *sphincter*) controlling the flow of material. Again we find a much more complex arrangement in the herbivores and the stomach reaches its peak of complexity in ruminants such as deer, which have a four-chambered stomach designed to assist the chewing of the cud. In rats and mice, the stomach is kidney-shaped and, because of their much more varied diet, more simple than that of ruminants. In other herbivores, the stomach is far simpler than you would expect for animals which eat hard-to-digest vegetation, but they have tackled the problem literally from the other end. In horses and the lagomorphs, there is a large blind-ended caecum positioned between the large and small intestines.

The impact which efficient and persistent herbivores can have on vegetation is well-documented and it is now believed that this pressure has been an important factor in the evolution of plants. The grasses (family Gramineae), consisting of some 9000 species, are thought to be the pinnacle of plant evolution and significantly their origins date back, as do those of the mammals, to the Cretaceous period. Grasses once grew from the tip of the leaf blade but they now grow from the base. This means that the non-growing portion is at the top and can be removed without stopping growth.

Most grazing animals are not able to crop close enough to the ground to remove all the succulent growing parts but the evolution of the muzzle of many species has enabled them to crop deeper and deeper. Grass evolution then responded by developing a growing area even closer to the ground and even by resorting to a subtle form of chemical warfare.

Plant cells are all protected by a rigid cell wall made of cellulose (related to the starches) and, to get at the nutrients within, the herbivores are faced with the difficult task of rupturing this case. Grasses have added to their defensive capacity by incorporating silica into the cell wall; this has been one of the driving factors in the evolution of the teeth of herbivores, which have become hard and ridged to cope with what amounts to a lifetime of grinding particles of sand!

Cellulose has so far proved resistant to mammalian chemical digestion and thus ruminants have resorted to 'symbiotic' liaisons with micro-organisms, an arrangement vital to their feeding. In exchange for an even temperature and safety from predators deep in the body of the mammal, bacteria break down the cellulose as part of their own nutritional process, but plenty is left over to supply the unknowing host. As their numbers build up, some of the bacteria are pushed out into other areas of the gut where they are digested. The most efficient arrangement is to carry out this process in the stomach (*forestomach fermentation*) from whence the material can pass into the rest of the digestive system. In some animals, the bacteria act on the food in the caecum (*caecal fermentation*) after the food has passed through the small intestine and other species, including the lagomorphs, to ensure that they get the maximum value from their food, eat some of their own faeces, which they deposit in the safety of burrow or bush (see Chapter 5).

RESPIRATION AND CIRCULATION

The basic breathing apparatus of mammals consists of a pair of lungs connected to the atmosphere by means of a windpipe (*trachea*). The lung structure varies from species to species but, as a general rule, the right lung has four lobes while the left shows considerably more variation. In the fox, for example, there are three lobes, while in the insectivores there is only one. This arrangement has evolved in conjunction with a terrestrial mode of life and both bats and seals have evolved variations to suit their life style (see Chapters 4 and 11).

In mammals, as well as in birds, the respiratory apparatus serves a secondary function—sound production—effected by driving the air out of the lungs using the muscular diaphragm (a typically mammalian feature) and passing it over the string-like structure of the larynx.

Assuming that a mammal obtains sufficient food and has access to a reliable supply of oxygen with which to 'burn' this fuel and release energy, there still remains the problem of ensuring that these raw materials reach each living cell and that any waste metabolic products, such as carbon dioxide and urea, are removed. These vital functions are carried out by the

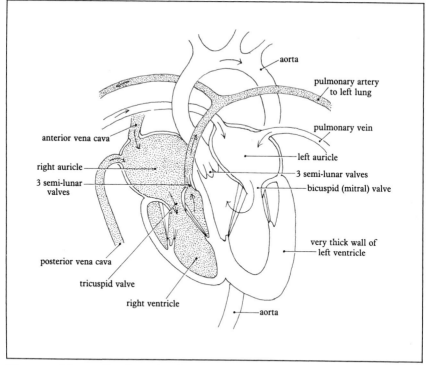

Figure 7. Mammalian four-chambered heart.

vascular (circulatory) system which consists of a four-chambered heart (Fig. 7), pumping blood into a closed system of vessels. Arteries carry blood at high pressure from the heart, veins return the blood to the heart at a much reduced pressure, and networks of capillaries connect the two (Fig. 8). The unique and invaluable feature of the mammalian heart is the separation of the two ventricles, thus producing two separate pumps and preventing the mixing of the oxygen-rich blood returning from the lungs and the blood going to the lungs to pick up oxygen. Thus all blood going to the body is rich in oxygen and allows the animal to function at a higher metabolic rate than its reptilian ancestors. The red blood cells contain the iron-rich pigment, *haemoglobin*, which is able to enter into a loose combination with oxygen to produce *oxy-haemoglobin*, which is bright red in colour. When this compound comes into contact with the carbon dioxide generated by all hard-working cells, it breaks down to release oxygen and the haemoglobin (which is dull purple) is returned via the veins to the heart and thence to the lungs, where it picks up another load of oxygen. Work done on the wood mouse, (*Apodemus sylvaticus*), by Kalabuchov in the Caucasus during the 1930s showed that the blood of individuals living above 1500 m (nearly 5000 ft) had a higher concentration of haemoglobin than those living at lower altitudes, a phenomenon also noted in our own species.

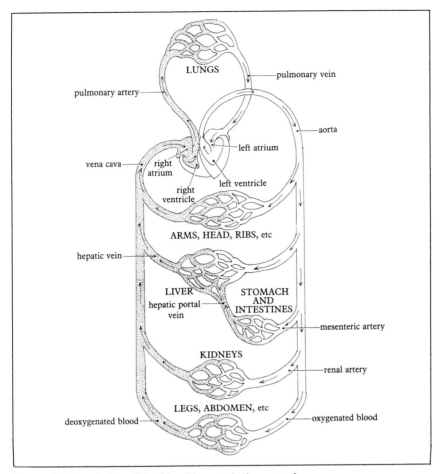

Figure 8. Circulation of the blood in a typical mammal.

IRRITABILITY: THE SENSE ORGANS

Anyone looking at a wild mammal cannot fail to notice how alert it is, how quickly it reacts to the threat of danger, and how well co-ordinated it is as it flees for cover. Obviously a complex system of co-ordination is at work here, but when we look closely we find two inter-meshing systems at work. The central nervous system functions as a series of electrical impulses co-ordinated by the brain, which acts rather in the manner of a telephone exchange. The hormone (*endocrine*) system on the other hand involves the production of chemical messengers which are carried around in the blood stream. The brain also plays its part since the pituitary gland, situated deep in the organ, acts as the master gland, triggering and controlling the activities of other glands which affect growth (the thyroid), sexual development (the gonads), the emotions (adrenalin and cortisone produced in the adrenals and kidneys respectively). The position of the main glands is shown in Fig. 9.

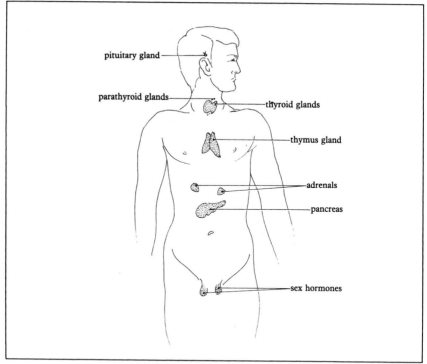

Figure 9. Positions of the main endocrine glands.

Man, a primate, is an arrogant species with binocular colour vision, a poor sense of smell and rather inefficient hearing. This arrogance leads to the assumption that all other 'lesser' beasts have a similar but much less efficient system. Nothing could be further from the truth! What about the small mammals which are so vulnerable when caught in the open in the full glare of daylight? They must live either beneath concealing vegetation, in hollow trees or walls or in underground runs. In these conditions, sophisticated eyes would be useless and, instead, they rely on efficient hearing, a refined sense of smell and a very delicate appreciation of touch, especially on the nose and via the sensitive vibrissae (all of which are lacking in Man). In many species, especially rodents and some insectivores, even the long sensitive tail can act as an early warning system.

In larger, more predatory species, eyes (Fig. 10) play a vital role but usually work in conjunction with equally efficient senses of hearing and smell. Furthermore, most wild mammals are either nocturnal or crepuscular (active at dawn and dusk) and so function best at times of low light intensity when colour vision is not important. They therefore tend to have little or no colour vision, but they do have a sort of image intensifier called the *tapetum*. One can find out if a particular species has colour vision by investigating the shape of the cells making up the sensitive retina (see Fig. 11). Some cells are rod-shaped while others are conical in section. Only cones are sensitive to

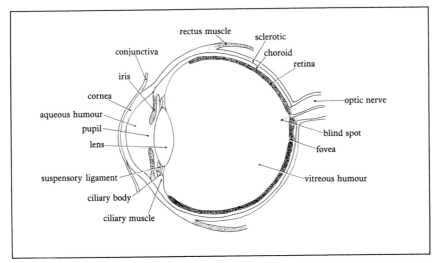

Figure 10. Cross-section of a mammalian eye.

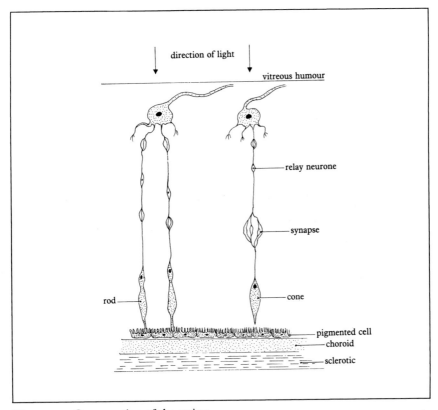

Figure 11. Cross-section of the retina.

coloured light, while the rods respond to light of low intensity. Thus, by working out the relative abundance of these cells, the degree of colour vision can be accurately calculated. The function of the tapetum as a light intensifier is seen when the headlights of a car or a naturalist's flashlight strike the eyes of a cat, which gleam shining silver, or those of a fox which smoulder red as the light is reflected. The tapetum consists of a layer of mirror-like cells which serve to reflect light within the eyeball so that it strikes the retina again and again, rather like the action of a pin-ball machine, and this makes sure that each photon of light has several chances to register on the retina.

The ears of mammals (see Fig. 12) serve the two equally important functions of balance and hearing. The ear consists of three regions—the outer, middle and inner ears. The outer ear is not important in man but in many mammals, including rabbits, foxes and deer, it functions as an ear trumpet to focus sounds into the ear drum. The two ears can be used together to ascertain the direction from which a sound is coming, which often means the difference between life and death to a hunted animal. The sound waves strike the ear drum and this in turn vibrates the three ear bones which make up the middle ear. These function in the same way as an amplifier and, eventually, the cochlea is stimulated and it passes on the message to the auditory nerve and thence to the brain.

Balance is controlled as a result of signals received from the three semi-circular canals. These are set at right angles to one another, one in each plane. They are full of a liquid (*endolymph*) in which float small particles of calcium carbonate. When the head is tilted, these particles roll about and stimulate nerve endings which enable the animal to re-orient itself.

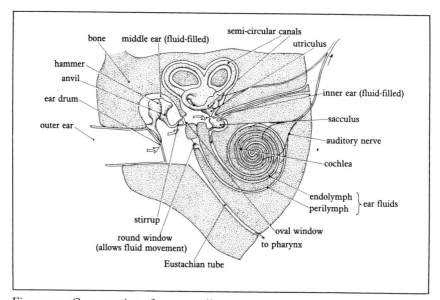

Figure 12. Cross-section of a mammalian ear.

The sense of hearing may be considered to be of a physical nature which contrasts sharply with the chemical senses of smell and taste. The mucous membranes in the area around the snout are sensitive to chemicals in solution. They arrive in the air, are breathed in and dissolve in the liquid of the mucous membrane—this is why a dog's nose is wet, a feature shared with many mammals. Thus the chemicals have to be in solution before they can be detected and the same applies to the sense of taste. The dissolved chemicals stimulate receptors which send nerve impulses to be brain. Biologically, this sense enables animals to have a preview of a potential meal before deciding whether or not to risk eating it.

No account of the nervous system of a mammal would be complete without reference to the skin and the hairy covering which is unique to this class of vertebrate. The major areas are the *epidermis* and the *dermis* (see Fig. 13), which rest on a bed of subcutaneous tissue called the *hypodermis*, which overlies the muscles and the bones. From the skin arise replaceable hairs and in it are *sebaceous glands* which produce oil and, often, chemicals called *pheromones*. The smell of these substances serves to keep herds together, warn off enemies and attract mates. The mammary glands, from which the class derives its name, are formed from the skin and its associated glands. More often than not, the number of feeding teats are constant both in number and pattern. In primates, for example, they are on the chest while in shrews, deer, sheep and cows they are in the groin. In the hedgehog, they extend like rows of buttons from neck to groin. Some workers have suggested a 'nipple formula' similar to the dental formula (see p. 38) but this does not seem sensible to me since there is just a little too much variation and such a formula could never be totally reliable.

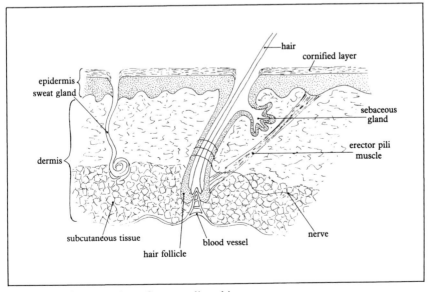

Figure 13. Cross-section of mammalian skin.

The skin is a vital organ in the control of body temperature which is such a vital feature in the success story of mammals. Nearly all mammals are fur-bearing, and the layer of air trapped in the fur acts as an insulator. Each separate hair has its own muscle, the *erector pili*, and this can alter the angle of the hair so that heat can be held in or allowed to escape, depending upon the animal's body temperature. *Homo sapiens* has lost most of his body hair but the erector pili muscles remain and, when they contract in cold weather, they 'bulge' to produce 'goose-pimples'. Many mammals, including our-selves, have sweat glands which open onto the surface and, as water evapo-rates from these, the skin is cooled. Species which lack sweat glands, such as the dog, cool themselves by losing heat from their lolling tongues. The skin also acts as a method of controlling the water and salt content of the body fluids, a function which it shares with the kidneys.

EXCRETION

In mammals, unlike other vertebrates, the only connection between the urinary and reproductive systems is the tubes which lead out from the body;

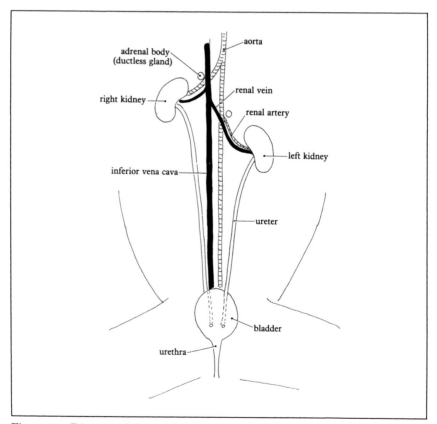

Figure 14. Diagram of the renal system of the rabbit.

these are actually united in males and very close together in females. Apart from the Cetacea, which, being fully aquatic, face special problems concerning their water balance, mammals have similar paired kidneys (see Fig. 14). These are provided with a blood supply from the renal arteries. Once inside the kidney, these divide into tiny arteries and then into capillaries, which make contact with one of a huge number of kidney tubules (*nephrons* or *uriniferous tubules*). These are the structures which filter out the urine from the blood by a complex mechanism, the net result being that the blood leaving the kidney has a regulated amount of water and salts dissolved in it. Unwanted fluid is passed from the kidneys to the bladder, which is designed to be emptied at regular intervals under the control of the animal itself rather than permitting the urine to leak out under the influence of gravity. This control over urine flow has allowed a secondary use to evolve; glands add their contents to the urine and these can serve as signals of offence and defence, both to their own species and to others. Anyone unfortunate enough to live close to a tom cat when a queen is on heat, despite the imperfection of the human sense of smell, knows what a powerful signal this is. A dog sniffing at or making his mark on a tree can learn as much about its environment as we can by purchasing a town guide. This signalling is a vital part of the breeding cycle of many mammals.

DEATH, GROWTH AND REPRODUCTION

Strange as it may seem one characteristic of life is death, since what has never been alive does not die. Following birth comes growth and maturation and reproduction, a vital requirement to replace the dead if the species is not to become extinct.

The general pattern of the male reproductive apparatus in the British placentals differs very little, but there is considerably more variation in the female system (Fig. 15). The ends of the paired oviducts are partially fused to form a vagina and, in each oviduct there is a muscular, highly vascularised area—the *uterus*. In higher primates, such as the human female, the two uteri are completely fused but, in the more primitive condition, found in rodents and carnivores, the uteri remain almost distinct as right and left halves, only partially united to form a T-shape. The Fallopian tubes leading from the ovary to the uterus are usually the site of fertilisation, as the mobile sperm travels from the terminal end of the vagina (the *cervix*) through the uterus and along the Fallopian tube. The fertilised egg is then literally pushed back into the uterus by contractions of the walls of the Fallopian tube, where it then develops a connecting link with the mother by means of the placenta. In some mammals, including the pine marten, mink, badger, fallow deer, stoat and the common and grey seals, *delayed implantation* occurs; in this, development of the fertilised egg is arrested at the *blastocyst* stage in a sort of suspended animation. This phenomenon enables an animal with a short gestation period to mate in the autumn but development of the young does not proceed until the spring, when the living is easier. In any

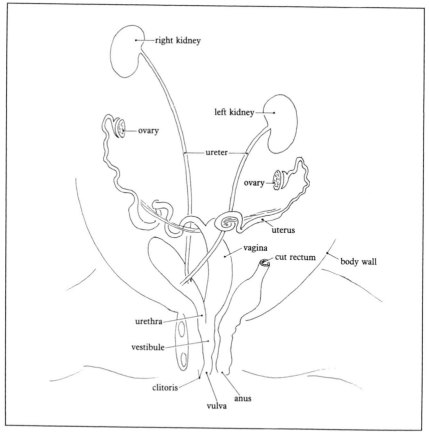

Figure 15. Urinogenital system of the female rabbit.

event, the placental development means that yolk and the protective tissues associated with eggs of birds are not needed and the mammalian egg is therefore very small.

The detailed structure of the placenta varies from species to species, but however complex, it originally developed from the amnion of the egg of the ancestral reptile. The degree of intimacy between the placenta and the uterus may be either entire (a *diffuse placenta*), as in the pig, or just a circular band of connective tissue, as in cats, an arrangement known as a *zonal placenta*. Limited intimacy may cause the occasional loss of developing young. Those species which have a really intimate placenta, such as the rabbit, have the advantage of a really efficient two-way exchange between mother and foetuses, but considerable damage is done to the uterus during birth. Placentation, controlled by complex hormonal activity, undoubtedly confers advantages on eutherian mammals. The female has no need to waste energy either in the production of eggs or in time guarding a vulnerable nest. The mother can move about at will and, in preserving her own life, she also saves the young. Following birth, the young are only helpless for a short time and the shortening of this period has been a crucial factor in the success story of placental mammals.

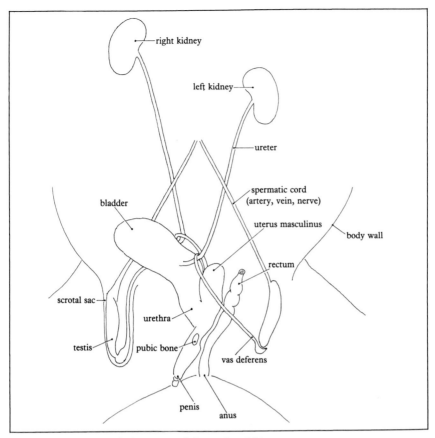

Figure 16. Urinogenital system of the male rabbit.

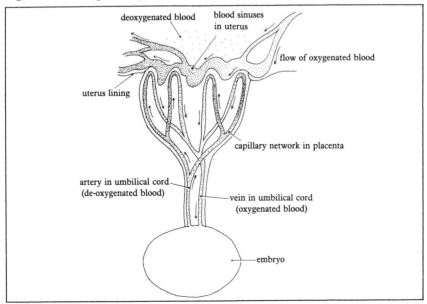

Figure 17. Mammalian placenta and associated blood vessels (simplified).

ADAPTABILITY AND MOVEMENT

Mammals are highly sensitive and therefore able to adapt very quickly to changes in environment. This is due to the highly efficient nervous system and an equally efficient locomotory system.

It is in the land mammals that the bony skeleton reaches its maximum efficiency. It has three functions: it supports the body, protects delicate organs and enables swift movement. These functions can be understood by reference to the skull, vertebral column and the limbs. The skull houses the brain, the main sense organs and the teeth and thus can be used to identify each and every species. All of these variations are based on a plan of thirty-nine bones. Shrews, for example, lack zygomatic arches and carnivores have huge temporal muscles connected to a saggittal crest on the top of the skull. The teeth, as we have seen, are particularly diagnostic, as are the vertebrae.

Each vertebra (see Fig. 18) has a central hole through which the nerve cord passes and between each is an *intervertebral disc* of cartilage which functions as a shock absorber. There are five groups of vertebrae. All mammals have seven neck (*cervical*) vertebrae and the top one, the *atlas*, is shaped to articulate with the skull. Below these come the *thoracic* vertebrae, which vary in number from eleven to twenty-one, depending on the number of ribs (there are twelve in man). The two to eight *lumbar* vertebrae (five in man) have the huge back muscles attached to them and then come the *sacral* vertebrae (varying in number from two to six, but often interlocked, or even rigidly fused, to form the *sacrum*). Finally come the *caudal* or tail vertebrae, of which Man has only one; in long-tailed species, especially rodents, these can often be quite numerous. In some cases, the number of caudal vertebrae can be important to the taxonomist and a subspecies of field vole (*Microtus*

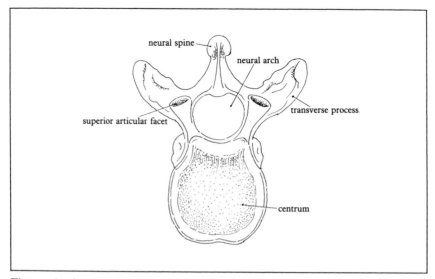

Figure 18. A generalised mammalian vertebra.

agrestis) has been recognised from the Isle of Muck in the Inner Hebrides on the basis of having one fewer vertebrae than the mainland type.

All mammals have two pairs of limbs (even in Cetaceans there are vestigial

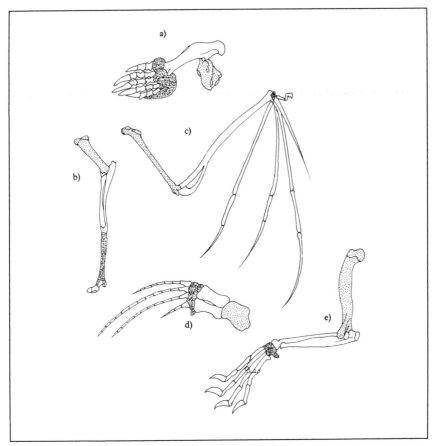

Figure 19. Variations on the pentadactyl limb in mammals: a) mole, b) deer, c) bat, d) whale, e) squirrel.

limbs present beneath the skin). All limbs have the same basic pattern (see Fig. 19): the upper part consists of only one bone, which articulates with the pelvic or shoulder girdle at one end and, at the other end, with the elbow or knee joint. The lower limb consists of two bones, but in many mammals one of these is much less substantial than the other and may even be reduced to a mere sliver attached to the larger bone. The lower end of these bones articulates with a mass of smaller bones which constitute the wrist or ankle and, at the extremity, there are the finger-bones or toe-bones. There is a considerable variation in the number and arrangement of these digits; the primitive number is five but in the horse, which has evolved for speed, only one is functional and even the 'toe nail' has developed substantially to form the hoof. Short-legged animals, whatever their body size, tend to walk flat-footed, placing all five digits on the ground, a method of locomotion termed *plantigrade*. Although we are bi-pedal, we also follow this pattern. Shrews are also plantigrade and, at the other end of the size scale, so is the massive bear. Plantigrade animals normally lack hair on the soles of their feet and, except for bears and primates, there are pads of hard skin which give the footprints a characteristic pattern. Those animals with longer limbs, such as the dog family, find it easier to walk on their toes and are known as *digitigrades*. Pads also occur in this group and produce characteristic prints which enable the field naturalist operating by day to discover which animals have moved over soft ground during the hours of darkness. The extreme case in the reduction of digits in found in the *ugiligrades* which run on their toe-nails; the deer, in addition to the horse already mentioned, are good examples of this.

Having given a brief account of mammalian biology we can now focus a more understanding eye on the individual species which make up the British list.

2 Marsupials: the Red-necked Wallaby

It might seem strange to begin a history of British mammals with a description of a marsupial, a group which is naturally restricted to Australasia and the Americas (mainly South America). Nevertheless, the species described below has successfully established itself in the wild in Britain and Europe.

The Red-necked Wallaby *Macropus rufogriseus*

This animal is also known as Bennett's Wallaby and is indigenous only to Tasmania and an area from central Queensland to South Australia. The male, on average, is larger than the female, the length varying from 600–660 mm (24–27 in), to which must be added a tail of approximately the same length. Males weigh from 7–23 kg (15.5–50 lb) with females considerably lighter and often only half the size of the males. The skull is very diagnostic (see Fig. 20). On the upper jaw there are three pairs of incisor teeth arranged in a definite V-shape. On the lower jaw, there is only one pair of incisors which point directly forwards and, between the incisors and the cheek teeth, there is a wide gap—the diastema.

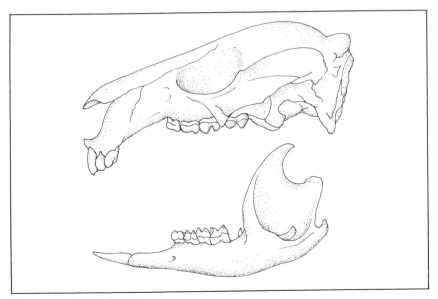

Figure 20. Skull of the kangaroo.

The introduction of the species into Europe, including Britain, follows a pattern which will become quite familiar as this book progresses. In the late nineteenth and early twentieth centuries, various landowners and zoological gardens began to introduce exotic species either for pleasure, profit or a combination of the two. Baron von Böselarger introduced two male and three female red-necked wallabies into an area of some 100 hectares (250 acres) of his estate near Helmerzheim in what is now within West Germany. Within 6 years, two lessons had been learned. Firstly, such introductions were quite likely to be successful since the population rose sharply to some forty animals. Secondly, it was discovered that wallaby meat is very palatable and the population was totally wiped out by poachers.

This was also the fate of the wallabies released by Prince Gerhard Blücher von Wahlstatt on Herm in the Channel Islands. This herd was thriving until British troops occupied the island and improved both their marksmanship and their rations by consuming every single beast. In Britain itself, two feral populations have established themselves, one in the Sussex Weald and the other in the Peak District of Derbyshire. The Derbyshire population originated from a private herd bred from Whipsnade Zoo stock, which was turned loose to fend for itself in 1940 because war rationing did not provide for their upkeep. They were not expected to survive for long but, despite some losses during bad winters, and frequent road accidents, the population has held its own at something like fifty animals. Deaths are balanced by successful single births, peaking during the months of April and May, but there are records of young born in every month of the year. The young have a 'pouch-life' of about 280 days.

A study of the animal's habitat requirements in Australia gives some clue as to how it has managed to support itself in Britain. The red-necked wallaby is a scrub-dwelling animal, emerging into grasslands to feed. In Derbyshire, it finds the birch woods which abut onto heather moors very much to its liking. Studies, particularly those by Yalden and Hosey (1971) have revealed heather as the staple diet of the animal. This constitutes some 50% of the food in summer, rising to 90% in winter, and is supplemented by grass, bilberry, pine and bracken.

OPPOSITE: The red-necked wallaby (*Macropus rufogriseus*).

3 Insectivores: the Hedgehog, Mole and Shrews

The insectivore family is the most primitive of all the placental mammals and, in Britain, is represented by the hedgehog, the mole and the shrews. Typically, they have five toes arranged in the plantigrade manner, i.e. they are flat-footed. In the case of the mole, there has been considerable adaptation of the fore-feet to provide the digging tools essential for an animal which burrows into the earth.

A look at the teeth reveals a resemblance to those of a carnivore: they are sharp and angular, an ideal shape for grappling with reluctant and slimy prey such as earthworms and slugs. The diet is almost entirely meat, but some vegetable material is taken attached to the food and possibly just a little is selected, no doubt to provide certain essential minerals and vitamins.

A few insectivores hibernate, the hedgehog being a prime example, but the majority are active throughout the year, as are the shrews and the mole. They occur in most regions of the world but are not found in South America or Australia, although the hedgehog has been successfully introduced into New Zealand.

The Hedgehog *Erinaceus europaeus*

Known also as the hedgepig, hotchiwichi, urchin and fuzzy pig, the hedgehog varies in weight from just over 100 g ($3\frac{1}{2}$ oz) when weaned to a maximum of 1100 g ($38\frac{3}{4}$ oz). It suffers a weight loss of up to 30% during hibernation. It ranges from 160–260 mm ($6\frac{1}{4}$–$10\frac{1}{4}$ in) in length and the males are larger than the females. There are two peaks to the breeding season: in May and September. The average litter size is five and the gestation period is about 33 days. The spines on the upper surface are a creamy brown colour. There is no regular seasonal moult but the spines are replaced at intervals of about 18 months. The normal hair on the ventral surface is a uniform brown.

The hedgehog is one of our most ancient indigenous mammals. Fossil remains found throughout Europe have been dated back to the Miocene period some 25 to 30 million years ago, but it is quite probable that the hedgehog is of even greater antiquity than this and the spiny beast was probably roaming about some 40 million years ago. So far as Britain is concerned bones dating back to Mesolithic times (some 12 000 years ago) have been found at Star Carr in Yorkshire and were described by Fraser and King in 1954.

The earliest evidence of folk recognising the hedgehog and its habits comes from ancient Athens about the middle of AD 400. In the region called

Agora, a figurine was discovered which quite clearly showed a hedgehog. Pliny was the naturalist of the period around AD 100 and from him, and also from contemporary writers, we find that pelts with their prickles directed outwards were used for combing out hemp before it was converted into cloth.

To the Anglo-Saxons, the hedgehog was known as *il*, which is a diminutive of the word *Igel*, its present-day name in German. In Norman French, it was *herichun*, which easily converted into 'urchin'—a name that it still retains in parts of Britain, especially in northern England and Scotland. The name 'hedgehog', originally spelt 'hyeghoge', does not appear until the beginning of the fifteenth century and the reason for this, I think, is very simple. The original home of the urchin was among the leaf litter of our originally vast indigenous forests. When these were gradually felled and the resulting fields ploughed and enclosed by hedges, the hedgehog, with its pig-like snout and accompanying grunts, found developments much to its liking and became a fixture in almost every British hedge, despite frequent attempts to eradicate it or even make use of parts of its body. (At one time it was thought that, if the right eye of a hedgehog was boiled in oil and kept in a brass vessel, it could be used as an ointment to enable people to see better at night.) It was only when hedges became an important part of our landscape, from the beginning of the seventeenth century, that the word 'hedgehog' appeared regularly in our language.

The distribution of the hedgehog has been well documented in recent years. Lydekker, in 1896, notes its presence over the greater part of Europe and parts of Asia. Since 1896, the range has widened to another continent, thanks to a successful introduction into New Zealand. Lydekker goes on to say:

In England it is generally distributed, although in many parts the fashion so prevalent of grubbing up hedgerows to make large fields [even in 1896!] *has resulted in a considerable diminution in its numbers. Abundant in the Lake District, it crosses the border into Scotland, where it is mainly characteristic of the southern and central counties, and some years ago it seemed to be chiefly confined to Clackmannan, Stirling, Dumbarton, and Perth, in the counties north of the Firths of Forth and Clyde. Now, however, according to Messrs. Harvie-Brown and Buckley, its range seems to be extending somewhat, probably owing to artificial introduction; but it is quite unknown in the Isles—that is to say, at least, as an indigenous animal.*

About 80 years later, this seems still to be the position, the natural distribution seemingly determined by the tree line, and introductions onto the outlying islands appear to have continued. Lydekker makes no mention of the distribution in Wales but it is well distributed there, again as determined by the tree line.

The hedgehog seems always to have been surrounded by superstition. An Anglo-Saxon bestiary, written in 1120, records that:

In the time of the wine harvest it mounts a tree where there is a cluster of grapes, knocks them down and sticks its prickles into them. When it is charged it carries its food to its children.

Its offensive nature is noted in a later bestiary, published in 1607 by the Reverend Edward Topsell and called *The Historie of the Foure-footed Beastes*. In it is written:

The hedgehog rowleth upon the serpent piercing his skin and flesh (yea, many times tearing the flesh from the bones) thereby he scapeth alive and killeth his adversary, carrying his flesh upon his spears like an honourable banner won in the field.

Thus we have two interesting suggestions concerning the feeding habits of the hedgehog. Miss Frances Pitt (1939) makes direct reference to the habit of impaling fruit on the spines pointing out that 'it is perhaps a pity to spoil a good yarn by mentioning that the hedgehog is not a vegetarian and seldom looks at fruit'. This is not true for the hedgehog is an opportunist feeder. I have seen a hedgehog eat apple and carrot and, on one occasion, in the Lythe Valley in the English Lake District, I saw a hedgehog with over-ripe damsons impaled upon its spikes, although I do not think that the animal had done this deliberately.

The skull and jaws of a hedgehog are very powerful, thus enabling it to cope with a variety of food, alive or dead. A convenient way of describing a mammal's teeth is in the form of a dental formula, which, for the hedgehog, is written:

$$2 \times \left\{ I\,\frac{3}{2} \quad C\,\frac{1}{1} \quad PM\,\frac{3}{2} \quad M\,\frac{3}{3} \right\} = 36.$$

The formula is multiplied by two since only half the jaw needs to be represented because the arrangement is symmetrical on each side of the mouth. Thus the hedgehog has, on each half of its upper jaw, three incisors, one canine, three premolars and three molar teeth. On each of the lower jaws

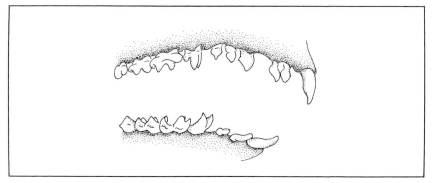

Figure 21. Teeth of the hedgehog.

The hedgehog (*Erinaceus europaeus*).

(the dentary bone), it has two incisors, one canine, two premolars and three molars, giving thirty-six teeth in the permanent dentition. A knowledge of dental formulae makes the identification of fossil remains very much easier. The premolars and molars together are often described as the cheek teeth. The actual arrangement of the hedgehog's teeth is unique amongst mammals (see Fig. 21) and makes the jaw easily recognised. They are 'snagged' and twisted in all directions, an arrangement which must make it easier to hang onto wriggling, twisting prey; this explains part of Topsell's description of the hedgehog and the serpent. Either Topsell himself, or his informant, must have been a competent naturalist since the hedgehog's method of dealing with an adder is just as he described it. Observing such a confrontation is somewhat similar to watching a contest between two skilled fencing masters. The hedgehog first erects its spines and charges; the adder strikes and damages its head on the sharp prickles. The hedgehog then backs off and the process is repeated many times until the snake becomes weakened by its exertions and loss of blood. Finally, the victorious hedgehog eats the writhing reptile alive, beginning at the tail. Just occasionally, the adder's fangs penetrate a vulnerable spot and the effect of the venom causes the hedgehog to break off the battle; such is the resistance of the tough little beast, however, that it may well recover. The quite fantastic resistance of hedgehogs, not only to poisons, but also to corrosive chemicals is well documented. Weight for weight, for example, it takes forty times the volume of snake venom to kill a hedgehog than it does to kill other mammals. They are said to be 7000 times more resistant to tetanus infection than are we humans. Blister beetles (*Lytta vesicatoria*) feature in the diet of the hedgehog. The beetles produce a poison called cantharidin which has been found to be 3000 times more dangerous to man than it is to master hedgepig.

So much then for the prey of the hedgehog, but in nature's scheme of things, the hedgehog has itself to withstand the attentions of predators.

Hedgehog attacking an adder and biting its tail.

PREDATORS OF THE HEDGEHOG

The spiky array of prickles, so formidable to the adder, is likewise a problem to potential enemies. Badgers and foxes are said to be able to unroll a hedgehog but this can never be an easy thing to do because the abdominal muscles are very powerful indeed. Some writers of the past have suggested that the crafty fox rolls the hedgehog towards the nearest water and, as Mr Prickles unrolls himself to swim, the fox sinks his teeth into the exposed and unspined belly. Like many stories about the fox, as we shall see later, we must allow for a considerable degree of exaggeration. Without doubt, the main enemy of the hedgehog has been *Homo sapiens* and our effect upon this humble insectivore can be considered under three headings: hunting it for food, killing it because it is regarded as vermin and, the latest and perhaps greatest threat, motor traffic.

THE HEDGEHOG AS FOOD

Still eaten and enjoyed by the Romany people, the hedgehog was, until well on into the nineteenth century, a favoured food of the agricultural worker. It can be prepared for the table in two ways: the spines may be burned off and the flesh basted on a spit or the carcase may be embedded in a ball of clay and roasted. When the clay is removed the spines come away with it. The taste is said to resemble chicken, while some people compare it favourably with veal. It is also believed that some gypsies preferred to find a dead hedgehog rather than to kill one since 'that which is killed by God is better than that which is killed by man'. The true gypsy, however, like the sensible chap he is, guards his secrets well and in his book *The Gypsies*, Dennis Harvey says:

> *The hotchiwichis are not baked in clay as the gaujas will have it. The spines are sheared off, the remaining hair singed, they are then opened out, cleaned out, and then soaked in salt water, later to be roasted on a spit or stewed.*

With the gypsies, it was a case of 'waste not want not' and the spiny skin was fastened to the shafts of a cart in such a position as to keep a restless horse looking forwards.

THE HEDGEHOG AS VERMIN

Hedgehogs have long been labelled as egg-stealers and secret suckers of milk from the udders of cows. Like the stories of the impaled fruit, which has doubtless been observed in a few cases, the tales of stealing eggs and sucking milk are probably true, but of very rare occurrence. It is probably significant that the hedgehog alone amongst our mammals has retained its juvenile sucking reflex into adulthood and teeth marks resembling the 'snagged' pattern found only in the hedgehog have been identified on cow's udders by veterinary surgeons.

Whatever the rights and wrongs of such a blanket condemnation of the hedgehog, a law was passed as early as 1564 labelling the species as vermin. A price was placed upon its head and the bounties paid can be seen by reference to the churchwardens' accounts from this date until well on into the nineteenth century.

HEDGEHOGS ON OUR ROADS

There is no doubt that the technique of rolling into a tight thorny ball, which has stood the hedgehog in such good stead for upwards of 30 million years, has, in the last half century, come unstuck. Fast-moving traffic simply squashes the beast flat, as the bloody blotches on our roads bear ample witness. There have been recent suggestions that the hedgehog is beginning to evolve a couple of strategies to ensure its survival. Firstly, it seems to be learning to use the verges of roads and to avoid crossing tarmac surfaces which are vibrating (there are even hedgehogs thriving in the central reservations of our trunk roads and motorways). Secondly, there is just a possibility of an advantageous genetic change having already occurred. In a letter to *The Field*, Conrad Wynstrom puts forward what may be a very significant observation:

So many hedgehogs have been killed on the road because at the approach of danger they roll into the mandatory defensive ball. A few, of course, run and these few live to face future dangers. Apparently now, the runners are becoming more than just a few because as the gene that says 'run don't roll' becomes more dominant then it is the rollers that will be the few.

The 'roller' hedgehog. Is this type on the way to extinction?

Perhaps it is rather too fanciful to suggest that evolution will work quickly enough to eliminate the rolling hedgehog before our road systems go the way of the canals and rural railways and give rise to a new form of transport less lethal to the hedgehog. Before leaving the history of the urchin, I must briefly mention recent discoveries with regard to its hibernation and to a unique piece of behaviour which has become known as 'self-anointing'.

HIBERNATION

It was thought at one time that a hibernating animal suddenly decided that it was time to go to sleep and found a suitable spot before dropping into a death-like slumber, only to wake up just as quickly when a shaft of warm spring sunlight penetrated its hibernaculum. It then trotted off as if nothing unusual had happened. Research over the last 30 years or so has shown that the hibernation period is nowhere nearly as continuous as previously thought, and the mechanisms involved are decidedly more complex than early workers imagined.

The onset is triggered neither by food shortage nor by falling temperatures, but by a gradual decrease in day length as autumn gives way to the long, chilly nights of winter. During late summer, fat begins to accumulate beneath the skin and around the body organs, and these fat deposits are of two distinct colours—brown and white. *Brown fat* is laid down mainly in the region of the neck, shoulders and chest, but its function remained obscure for some time, despite a clue provided in 1551 by the Swiss naturalist Konrad von Gesner. Working on the marmot (*Marmota marmota*), Gesner discovered a mass of brown fat just above the shoulder blades and this became known as the *hibernating gland*, a term which is frowned upon these days. The brown fat, however, does bestow two great advantages on the over-wintering hedgehog. Even during hibernation, extremely low temperatures would cause the animal's blood to freeze and its metabolism to be damaged beyond repair. In very cold weather, the hedgehog must therefore wake up and the brown fat, which has a high calorific value, provides the much needed heat very quickly and thus food can be looked for and a warmer hibernaculum discovered. Normally, the brown fat is only drawn upon gradually during the period of sleep and it is the depletion of the last reserves of this which acts as a trigger, awakening the hedgehog in spring.

White fat is also accumulated prior to hibernation and this is found under the skin and around most of the body organs. It does not provide as much energy per gram as does the rich brown fat and it is drawn upon in the early stages of hibernation while the latter is held in reserve.

In times gone by, country folk thought that there were two types of hedgehog, which they called *mutton* and the *beef*. A possible explanation is that the beef hedgehogs contained a lot of brown fat while mutton hedgehogs had a predominance of white fat, the former obviously being more common in the autumn.

It is absolutely vital that any hibernating animal conserves as much energy as possible and therefore its metabolic rate must be considerably slowed. A hedgehog's normal body temperature is something like our own (37°C = 98.6°F), but during hibernation this can fall as low as 4°C (39°F) without causing death. There is an equivalent reduction in pulse rate, blood pressure, kidney and other bodily functions. The hedgehog has provided the answer to another pertinent question, namely what happens to any food which may be present in the gut at the onset of hibernation? There is a movement of white blood cells which gather in the walls of the stomach and intestines and so act as a protection against a build-up of pathogenic bacteria. A lot of work has been carried out on the hibernating mechanisms of the hedgehog and also on comparable strategies evolved by bats, which will be discussed in Chapter 4. Whilst the minor details will vary in different species, the basic mechanisms involved appear to be similar.

SELF-ANOINTING

This term derives from the German *Selbstbespuchen* which translates literally as 'self-spitting'. The first mention I can find of this behaviour in the English language dates only from 1912 and, although frequent references to it have been made by continental workers, it was not until 1955 that Burton described the phenomenon fully. It seems that a hedgehog, on approaching a strong-smelling object, will produce copious amounts of saliva with which it coats the object; it then transfers the saliva onto its spines until it begins to look like a soapy scrubbing brush. The phenomenon occurs frequently enough and follows such a familiar pattern that it must have a function and many suggestions have been made as to what this may be, e.g. it keeps the spines supple, removes parasites from the body surface, or is even a part of the reproductive cycle.

In 1978, Dr Edmund D. Brodie Jr of Adelphi University, New York, carried out some very enlightening research. He presented a hedgehog with the skin of a poisonous toad and was rewarded with an exhibition of self-anointing, although the skin itself was not actually eaten. He next fed his captive on a toad after having removed the offensive skin and this was eagerly eaten, but there was no sign of self-anointing. Finally, Brodie gave his hedgehog a complete toad and it self-anointed, using the skin which it then removed before eating the food. This work has led to the suggestion that, during self-anointing, the spines are coated with poison from the toad's skin, thus adding to the hedgehog's own defensive mechanisms. This was underlined by a rather bizarre extension of this work. Student volunteers, and also the brave doctor himself, were pricked with normal hedgehog spines which resulted in little more than the initial pain of breaking the skin whilst the 'toady' spines caused great irritation. Thus it seems that self-anointing adds to the hedgehog's ability to protect itself and helps to ensure its survival.

The Mole *Talpa europaea*

Among the fascinating common names for the mole are mouldiwarp—from the Saxon *molde* meaning 'earth' and *werpen* 'to throw'—hence 'earth-thrower'; *maulewerf* (German); *muldvarp* (Danish); *mulle*, from which we get 'mole'; umpty-tumpt, doubtless from the mole hills; and *want*. The mole weighs between 70 and 130 g (2½ and 4¼ oz) and is 100 to 160 mm (4 to 6¼ in) long with a tail of 30 to 40 mm (1 to 1½ in). The male is larger than the female. There is a short breeding season, peaking during late May. The gestation period is 25 to 30 days and the litters average about four. Each baby weighs about 4 g (⅙ oz). They are looked after by the female but are self-sufficient at 5 weeks of age. The mole has dark velvety fur and moults three times a year—in April, July and November. This is useful for a burrowing animal. It has no pinnae to its ears.

Geologically, the mole is a relatively ancient species and fossils have been found in Norfolk which have been dated back to the Pliocene period. It belongs to the family Talpidae, which has representatives throughout North America and Eurasia. Altogether there seem to be about eleven species, the precise count depending on the authority consulted. In Britain, however, we have only one species and, like most other moles, it retains the dental formula typical of a primitive mammal namely:

$$2 \times \left\{ I\frac{3}{3} \quad C\frac{1}{1} \quad PM\frac{4}{4} \quad M\frac{3}{3} \right\} = 44.$$

In rare cases, the premolar teeth show a variation and can either be doubled or absent altogether.

A newborn mole. This baby will weigh only about 4 gm (1/6 oz).

The mole (*Talpa europaea*)—also known as the 'umpty tumpt'.

Throughout its range, the mole shows great variation in colour and albinism is common. Its distribution in the British Isles is interesting. It is unknown in Ireland, the Isle of Man and many of the Scottish isles, although accidental introductions were reported in 1896 by Lydekker in his account of its distribution:

Always more or less abundant in the Scottish lowlands, the Mole appears to have been formerly very rare or unknown in the more northern districts, but during the latter decades of the present century has been gradually extending its north-ward range. In Sutherlandshire, according to Messrs. Harvie-Brown and Buckley, it is still steadily on the increase, having been very rare about 1840 in Durness, where it is now common, as it is, in suitable localities, throughout Caithness. Although unknown in 1791 in the Lismore district, it subsequently made its way into the Kintyre isthmus of Argyllshire, and is now found in many parts of that county. The writer last mentioned further states that 'the Mole is said to have been accidentally introduced into Mull—where it is now quite common—about eighty years ago—say about 1808—in a boat-load of earth brought from Morven. The earth was a peculiarly fine loam, intended for making the floor of a cottage when mixed with clay and smithy ashes.' Quite

Trapped moles hanging on a wire fence.

recently it has made its appearance in the adjacent island of Ulva. It appears, however, still to be absent from the other islands. Similar testimony might be adduced as to the gradual spread of this animal in other northern counties of Scotland, but the foregoing is sufficient to show that ere long it will probably be found everywhere on the mainland, where suitable conditions for its peculiar mode of life exist. The increase of cultivation and of communication between remote districts will probably account for this widening distribution of the Mole; for it is almost impossible to believe that its introduction into certain districts can be due, as in the case of Mull, to accidental importation by human agency.

The present distribution bears out Lydekker's prediction and the mole is found throughout the mainland of England, Wales and Scotland, as well as on the offshore islands of Alderney, Jersey, Wight, Anglesey, Skye and, of course, Mull. It is still unlikely that deliberate introductions of moles would be made since, rightly or wrongly, it has long been considered a pest, and the mole-catcher has always been in great demand. The whole essence of the mole-catching profession is captured in John Clare's evocative poem, 'The Mole-catcher'.

When melted snow leaves bare the black-green rings,
And grass begins in freshening hues to shoot,
When thawing dirt to shoes of ploughmen clings,
And silk-haired moles get liberty to root,
An ancient man goes plodding round the fields
Which solitude seems claiming as her own,
Wrapt in greatcoat that from a tempest shields,
Patched thick with every colour but its own.

With spuds and traps and horsehair string supplied,
He potters out to seek each fresh-made hill;
Pricking the greensward where they love to hide,
He sets his treacherous snares, resolved to kill;
And on the will sticks bent to the grass,
That such as touched jerk up in bouncing springs,
Soon as the little hermit tries to pass,
His little carcass on the gibbet hangs.

And as a triumph to his matchless skill,
On some grey willow where a road runs by,
On the bough's twigs he'll many a felon tie;
On every common dozens may be met,
Dangling on bent twigs bleaching to the sun,
Whose melancholy fates meet no regret,
Though dreamless of the snare they could not shun.

On moors and commons and the pasture green,
He leaves them undisturbed to root and run,
Enlarging hills that have for ages been
Basking in mossy swellings to the sun;
The pismires too their tip-tops yearly climb
To lay their eggs and hunt the shepherd's crumbs,
Never disturbed save when for summer thyme
The trampling sheep upon their dwelling comes.

At one time, the pelts of moles had a ready sale to hatters and clothiers, who appreciated one unique feature of the fur—whichever way you stroke a mole the fur lies flat—an ideal adaptation for an animal which travels both backwards and forwards along a system of narrow tunnels. In order to cure the skins, they were impregnated with the salts of heavy metals, particularly those of lead and mercury. Modern research has proved that the compounds of both these elements can be absorbed into the human bloodstream through the skin and can therefore reach and cause permanent damage to the brain cells and so the term 'mad as a hatter' may well have been an accurate, if rather insulting remark.

The method of killing moles these days is often by poisoning with strychnine or gassing, but the two main types of trap used have not changed very much in recent times; these are the scissor trap and the duffus trap. The scissor trap has a pair of strong jaws, held apart by a metal plate; these are triggered by the passage of the mole which is quickly dispatched with little, if any, pain. The duffus trap is used mainly in Scotland and operates rather in the manner of a conventional mouse trap. I am surprised that the Scots want to kill the mole at all since, in the year 1702, King William III, whom they believed had usurped the Stuart throne, was thrown and killed when his horse stumbled over a mole hill. This led to the famous Jacobite toast which drank the health of 'the little gentleman in velvet'.

A somewhat ambivalent attitude towards the mole has been apparent for many years, as a search of contemporary literature clearly shows, and this is likely to continue for as long as we exist to argue about it. Two of the most debatable points concern the effects, beneficial or otherwise, of its diet and its burrows on agriculture, both amateur and professional.

Moles seem to take no vegetable food deliberately, although, in their eagerness to catch sufficient nourishment to maintain their high metabolic rate, they may take in the odd leaf or piece of root, along with the prey, which consists mainly of earthworms. This must make the mole an enemy of both farmer and gardener since worms are so beneficial to soil fertility by dragging leaves into the soil to plug their burrows and by improving drainage and aeration by their movement through the soil. The population of earthworms is, however, vast and the mole can hardly do more than dent the population. In any case, it also consumes huge numbers of the very destructive wireworm which can decimate a crop if not held in check. On this

Mole eating a worm. Recent evidence suggests that *Lumbricus terrestris* is a favourite species.

point, therefore, the mole may well be considered as neutral and the money spent on its destruction may well be money wasted.

There is quite a lot of evidence suggesting that moles collect surplus worms and bite them in such a way as to damage their primitive brain and cause immobility without actually killing them. Nineteenth-century naturalists were very much divided on this issue, but the majority opinion was expressed by Edward Jesse in 1853, who described the mole as hollowing out a sort of basin which 'will sometimes contain almost a peck [a dry measure of 2 gallons] of worms, bitten near the head but not killed'. This may be a way of obtaining a constant supply of worms. A.C. Evans, reporting the results of his work at Rothampstead in the 1940s, commented that the stores consisted almost entirely of one species of worm, *Lumbricus terrestris*, even when the mole had some half dozen species available; it must therefore be able consciously to select as well as to immobilise its prey.

There are records of moles being prepared to chase worms up to the surface and this is no doubt the reason for the appearance of mole remains in the pellets of birds of prey, such as the short-eared owl (*Asio flammeus*) and the buzzard (*Buteo buteo*). The buzzard is thought to be an expert mole-catcher and its *modus operandi* was described by Harting (1880), yet another competent nineteenth-century naturalist, who noted that a bird standing:

. . . in the vicinity of a mole-hill will take up a position on some tree, and watch until it sees a mole working near the surface, when it will instantly drop down and sieze it. In this way [i.e. by watching and jumping down] *buzzards destroy numbers of rats and other vermin, for which good service they deserve to be protected instead of being shot and trapped at every opportunity.*

Harting's spirited defence of the buzzard underlines the fact that all wildlife should be given a fair hearing before being declared 'vermin' and subjected to an extermination campaign.

This brings us to the second debatable point concerning the mole— namely its burrows and the damage they do, if any. Moles began life as woodland dwellers and they still live, apart from during the period of mating, a more or less solitary life, often in semi-natural burrows under the roots of trees. In this situation, very few mole hills are produced and all of our present-day deciduous woods have a healthy mole population. Once man became pastoral, he felled the forests, his cultivated fields were cleared of tough roots and the plough made progress much easier for the mole, it did not miss the opportunity and quickly became a field dweller, although it never deserted its primitive niche in the woodlands. Thus the potential conflict between mole and man began, becoming much more emotional once gardens, lawns and sports fields became part of our culture and farmers began to look more closely at their profit margins. While accepting that mole hills have no part to play on a cricket wicket, tennis court, bowling green or suburban lawn, there are two schools of thought regarding its effect on agriculture. The first witness for the prosecution in the case of mole versus the people is one John Worlidge, whose statement appeared in his book *Systema Agricultura: The Mystery of Husbandry Discovered* (1697). Part of it reads:

Moles are a most pernicious Enemy to Husbandry, by loosening the Earth and destroying the Roots of Corn, Grass, Herbs, Flowers etc and also by casting up hills to the great hinderance of Corn, Pastures etc.

It might seem to the jury that this statement contains much hearsay and little if any factual evidence on which to convict mole. Still the prosecution has not yet rested its case and is about to call J.P.E. Bell, whose statement was recorded in 1904 in the *Agricultural Gazette*:

When seeds and clover fields are badly infested with moles, great destruction necessarily follows. The soil is disturbed, and the tender rootlets become more susceptible to frost and drought, and a number of the plants will die off altogether. Wherever mole hillocks are thrown up, the plants are positively uprooted, and die as a matter of course, whilst on the surface runs far greater damage is caused than farmers are generally aware of. To a casual observer these are not always easily detected, but they are very apparent to the eye of a naturalist. Whilst moles play sad havoc on pasture land, their depredations are infinitely worse on land under tillage. In newly sown cornfields, especially when laid down with seeds and clover, the damage done by moles is sometimes enormous and amongst mangel and turnip drills the losses occasioned by these hardworking little animals are almost incalculable.

Thus the case against mole builds up and, unless council for the defence works hard on his brief and comes up with a pretty effective witness, poor old mouldiwarp will soon be looking tearfully at the black cap. Let us now call Edward Jesse, whose writings on the mole have already been referred to in the course of this chapter. In 1853, in *Scenes and Occupations of Country Life: with Recollections of Natural History*, he gives the defence a valuable statement:

So far from the mole being an injurous, it is a most useful animal to the farmer. It produces hillocks of fine rich mould which are extremely beneficial when spread over the ground—a top dressing of it will invigorate young wheat, whilst the hillocks will suffocate plants, the hills should be scattered more promptly by the farmer. The tunnels keep the soil drained. The mole devours the larvae of the cockchafer, flies, beetles and wireworms, and when we hear as we often do, of the ravages of the wireworm, we may wonder that the very instrument appointed by the Almighty to prevent these ravages should itself be destroyed by man.

At this point I feel sure that no jury could come to a verdict and the case against the mole must be dismissed for lack of evidence but his activities should be kept under close surveillance in future.

There have, however, been some interesting attempts to study the mole in a scientific manner, in particular, by a Frenchman M. Le Court. He inserted lightly constructed flags into the mole's run and then proceeded to blow a horn at the end of the tunnel; all that had to be done then was to measure the speed at which the flags tumbled. Nowadays we must regard it as a good attempt but sceptics have observed, not I think, without good reason, that the horn itself could have disturbed the flags by the sudden increase in air pressure produced as it was blown! At least Le Court was trying to be logical, which is more than can be said for some of his contemporaries who believed that a person carrying the paw of a mole in the pocket would never suffer from cramp and that moles could be killed by placing bramble twigs into the burrows. It was reliably reported that any mole which blundered into the thorns would bleed to death within the hour.

This brings us to the point where we must consider the eyesight of a mole—can it make out shapes if sufficient light is present? The mole has tiny but perfectly formed eyes. Vision does not play a great part in its life, but it is interesting to note that it is the increasing hours of daylight during the spring which brings the species into breeding condition. Thus the animal must spend sometime on the surface and be able to appreciate and measure daylight while it is there.

It is convenient to conclude this section on a point of agreement between ancient folklore and modern fact; a sharp blow on the snout will kill a mole. The snout is hairless and can be enlarged by blood being pumped into it by a mechanism similar to that used to erect a penis. In the erect position, the snout can be seen to be covered with tiny raised nerve cells which have been named 'Eimer's organs.' It is these which are so sensitive and these whose function biologists are still attempting to discover. Two ideas put forward to explain the function are exciting and a combination of both appeals to me enormously. Eimer's organs may be sensitive to smell, which would be invaluable to an animal spending most of its life in the dark, but they could also be what have been termed 'teletactile' receptors. The best way of understanding how these might work is to imagine yourself in a tube station and to make a further assumption that it was pitch dark. Even if you were deaf, the wind on your face would tell you that a train was coming and from which direction; this is possibly what Eimer's organs do for the mole by telling it that there is someone in its run, how large the intruder is and how fast it is advancing—vital information indeed. Extreme sensitivity seems but a small price to pay for such a valuable source of information.

SHREWS

The shrews are widespread and typified by a narrow pointed snout, a diet of invertebrates and young who do not have a complete set of milk teeth, although such teeth may be present in the foetus. Worldwide, there are about a hundred species arranged into twenty genera, but the precise classification depends upon the authority consulted. The British list consists of five species but only three are common. The position is summarised in Table 3.

Table 3 BRITISH SHREWS

Common Name	Other Common Names	Scientific Name	Approximate Body Length	Distribution
common shrew	erd, shrew mouse, ranny	Sorex araneus	70 mm (2¾ in)	General except for outer isles of Scotland, Isle of Man, Ireland and Scilly Isles.
pygmy shrew	lesser shrew	Sorex minutus	50 mm (2 in)	Present throughout, including islands.
water shrew	lavellan	Neomys fodiens	125 mm (5 in)	Absent from parts of N. Scotland, Isle of Man and Ireland.
greater white-toothed shrew	house shrew	Crocidura russula	80 mm (3 in)	Restricted to Channel Islands.
lesser white-toothed shrew	—	Crocidura suaveolens	65 mm (2½ in)	Restricted to Alderney, Guernsey, Herm and the Scilly Isles.

So far as most of our islands are concerned only two, or perhaps three, species of shrew occur, all typified by a certain amount of red on the teeth about which more will be said later (p. 60). It is certain that, to our superstitious ancestors, the common and pygmy shrews were not distinguished and the folklore refers equally to both species. The two were, however, distinguished by Linnaeus as early as 1766.

The Pygmy Shrew Sorex minutus

As previously stated, the pygmy or lesser shrew was usually not distinguished from the common shrew, but there are significant differences with regard to both distribution and anatomy. Throughout mainland Britain, it is not so common as *Sorex araneus*, but both species are notoriously difficult to census. The lesser shrew is found from sea level to mountain top, but its preference is unequivocally for woodland. In Ireland and the outer isles, *Sorex minutus* is the only species of shrew which occurs. Anatomically this species is smaller than the common shrew (see Table 3) and the length of the tail is greater in proportion to that of the head and body. The colour of the back is lighter than the common shrew and there seems to be no seasonal variation of colour.

There is one very significant behavioural difference between the two species in that pygmy shrews never construct their own runways through the vegetation, but simply move in to those of other species, including the common shrew. Direct competition between the two seems to be avoided due to the fact that they have different periods of activity. Although both species are active day and night, the pygmy shrew tends to be more diurnal. Its fossil remains in eastern Ireland would appear to date back as far as the beginning of the Pleistocene. Outside Britain, the lesser shrew extends its range across central Europe and Asia to the borders of the North Pacific but it does not penetrate into North America.

Pygmy shrews breed between April and August of the second year of their life and the females produce several litters of between four to seven young; thus populations can build up very rapidly. The precise gestation period is not known for certain but is probably about the same time as the lactation period, which is about 22 days. It would seem that the occasional precocious individual breeds during its first year.

The Common Shrew *Sorex araneus*

There is only a slight superficial resemblance between shrews and mice, which are rodents having a totally different dental formula reflecting their contrasting diet. The dental formula for the common shrew, also known as the erd, shrew mouse or ranny, is:

$$2 \times \left\{ I\frac{4}{2} \quad C\frac{1}{0} \quad PM\frac{2}{1} \quad M\frac{3}{3} \right\} = 32.$$

The pygmy shrew (*Sorex minutus*).

OPPOSITE: The common shrew (*Sorex araneus*).

One very mystifying aspect regarding the common shrew and the pygmy shrew (*Sorex minutus*) is the large number of dead animals found on paths and this has led to some quaint superstitions; these go back at least to the time of Pliny whose explanation was that 'if they fall into a cart-road they cannot get forth again'. Another idea was that the smell of a human being was fatal to them and, if a shrew so much as crossed a human footprint, it was doomed. One scientific clue towards an understanding of this puzzling mortality comes from the fact that the bodies are most often found in late summer and early autumn, when the population is at its highest. It has been suggested that predators catch many shrews at this time, but they find the flesh unpalatable and leave the body uneaten. The search for knowledge by Victorian naturalists, led by the eccentric Frank Buckland, knew no bounds and he pronounced from experience the flesh of shrews as both 'acid' and 'bitter'! This still does not account for the seasonal distribution of corpses, however, and the most likely explanation seems to be that shrews do not live very long and fail to survive beyond their second autumn; the old, tired and often dying adults are driven from their grass-covered territories by their stronger offspring. They die in peace on the paths which no self-respecting shrew would include in its territory. The 'autumnal epidemic', as the old naturalists called it, would seem to be due to old age, since juvenile shrews undergo a complete moult whereas those older than 1 year do not have a

The common shrew (*Sorex araneus*): a young specimen disturbed from its nest.

moult and the great majority of them do not survive the autumnal fall in temperature. It has also been suggested that open spaces and the danger of being caught in such a dangerous place by a predator such as a cat may sometimes be enough to frighten the poor beast to death!

The shrew was once described as:

... a kind of field mouse of the bigness of a cat and colour of a weasel, very mischievous to cattle which going over the beast's back, will make it lame in the chine, and the bite of it causes the beast to swell of the heart and die.

This statement proves two things—that the countryman's inbred fear of the shrew was profound and also that his knowledge of accurate recording of natural things was much less so. This fear is further underlined by Edward Topsell in 1607 in *Historie of the Foure-footed Beastes*:

It is a ravening beast, feigning itself gentle and tame, but, being touched, it biteth deep and poysoneth deadly. It beareth a cruel minde, desiring to hurt anything, neither is there any creature it loveth, or it loveth him, because it is feared by all. The cats do hunt and kill it, but they cannot eat them, for if they do they consume away and die. They are fraudulent and take their prey by deceit and many times they gnaw the oxes hooves in the stable.

Farmers were convinced that the bite of a shrew was poisonous (see p. 58) and if they noticed any of their cattle with a sore limb, the shrew was automatically held responsible. This idea can be traced back to the time of the Greeks in general, and Aristotle in particular, who stated that a shrew bite caused both ulcers and cancerous growths. Agricola weighed in for the Romans by postulating that the shrew injected venom into the wound (it was called *musaraneus*—'poisonous mouse'—for this reason) and he added that its effect was more pronounced in hot countries.

Any problem of this nature facing 'primitive' folk with no patent medicines and antiseptics at their disposal was to seek an antidote. Agricola had a sort of 'hair of the dog' remedy by recommending that the shrew should be cut in pieces and its flesh applied to the wound. The British countryman had a much less messy but just as cruel a method and this is faithfully recorded by Gilbert White (1789) in his *Natural History of Selbourne*:

There stood about twenty years ago a very old, grotesque, hollow, pollard ash, which, for ages, had been looked on with no small veneration as a shrew ash. Now a shrew ash is an ash whose twigs and branches, when gently applied to the limbs of cattle, will immediately relieve the pains which a beast suffers from the running of a shrew mouse over the part affected; for it is supposed that the shrew mouse is of so baneful and deleterious a nature, that whenever it creeps over a beast, whether it be horse, cow, or sheep, the suffering animal is afflicted with cruel anguish, and threatened with the loss of the use of its limbs. Against this accident, to which they were continually liable, our provident forefathers always kept a shrew ash at hand, which, when once medicated, would maintain its virtue for ever.... A shrew ash was made thus; into the body of the tree a deep hole was bored with an auger, and a poor devoted shrew mouse was thrust in alive, and plugged in, no doubt with several quaint incantations long forgotten.

Our ancestors' interest in the shrew ash did not stop at this point and they cut branches (I wonder if they were rationed) from the tree, keeping them ready to deal with a shrew should it creep up and attempt to do a mischief without warning. If a 'shrew-struck' man or beast had no access to a shrew ash then a bramble branch could be bent over into a hoop and the sufferer dragged beneath it. This was even recommended for the treatment of horses which were allegedly struck 'numb' by shrews. I would love to have seen a petulant horse with a lame leg being pulled through a bramble loop!

Apart from Man, the shrew does have many natural enemies, despite its unpalatable flesh. Birds of prey in general, and owls in particular, have little or no sense of smell and swallow their prey whole. The bones and fur are compounded together in the form of a pellet. The jaw bones of small mammals can almost always be retrieved intact and identification, based upon dental formulae and bone dimensions, is easily accomplished.

The Water Shrew *Neomys fodiens*

This species, also known as *lavellan* in Caithness, occurs on many river banks and shows a preference for areas of lush vegetation, such as watercress and water crowfoot. The entrance to the burrow system is usually just below the water level, but the system is quite extensive and runs both inland and parallel to the water course, each animal having a home range of some 150 m (165 yd). It is more common in England and Wales than it is in Scotland and does not occur at all in the Isle of Man, the outer isles of Scotland or Ireland.

Water shrews sally forth to hunt for prey at night and, although the bulk of their diet consists of earthworms, other annelids, molluscs, crustaceans, fish and amphibians may be taken. The prey may be taken on land but, if overwhelmed in water, it is carried to the bank to be eaten. A poisonous secretion is produced in the sub-maxillary glands and this can cause death to the prey, but in any event it certainly slows them down. Lydekker has this to say regarding the diet of the water shrew:

In the spring it appears to be specially fond of the larvae of the Caddis-fly; and in searching for fresh-water Shrimps the animal is in the habit of turning over the stones at the bottom of clear streamlets. It will also prey at times on the fry of fish, one of the Duke of Sutherland's gamekeepers having watched one of these Shrews attack a shoal of young Salmon which had just been liberated from the hatching-house into a small brook. This fish-eating propensity is likewise proved from the observations of Mr. Buckley; while there is also evidence that this Shrew will at times eat the flesh of dead mammals or birds. Mr. Trevor-Battye tells me that a colony of these animals, which he found in Kent, inhabited a garden-pond for a great number of years, where they showed a great partiality for frog-spawn.

Although mammals are not listed as prey items in *The Handbook of British Mammals*, the injection of 'water shrew venom' into laboratory animals has been found to affect adversely the nervous, respiratory and vascular systems. For this reason, great care must be exercised when handling the water shrew, which is bound to attempt to bite when put under stress and, in any event, does not do well in captivity (although several workers in recent years refute this statement). Sebek and Rosicky (1967) reported that, in Czechoslovakia, the three shrew species so far discussed are vectors for an

The water shrew (*Neomys fodiens*). Like other red-toothed shrews, this species has a poisonous bite.

The lesser white-toothed shrew (*Crocidura suaveolens*).

organism called *Pneumocystis carinii*, which can cause a type of pneumonia in children although this does not seem to occur in Britain.

Thomas Bell (1837) was well aware of the contrast between this species and its two smaller relatives. He wrote:

Specific Character.—*Nearly black above, white beneath, the colours distinctly separated; tail two-thirds the length of the body; feet and tail ciliated with strong white hairs ... the addition of stiff cilia to the sides of the toes, and the greater breadth of the feet, together with the fringe of hairs on the under surface of the tail, show that its ordinary pursuits require the use of oars and rudder....*

Bell also makes reference to another British mammal, the oared shrew. He applied the scientific name of *Sorex remifer* to it and described the beast as being blackish above with a pale grey colour beneath and the throat as having a yellowish ash colour. The oared shrew was also listed by Yarrell, but Lydekker, writing in 1896, sorts out the confusion thus:

The great variation in the colouring of the Water-Shrew gave rise to the idea that there were two British representatives of the genus, although it is now well ascertained that such variations are merely individual.

The water shrew occasionally breeds during the first year of its life, but it is usually during the second year that the species first comes into breeding condition. The breeding season can extend from mid-April to October but it peaks during early June. Following a period of some 24 days' gestation a litter of between three and eight young are born, each weighing only about 1 g (less than $\frac{1}{20}$ oz). At the time of weaning, some 37 days after birth, the youngsters weigh about 10 g (less than $\frac{1}{2}$ oz). There are two litters a year and, during the autumn, a longer winter coat develops and is replaced the following spring by a shorter coat. The water shrew's lifespan is short and, although it may approach 2 years, it never survives beyond the second.

The White-toothed Shrews *Crocidura russula* **and** *C. suaveolens*

To the vast majority of British naturalists, the white-toothed shrews will remain 'theoretical animals' since their distribution is restricted to the Channel and Scilly Islands; the greater white-toothed shrew (*Crocidura russula*) just reaches the Channel Islands but the lesser white-toothed shrew (*Crocidura suaveolens*) penetrates as far as the larger islands of the Scillies. On a global scale, the genus occurs commonly in the southern part of the Palaearctic zoogeographical region and throughout the Ethiopian and Oriental regions. They are distinguished by having unpigmented teeth, hence the vernacular name of white-toothed shrews, and *The Handbook of British Mammals* points out that the two species occurring in Britain are difficult to distinguish but have not so far been found on the same island. Head and body length in *Crocidura russula* varies from 60–90 mm ($2\frac{1}{4}$–$3\frac{1}{2}$ in), compared with a figure of 50–75 mm (2–$2\frac{3}{4}$ in) for *Crocidura suaveolens*; the former is often found around houses, which accounts for its continental vernacular name of 'house shrew', and it is pointed out that members of this genus are easier to maintain in captivity than those of the genus *Sorex*, a factor which may enable more accurate information to be gathered in the future than has been possible in the past.

It would seem that white-toothed shrews are less aggressive towards each other than the red-toothed species. The female, even when pregnant, often allows the male to share the breeding nest. White-toothed shrews also exhibit a form of behaviour which has become known as 'caravanning'—the young attach themselves to the tail of the mother or a sibling and they all go around in a sort of conga-line. This behaviour does not usually occur in red-toothed shrews but was reported, probably relating to the common shrew, in the *Journal of Zoology* in 1977.

4 Chiroptera: the Bats

About 900 species of bat occur in the world at present and they are placed in their own order—the Chiroptera—which translates literally as 'hand-wing'. They are assigned to one of two suborders: the flying foxes (Megachiroptera), accounting for about 150 species, and the rest which are classified as true bats (Microchiroptera). The Microchiroptera is divided into eighteen families, but only two of these (the Rhinolophidae and the Vespertilionidae) occur in Britain; all microchiropterans live on a diet of insects, there being no fruit-eaters or blood-suckers. The Rhinolophidae has two British representatives, the greater and lesser horseshoe bats, while the Vespertilionidae includes sixteen British species, belonging to seven different genera. Since in Britain there is a total of only sixty-eight mammal species, eighteen of which are bats, then the Chiroptera, which comprises 26.4% of the total, must be the dominant mammalian order in these islands. Although many of them have a very restricted distribution, we most certainly cannot ignore them. The British bats are summarised briefly in Table 4.

ORIGINS

We are pretty safe in assuming that bats evolved from primitive insectivorous mammals, which were probably also the ancestors of the shrews, and some workers believe that shrews use a rudimentary form of echolocation, based on the system perfected by the bats. The mode of life of the majority of Chiroptera is not conducive to the production of fossils, but a few cave systems, such as that at Querçy in France, have produced Eocene remains of five extant families and, in Wyoming, USA, an Eocene deposit has yielded a fossil which has been named as *Icaronyceteris*, the oldest bat remains so far described and dated at about 50 million years. Three aspects of bat natural history are of particular interest: echolocation, flight and hibernation.

ECHOLOCATION

In the Microchiroptera the eyes are merely vestigial but the flying foxes are just as dependent upon vision as terrestrial mammals or flying birds. All the smaller bats rely on sound pulses, a phenomenon which has puzzled naturalists for centuries and has only recently been accurately described. Bell (1837), summarises the state of knowledge at that time and from his description we can see how near they were to the correct solution:

Table 4 A SUMMARY OF THE MAJOR BRITISH BATS

Common Name	Scientific Name	Distribution	Habitat and Comments
greater horse-shoe bat	*Rhinolophus ferrumequinum*	Now restricted to S.W. England and S. Wales. Older records up to 1900 but range since diminished.	Caves, mines, cellars (winter); large roof spaces, barns (summer). Largest roosts in sheltered well-wooded valleys. Head and body always exceeding 55 mm (2 in).
lesser horse-shoe bat	*Rhinolophus hipposideros*	In Britain not clearly known but mostly S.W. England throughout Wales, northwards to Yorkshire with records from S.E. England. Also in western Ireland.	Similar to *R. ferrumequinum* but often found in small tunnels, hanging near the ground (winter) and in small attics (summer). Head and body not exceeding 40 mm ($1\frac{1}{2}$ in).
whiskered bat	*Myotis mystacinus*	Difficult to establish due to confusion with Brandt's bat. Positive records from Devon, Wiltshire and Sussex, north to Yorkshire, including Wales and Suffolk; probably throughout England and Wales.	Wooded and open country. Roosts in trees and buildings (summer) and sometimes in caves (winter).
Brandt's bat	*Myotis brandtii*	Positive records, mainly southern counties but also Yorkshire and East Anglia.	Wooded country. Caves (winter) and buildings (summer).

The flying membrane is not the only part which indicates a tendency to an extraordinary development of the cutaneous system. The ears and the nose exhibit in many cases a curious conformation, consisting of the great expansion of the former, and some remarkable appendages to the latter. The ears are, in all the British Bats, of considerable extent; and the tragus is of large size in those in which the nasal appendages just alluded to do not exist: in the Long-eared Bat, the ear is nearly as large as the body, and the tragus very long; but in the Rhinolophus, *or Horse-shoe Bat, though the ears are large, the tragus is not perceptible; and there are certain very curious foliaceous appendages to the nose .... Spallanzani had found that Bats, when deprived of sight, and, as far as possible, of hearing and smelling also, still flew about with equal certainty and safety, avoiding every obstacle, passing through passages only just large enough to admit them, and flying about places previously unknown, with the most unerring accuracy, and without ever coming into collision with the objects by which they passed. He also stretched threads in various directions across the apartment with the same result. So astonished was he at these curious facts, that he was led to attribute the phenomenon to the possession of a sixth sense ....*

Leisler's bat	*Nyctalus leisleri*	England but not Scotland. Seems plentiful in Ireland.	Forest bat preferring tree holes, but in Britain and Ireland known in buildings.
noctule	*Nyctalus noctula*	Throughout England and most of Wales. No recent records from Scotland and none at all from Ireland.	Tree and forest but in suburban parks if trees are present.
pipistrelle	*Pipistrellus pipistrellus*	Widespread in Europe. Throughout British Isles, including some offshore islands.	Very adaptable. Prefers to roost in trees or walls. Occurs over water, obviously in search of insects.
barbastelle	*Barbastella barbastellus*	Throughout Europe, stretching to 60°N and eastwards into Russia. England and Wales. Not Scotland and Ireland. It is, however, not well-recorded.	Wooded river valleys. In cold weather has been known to hibernate in caves. Solitary and low-flying.
common long-eared bat	*Plecotus auritus*	Ireland to Japan north to 63°N. British Isles including Ireland. Absent from N. Scotland and outer isles.	Sheltered woody areas. Roosts in trees and buildings, occasionally caves.
grey long-eared bat	*Plecotus austriacus*	First recognised in England in 1963. One known colony: house roof in open. Exact location not given.	Associated with villages and small towns.

tragus

Generalised bat showing the tragus.

Spallanzani, working at the end of the eighteenth century, came very close to discovering the bat's radar system. He could never have proved its existence, however, without the use of the 'sophisticated' sound-receiving equipment available today. It is small wonder, then, that his immediate successors sought an explanation for the skilful flight patterns by a close examination of more obvious parts of the chiropteran anatomy. Bell goes on:

Cuvier was the first to appreciate the real value of these experiments, as affording a proof of the existence of a vast expansion of the most exquisite sense of touch over the whole surface of the flying membrane . . . . From this view, therefore, it would appear, that 'it is by means of the pulsations of the wings on the air that the propinquity of solid bodies is perceived, by the manner in which the air reacts upon their surface.'

Thus Cuvier thought that the wings detected columns of air bouncing back off solid objects, an explanation quite similar to the modern theory of sound waves being produced from the mouth or nose leaves and rebounding back from solid objects to be picked up by the large and sensitive ears. Like Man's radar, bat sonics can be employed for defence or offence and their insectivorous food is located by these mechanisms. It has recently been discovered that some moths are capable of producing high-pitched squeaks which effectively 'jam' the bat radar; so the similarity to the techniques of modern warfare is continued.

FLIGHT

Naturalists are often inclined to write off the flight of bats as inferior to that of birds. Quite correctly, they point out that birds have not had to sacrifice the use of their hind limbs; also, in birds, the feathers are replaced during the annual moult whereas the flight membrane of bats (called the *patagium*) is a permanent double-membraned area of stretched skin and, should this be damaged, the animal's flying efficiency can be permanently impaired. It should not be forgotten, however, that the annual moult of a bird is a time of great physiological and psychological stress, requiring the intake of a lot of energy and, during this period, the inevitable loss in flying efficiency means that birds are particularly vulnerable to predators. Bats, like all vertebrates, are possessors of a modified pentadactyl limb; the primitive five-digit structure is reduced to four very long fingers. The patagium is stretched between them and also attached along the sides of the body and between the legs and, sometimes, along the length of the tail. A spur-like structure called the *calcar* may project from the ankle and assist in the support of the tail membrane. The patagium varies from species to species and a detailed description of its anatomy can be of invaluable assistance to the taxonomist.

One further disadvantage of the chiropteran patagium compared with the avian wing should be mentioned. The area of naked skin inevitably results in losses of heat and water, factors which do not apply to the bird's insulating and almost waterproof feathers. This means that bats must roost in hollow trees and caves to reduce these losses and this may well be one of the main reasons for their nocturnal habits and the fact that those bats occurring in temperate climates have been obliged to hibernate.

HIBERNATION

The hibernation versus migration question has probably been responsible for more heated arguments among natural historians than any other single issue. If we turn to Bell's *History of British Quadrupeds* we find:

Do our Bats ever migrate? or do Swallows ever hibernate? To both these questions I doubt not the same unqualified negative must be given. Their winter absence from the scenes which their summer presence and activity had enlivened, must be attributed to exclusively distinct causes. The Bats hibernate; the Swallows migrate. The hibernation of these animals is indeed one of the most interesting points in their economy. At an earlier or later period of autumn, according to the species, they retreat . . . . The retirement of the different species takes place at very different periods of the year. The Noctule is seldom seen abroad much later than July; and the Pipistrelle, the most common of our indigenous Bats, will sometimes make its appearance, in fine mild weather, in almost every month in the year; it does not even restrict itself to the obscurity of evening, but may now and then be seen flitting about in the bright sunshine of a December day, in search of the few insects which the unwonted influence of his rays has called into a short-lived activity.

Thus the idea that hibernation of mammals was not just a question of falling into a deep trance for the duration of the winter is at least 150 years' old. Obviously the choice of hibernaculum is crucial and two main habitats are open to bats: trees and caves. The latter are much more constant in temperature and species which habitually choose caves, such as the horse-shoe bats, tend to be much less hardy than those choosing hollow trees. These tougher types include the pipistrelle, the serotine and the noctule (see Table 4). It has been found that bats can be aroused from hibernation either by rising or falling temperatures, the former being much less surprising than the latter contention. Rapidly falling temperature can cool the body tissues below the level at which an acceptable metabolic level can be maintained and, in this case, the obvious survival value of arousal can be seen as a necessary risk. Many bats can be aroused from hibernation by thoughtless human disturbance and this very often results in the death of the unfortunate animals which have been thus forced to use up vital supplies.

Leaving aside 'accidental' disturbances, what is it that actually arouses bats from hibernation at the end of the winter? The answer seems to be open to debate but two attractive theories, in addition to a rise in the ambient temperature, seem worthy of consideration. During the winter, there must be some gradual, even if slow, accumulation of waste materials and these

The whiskered bat (*Myotis mystacinus*) hibernating. Note the condensation which has formed on the fur.

may build up to a threshold level beyond which the animal wakes up. The injection of urea into a hibernating bat causes it to wake up but it is impossible to be sure whether this is due to the injection itself or the urea entering the blood stream. In the chapter on the hedgehog, I pointed out that arousal from hibernation may be effected by the relative amounts of brown and white fat and, as both these substances are found in bats, it may well be that a similar mechanism is in operation.

The greater horseshoe bat (*Rhinolophus ferrumequinum*).

The Greater Horseshoe Bat *Rhinolophus ferrumequinum*

The first of the scientific names has Greek roots deriving from *rhis*, which means 'a nose', and *lophos* meaning 'a crest', thus producing an accurate description of the nose leaves. The specific name *ferrumequinum* has Latin roots. *Ferrum* obviously means 'iron' and *equinum* relates to horses and thus we can explain the name 'horseshoe bat'. The works of Bell and Lydekker throw a great deal of light on the occurrence of this species in Britain. In 1837, Bell wrote that the greater horseshoe bat:

... forms one of the numerous additions which were made by Daubenton to our knowledge of European Cheiroptera. It was first ascertained to be British by the venerable Dr. Latham, by whom it was communicated to Pennant, who published it in the fourth edition of his British Zoology. Dr. Latham's specimen was taken in the saltpetre-houses belonging to the Dartmouth powder mills. It has since been found in many localities; in Bristol and Rochester Cathedrals, in caverns at Clifton, at Colchester, and some other places. Montagu found it in considerable numbers, in company with the Smaller Horse-shoe Bat, in the well-known cavern near Torquay, called Kent's Hole ....

Lydekker (1896) points out that this species had probably been present in this particular cave system since the days of the mammoth, his evidence being based upon the discovery of fossilised bones. Lydekker also discusses its wide geographical distribution over most of Europe, Africa and Asia north of the Himalayas, but points out that the greater horseshoe bat in Britain is a southern species, rare in the Midland counties and absent from the north and Scotland and Ireland. This is still true today, but the range appears to have contracted still further and traditional sites in both Kent and the Isle of Wight have long since been deserted.

With such a restricted distribution in Britain, the few colonies remaining assume a greater importance and some concern has rightly been expressed with regard to the future status of the greater horseshoe bat. During hibernation, it is very sensitive to disturbance, both to noise and to sources of artificial light.

This should be carefully considered by naturalists who wish to study it—we have had quite enough examples of species being scientifically studied into extinction. It is, however, encouraging to find that the Royal Air Force, who owe so much to bats, are making some effort to redress the balance. Early in 1982, they put out the following press release, which is worth quoting in full:

RAF 'BATMEN' LOOK AFTER THEIR OWN
Bats in Britain are a threatened species—except, perhaps, for one colony the RAF has taken under its wing in Wiltshire.

Another bat earns its wings—Wing Commander Tony Howells enrols one of nature's night fliers during the annual bat count in the caves at RAF Chilmark.

At the storage depot RAF Chilmark, a disused stone quarry has become one of the most important sites for bat studies in Southern England, where several varieties are now very rare.

Not that the RAF has any special interest in bats, though it is well known that the little furry night-fliers developed their own form of radar navigation long before we did . . . .

In fact, most RAF stations in Britain have formed conservation groups to protect local flora and fauna—and Chilmark's bats need all the protection they can get.

The commanding officer, Wing Commander Tony Howells, revealed that a recent count included one resident, the Serotine bat, never before found living in a cave in this country.

In addition, there were 25 Greater Horseshoe bats. A century ago there might have been 150–250,000 of them in Southern Britain alone, where now they had all but completely disappeared.

'We have no reason to go near their caves, so we don't—except to make sure the entrances are clear of foliage,' said Wing Commander Howells.

'They are no trouble to us and we're happy to be able to leave them in peace.'

Dr Bob Stebbings, newly appointed by the Nature Conservancy Council as Britain's first official 'batman', said Chilmark was a fitting sanctuary in more ways than one.

'Bats hibernate from October to May and they don't like being disturbed, so these caves are an ideal winter home.

'Ironically, the decline in numbers may be partly due to eviction from their former roosts in the South's old churches—and 700 years ago Chilmark was the quarry that supplied the stone to build the cathedrals at Salisbury and Winchester.'

Dr Stebbings is a biologist employed by the Institute of Terrestrial Ecology and based at the Monkswood Experimental Station, Huntingdon. He has been interested in bats from the age of ten.

It has been suggested to him that bats were just the sort of macabre hobby that would appeal to a boy of ten . . . .

'Actually, bats no longer get such a bad Press as they once did. I still do get calls from people who want to know how to get rid of them—but more often they seem to be interested in ways of protecting and enhancing any colonies bound on their property. They have almost become a sort of status symbol.

'But the bad June weather of 1979 and 1980 hit them hard. It was cold and wet during a vital time in the breeding season and whole colonies abandoned their young just after birth. Horseshoe bats showed a decline of 56 per cent during these two years.'

Counts at Chilmark, begun in 1974, continued to give encouragement, however. Last year saw the highest number in residence to date. Why worry—what use are they? Well, that is hardly a consideration to weigh heavily with the true nature lover, but believe it or not, bats really are worth having around.

British bats are also completely harmless, insists Dr Stebbings. We don't have the blood-sucking vampires, which go out at night to feed off livestock.

'Actually, they eat a number of insects which are crop pests, including the cockchafer beetle which can damage valuable pasture. We must hope people will continue to take an enlightened view of their presence here.'

Meanwhile, back at Chilmark the watch continues. The bats are left strictly alone—but the Chilmark Ravine, a scheduled site of scientific interest, is also a treasure trove of undisturbed flora and fauna, containing many species that died out elsewhere 80–90 years ago.

Security restrictions are a bar to casual sightseers—which is just as well, of course—but anyone with a genuine interest can sometimes gain permission for a visit under escort. [Details may be obtained from Public Relations (Royal Air Force), Ministry of Defence, Main Building, Whitehall, London SW1A 2HB]

Greater horseshoe bats are sturdily built, the female weighing about 28 g (1 oz) more than the male, which is almost always the smaller. Head and body measurements reach just over 100 mm (4 in), to which must be added a tail length of 30 mm (about $3\frac{1}{4}$ in). Hibernation can commence as early as October but in most years it is probably November. Even in a torpid state, they are able to detect danger, a situation known to Charles Oldham, who wrote:

Even when sunk in winter sleep they appreciate man's approach. Their eyes are, of course, then shrouded by the wings and the sense of danger must be conveyed to them either by hearing, smell, or, as seems to be most probable by the exercise of their extraordinary tactile sense which enables them to actually feel the approaching danger.

R.H. Ransome, an acknowledged expert on the species, has established that the behaviour of the greater horseshoe bat is greatly affected by temperature, a factor which not only determines onset, duration and conclusion of hibernation but, because of the bat's sensitivity, may also warn it of the approach of a warm-blooded organism such as a human observer.

The Handbook of British Mammals describes the wings as broad with rounded tips and the flight as butterfly-like and low (under 13 m or 43 ft) alongside hedges and riversides. It is unable to crawl on level surfaces and so its roost requirements must be modified accordingly.

The horseshoe bats are distinguished from other species by the absence of a tragus and the presence of a nose leaf. This latter structure consists of an outgrowth of naked skin in the region of the muzzle and the area around the nostrils. The front part of the nose leaf is shaped like a horseshoe. The sound pulses are emitted via the nostrils, rather than via the open mouth as in other bats, and the nose leaf functions rather in the manner of a megaphone, allowing the sound to travel further with no additional expenditure of energy being necessary. Apart from the actual act of mating, the two sexes seem to remain in discrete units, with females, their nursing young and juveniles roosting separately from the adult males, which are found in more scattered colonies. Hibernation among males seems to be less complete than among females and they are active on many days during the winter. The greater horseshoe bat matures at about 3 years of age and can live for longer than 20 years, but the nursing colonies seem easily upset by disturbance and the species is now protected by the Conservation of Wild Creatures and Wild Plants Act (1975). Let us hope that this essential legislation has not come too late and that other associations will follow the example of the RAF.

An adult lesser horseshoe bat (*Rhinolophus hipposideros*) and young.

The whiskered bat (*Myotis mystacinus*) in flight.

The Lesser Horseshoe Bat *Rhinolophus hipposideros*

A comparison between this and the previous species can be seen in Table 5. The range is not quite so extensive as that of the greater horseshoe bat, but it is found in more northerly latitudes, reaching as far as the Baltic. It was first recognised as an English species in Wiltshire and is still mainly a southern species, although it has been recorded from Yorkshire and in Ireland, especially counties Clare and Galway. In the latter county, it has been recorded as hibernating in caves among plantations and a typical site is a cave with an entrance fringed by vegetation. Once more there is a distinct tendency for males and females to be concentrated in separate colonies. Both species have the same dental formula:

$$2 \times \left\{ I\,\frac{1}{2} \quad C\,\frac{1}{1} \quad PM\,\frac{2}{3} \quad M\,\frac{3}{3} \right\} = 32.$$

Table 5 COMPARISON OF SIZE OF GREATER AND LESSER HORSESHOE BATS

Common Name	Scientific Name	Length of Forearm	Length of Head and Body
greater horse-shoe bat	*Rhinolophus ferrumequinum*	More than 50 mm (2 in)	50–70 mm ($2\frac{3}{5}$ in)
lesser horse-shoe bat	*Rhinolophus hipposideros*	Less than 45 mm ($1\frac{4}{5}$ in)	Less than 40 mm ($1\frac{3}{5}$ in)

The Whiskered Bat *Myotis mystacinus*

Looking at *The Provisional Atlas of Mammals*, produced for the Institute of Terrestrial Ecology by H.R. Arnold in 1978, it would appear that this species is very rare in England and Wales with no records at all for Scotland and Ireland. This is due, I think, to two factors. Firstly, there is a distinct shortage of interested and competent observers and, secondly, it is often extremely difficult to distinguish *Myotis mystacinus* from *Myotis brandtii*

Map 1.   Distribution of the whiskered bat in the British Isles. (Circles: records before 1960. Dots: records since 1960.)

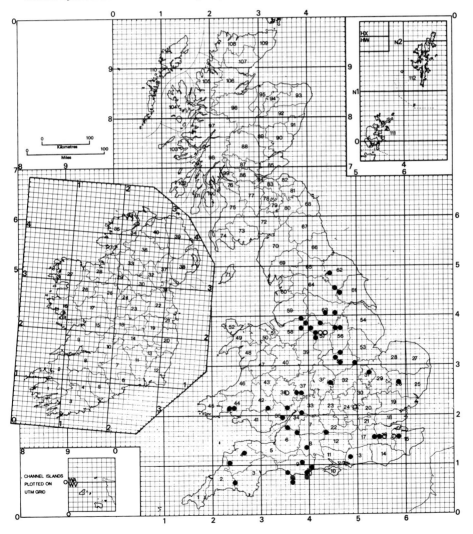

(Brandt's bat). Even *The Provisional Atlas* publishes three separate maps, one for each species and one pinpointing those records from which the two species cannot be separated reliably (see Maps 1 to 3).

It is reliably stated that whiskered bats have more pointed ears and a longer tragus while, in adult males, there are differences in penis structure which may be an important factor preventing interbreeding between whiskered bats and Brandt's bats. In whiskered bats, the penis is quite thin and parallel-sided while, in Brandt's bat, it is clearly club-shaped. Examination of the respective dentitions will also reveal a difference since Brandt's bat

Map 2. Distribution of Brandt's bat in the British Isles. (Circles: records before 1960. Dots: records since 1960.)

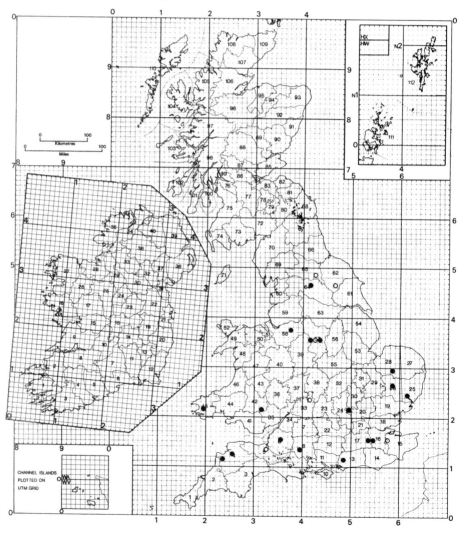

has an obvious cusp on the inner side of the upper premolar tooth which is not present in the whiskered bat. These differences are, however, not relevant to observers of bats in the field, hence the difficulty in assigning sight records to a particular species.

Whiskered bats are found in both wooded and open country and they often have their own favourite hunting beat which they patrol throughout the night and, in spring and autumn, when food must be gathered, they may also be seen hunting by day usually up to 20 m (72 ft) above ground level. In appearance, the whiskered bat lives up to its name, having hairs around its

Map 3. Distribution of the whiskered bat and Brandt's bat in the British Isles. (Circles: records before 1960. Dots: records since 1960.)

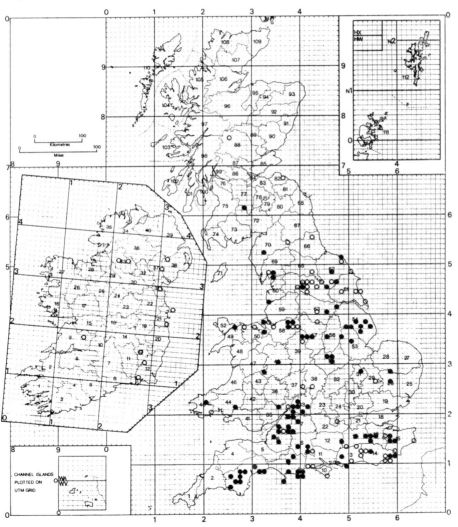

lips forming a moustache as well as other groups of bristles along the forehead and chin. Again the female is slightly larger than the male but, with a head and body measurement of 35–50 mm ($1\frac{1}{2}$–2 in), it is just a little longer than the lesser horseshoe bat.

Brandt's Bat *Myotis brandtii*

This species was only separated from the whiskered bat by Eversmann in the year 1845. It does not even warrant a mention by Lydekker (1896), Sir Harry Johnston (1910) or by Harrison Mathews (1962). A full description is given in *The Handbook of British Mammals*, which points out that:

Since its recognition it has been recorded from most European countries. In Britain positive records have been made in North Devon, Somerset, Wiltshire, Gloucestershire, Suffolk, Norfolk, Surrey, Kent, Staffordshire and Yorkshire.

This last record was only noted in 1971 and doubtless more records will come to light as field workers become more familiar with it and learn to distinguish it from the whiskered bat.

Brandt's bat (*Myotis brandtii*).

Natterer's bat (*Myotis nattereri*).

Natterer's Bat *Myotis nattereri*

At one time the English vernacular name for this species was 'reddish grey bat' obviously in reference to its colouration. The scientific name, according to Bell's publication of 1837, was *Vespertilio nattereri* and he points out that it was first described by Kuhl and named after the celebrated Austrian naturalist, Dr Natterer. There is evidence to suggest that some taxonomic confusion may have arisen due to the pronounced sexual dimorphism occurring in this species, the female being significantly larger than the male. Lydekker also follows Bell's terminology, although he does disagree regarding the distribution of the species, pointing out that it is exclusively European; we now know this not to be true, however, since specimens have been observed in Japan. It is therefore best described as a southern

Palaearctic species, stretching from Ireland in the west and Finland in the north. Lydekker's description of its British distribution is of some interest:

In England, although somewhat local, it appears to be not uncommon in several of the southern and midland counties, but seems to get scarcer as we go north. It is recorded by Bell from near London, Essex, Cambridgeshire, Hampshire, Kent, and Norfolk; Mr. Montagu Browne notes its presence in Leicestershire; and in the Lake District a colony was discovered, according to the Rev. H.A. Macpherson, in the summer of 1886, in an old outhouse at Castletown. In the second edition of Bell's 'British Quadrupeds,' this species was said to be unknown in Scotland, but there is a specimen in the British Museum from Inverary, Argyllshire, presented by the Duke of Argyll, showing that the statement in question is incorrect. In Ireland it has been taken at least in the counties of Dublin, Cork, Longford, and Wicklow, but is very rare.

Since this publication in 1896, the distribution of the species has changed little and, since it has a number of unique features, it is not likely to be confused with any other species. These include a fringe of hairs along the edge of the inter-femoral membrane. The wings are both broad and pointed and some workers have suggested that its mode of flight can be used as a point of identification. Montagu Brown compared the flight with that of a pipistrelle. Natterer's bat, he said, had a more sustained flight, slower and much more direct than the twisting motions of the pipistrelle. *The Handbook of British Mammals* adds that the high-speed photography of Eric Hosking and S.C. Bisserôt has shown that, during flight, the tail of this species tends to be carried straight behind and not downwards and at an angle as in other species.

Bechstein's Bat *Myotis bechsteini*

Fossil evidence relating to this species goes back some 4000 years having been excavated in the region of Grime's Graves in Norfolk. The surrounding area at this time, along with most of Britain, was heavily forested and was an altogether more suitable habitat for Bechstein's bat than is the case at the present time. With the reduction of forests, and also probably climatic changes, it may well be that the range of this species is gradually contracting. Even in 1896, Lydekker expressed some doubts as to whether it should be included in the British fauna but Bell is in no doubt, pointing out that:

This handsome and striking species is rare in this country, being only known as British from the occurrence of specimens taken by Mr. Millard in the New Forest, and now in the British Museum. This locality corresponds with its habits as detailed by the Continental naturalists, who state that it resorts exclusively to the hollow trees in the midst of forests, never approaching towns or retiring to buildings. It shuns even all association with other species of Bats, congregating in small groups of about a dozen, the largest number observed together being thirteen, all of which were females.

Bell also mentions the resemblance to Natterer's bat, but notes certain differences: the inter-femoral membrane, which is not fringed with hairs, and the ears, which are longer than those of *Myotis nattereri*. Bechstein's bat is truly a European species, extending as far as the Caucasus, but nowhere is it common, although it appears to be more abundant in Germany than elsewhere. There are less than thirty records in Britain, of which sixteen relate to the county of Dorset and none have been found further north than Shropshire.

The Mouse-eared Bat *Myotis myotis*

As is usual in bats, the female is somewhat larger than her partner and, at an average of nearly 65 mm ($2\frac{1}{2}$ in), for the head and body, plus an additional tail length of almost 40 mm ($1\frac{1}{2}$ in), we have a very large bat indeed. At one time it was known in scientific circles as *Vespertilio murinus* and it is under this name that Bell gives us a graphic description, in which he is at pains to point out why the species does not earn the title of the common bat of Great Britain:

On the Continent, indeed, this species is very generally met with. It was probably the species known to the Greeks by the name of Νυκτεξίς, and may be considered as one of the most frequent in Germany, as well as in France and in many other parts of Europe: but in England it is one of the rarest species yet discovered to be indigenous to the country, and has, I believe, hitherto only been taken in the gardens of the British Museum.

An appraisal of the species is given by Sir Harry Johnston (1903), who gives it the vernacular name of 'common continental bat'. He says:

The Common Continental Bat is supposed to have been captured in a Bloomsbury garden in the early part of the nineteenth century, and it is thought that the British type in the possession of the Natural History Museum at South Kensington is one of the bats caught in the vicinity of the British Museum in Bloomsbury. Only one other certain instance occurs of its presence in England— about fifteen years ago, in Cambridgeshire—though it has been reported, on probably mistaken evidence, to exist in Dorsetshire and the Isle of Wight. It is such a common bat in France, that, as it is quite able to fly across the Channel at its narrowest, there is no reason why it should not be found in the south of England. It is met with in most parts of Europe and in North Africa, and over the greater part of Temperate Asia. This bat is the Vespertilio murinus *of Blasius, Dobson, Lydekker, and other authorities prior to 1898. It is now re-named* Myotis myotis.

Being such a large species, it is easily recognised and, in addition, it has large eyes and ears and the origin of the inter-femoral membrane is very close to the base of the toes. The upper surface is brownish and contrasts with the greyish under-surface. As a species, it is extremely aggressive and not only bullies smaller species but, according to Lydekker, has definite cannibalistic tendencies.

Some corrections have been made in recent years to Sir Harry Johnston's work on this species. Dr V. Aellen informed the editors of *The Handbook of British Mammals* that the Cambridge specimen was not *Myotis myotis* but *Myotis blythi*, the evidence for this being its very small size. The balance is, however, somewhat restored by two recent records from Dorset and Sussex. We are still, however, dealing with a species which, although entitled to be called a British mammal, is nevertheless a very, very rare animal.

Daubenton's Bat *Myotis daubentoni*

Daubenton's bat tends to roost on its own among trees and is certainly not inclined to be gregarious. It has often been referred to as the water bat because of its habit of hunting insects over water. The Rev. H.A. MacPherson, who noted specimens on the Carlisle Canal of 1853, and near Ullswater in 1863, has this to say about the association of the species with water:

They flew actively over the water, frequently dipping, sometimes two or three times in succession, apparently feeding, their shadows being reflected as they hovered over the water, and the motion of their wings recalling the flight of the Common Sandpiper. They flew uniformly low over the water. Sometimes one would approach the margin of the lake, but they seemed to obtain most of their prey in the centre of the latter.

Sir Harry Johnston, basing his account on the history compiled by Bell, Lydekker and others, notes that Daubenton's bat was frequently observed in the western Midlands and the Lake District and also mentions records from Scotland and Ireland. His basic picture of the distribution seems to be similar to the modern view but, with an increasing number of competent recorders, the species has now been logged from most of Britain save the Isle of Man, the Scottish islands and the extreme north of mainland Scotland. It was while researching this present volume that I obtained a specimen taken on the towpath of the Leeds to Liverpool canal on the outskirts of Burnley. It is also present over much of Ireland. Anatomically, the species can be separated from other bats by means of the following characteristics: the margin of the inter-femoral membrane is naked and attached almost to the base of the toes while the wings themselves are broad and almost black in colour; the length from nose to tail is some 87.5 mm ($3\frac{1}{2}$ in) while the ears are about 25 mm (1 in), which is quite short when compared to other species in the genus; the tragus is about 8.4 mm ($\frac{1}{3}$ in) and is scimitar-shaped; the nose

Daubenton's bat (*Myotis daubentoni*).

is quite narrow and depressed in the middle whilst the gape is very wide, an obvious result of the fact that all the insect food is taken on the wing.

The Serotine Bat *Eptesicus serotinus*

The serotine bat belongs to the genus *Eptesicus* and has the dental formula:

$$2 \times \left\{ I\, \frac{2}{2} \quad C\, \frac{1}{1} \quad PM\, \frac{1}{2} \quad M\, \frac{3}{3} \right\} = 30.$$

In Britain, its distribution is confined to the south and east; it is absent from Devon and Cornwall and prefers to hibernate in trees. So far as the general distribution of the species is concerned, it is thought to be fairly widespread throughout the Palaearctic region south of Denmark. In the early histories of mammals, typified by Bell's *History of British Quadrupeds*, the details of the serotine were often copied directly from continental workers:

The serotine bat (*Eptesicus serotinus*) carrying young.

THE SEROTINE, notwithstanding the clear and intelligible description of Daubenton, was mistaken for the Noctule by Geoffroy, who described the one for the other. It was discovered by Daubenton, and forms one of the subjects of his excellent paper on the Bats in the Memoirs of the French Academy for 1759. It was also described and well figured in the eighth volume of Buffon's great work.

It appears to have very much the habit of the Noctule, at least as far as regards its late appearance in the spring, its sound and long-continued slumber. It flies from evening till morning, when the state of the atmosphere is favourable. In France, where it is far from being rare, it frequents forests, where it flies amongst lofty trees; it is also commonly found amongst the huge piles of wood in the timber-yards of Paris, seeking its place of repose on the tops of the highest piles. With us it appears to be a rare species, not having hitherto been found anywhere but around London.

Mouse-eared bats (*Myotis myotis*) roosting.

A group of Bechstein's bats (*Myotis bechsteini*).

Since Bell's time a few more sightings have been made but they are still very much biased to the south and east. To look at, the serotine is quite a large dark brown bat, with a head and body length of about 75 mm (3 in). Some confusion with the noctule is understandable but the serotine has proportionally longer ears and the tail juts out beyond the inter-femoral membrane and, in addition to the teeth being larger, the noctule has a different dental formula namely:

$$2 \times \left\{ I \frac{2}{3} \quad C \frac{1}{1} \quad PM \frac{2}{2} \quad M \frac{3}{3} \right\} = 34.$$

There is also a structural difference in the tragus, which is described as being broader at the tip than at the base in the noctule while *The Handbook of British Mammals* says that the tragus of the serotine is 'bluntly pointed'.

Leisler's Bat *Nyctalus leisleri*

This species, formerly known as the hairy-armed bat, can also be confused with the noctule bat (*Nyctalus noctula*), the distinction being made partly on size (see Table 4), by slight differences in skull size and by smaller lower incisor teeth, although the dental formula of the two species is the same. This once more underlines the difficulty of working with British bats, since their fly-by-night activities mean there are few contrasting colour patterns and few opportunities for observation. Lydekker, in discussing the similarities between Leisler's bat and the noctule points out:

> *In common with the Noctule, the present species has a band of fine short hair running down the under side of the fore-arm to the wrist, and it is from this character that the Hairy-armed Bat derives its common English name.*

This old vernacular name could be very misleading since the noctule could just as easily be described as hairy-armed. Leisler's bat is to some extent migratory and does tend to be very secretive, so it may be more common than confirmed reports indicate. In England, it reaches Cheshire and Yorkshire, but its stronghold is once again in south-eastern England. It is apparently well represented in Ireland and it is interesting that, so far, the noctule has not been recorded from there. We must wonder if the noctule may have been missed and whether the species may yet be discovered.

The Noctule *Nyctalus noctula*

Known to early writers as the great bat, the noctule is certainly an impressive beast with a wing span approaching 400 mm (16 in). The species is given prominence in the works of Bell and Lydekker. Bell (1837) provides us with a good introduction to its history, in which it is described under the name of *Vespertilio noctula*:

IT is to Daubenton that we are indebted for the discrimination of this fine species of European Bat. He has described it and given a figure of the head, in the Memoirs of the French Academy for 1759; and Buffon subsequently gave it a place in his great work. The first notice of its occurrence as a British species is in White's Natural History of Selborne, in which it is repeatedly mentioned. This writer gave it the name of altivolans . . . .

The Noctule is gregarious in its habits, associating in considerable numbers, and seeking its retreat sometimes in the hollows of trees, at others under the roofs and eaves of houses. Pennant states that he was informed by the Rev. Dr. Buckhouse, that he saw taken from under the eaves of Queen's College, Cambridge, one hundred and eighty-five in one night: but as there is no reason to believe that these were all submitted to the rigid examination necessary to detect the specific distinctions of these animals, it is probable that other species were mingled with them in this great congregation. It is however particularly stated, that of all those which were measured, the extent of the wings was fifteen inches. In the second night, sixty-three were taken. The flight of this Bat is remarkably high and rapid, and its cry when on the wing is sharp and harsh. It was observed by White to emit a very offensive odour. It remains in activity for a shorter time than any other, coming abroad later and retiring earlier: White says that he never saw it till the end of April, nor later than July. This difference between the hibits of the Noctule and the Pipistrelle is the more remarkable, as in their zoological character they strikingly resemble each other, excepting in size.

So far as its present distribution is concerned, the noctule is mainly restricted to England and Wales, although the possibility of confusion with Leisler's bat (to which I referred above) was also noted by Lydekker (1896) in his appraisal of the noctule. He notes:

The most northern locality which Bell was able to ascertain for this species was Northallerton, in Yorkshire, but it has been recorded by the Rev. H.A. Macpherson from Carnforth, on the coast of Lancashire, and it is possible that certain large Bats observed at Bowness-on-Solway during the summer of 1888 may have pertained to the present species . . . it is not recorded by Thompson among the Mammals of Ireland. There is, however, reason to believe that it is an inhabitant of the latter island, as may be gathered from the following extract from a paper on Bats by Mr. Harting, who writes that in the Zoologist *for 1874 'Mr. Barrington gave a very interesting account of the discovery, in June, 1868, of a colony of large Bats in the demesne of the Duke of Manchester at Tandragee, county Armagh, and of the subsequent capture of several (presumably of the same species) at the same place in May, 1874. Mr. Barrington identified them as* V. leisleri, *observing "they were all of the hairy-armed species. I have presented two specimens to the British Museum." These two specimens were examined by Dr. Dobson in 1876, and he pronounced them to be immature examples of* V. noctula.' *This seems to establish the occurrence of the latter species in Ireland, where, however, it may well be accompanied by the Hairy-armed Bat.*

This must give some room for doubt but neither *The Handbook of British Mammals* nor *The Provisional Atlas of the Mammals of the British Isles* allow any Irish records and this situation must for the moment be accepted.

The Pipistrelle *Pipistrellus pipistrellus*

The genus *Pipistrellus* is represented in Britain by two species, one being our most common bat, the other probably the rarest and added to the British list on the strength of a single record from Dorset in October 1969 and reported by Stebbings. This is Nathusius' pipistrelle (*Pipistrellus nathusii*) but, apart from noting that the taxonomic distinction from the common pipistrelle is made on the basis of tooth shape and position, we may say little about it. Both species have the same dental formula of:

$$2 \times \left\{ I \frac{2}{3} \quad C \frac{1}{1} \quad PM \frac{2}{2} \quad M \frac{3}{3} \right\} = 34.$$

Leisler's bat (*Nyctalus leisleri*): females in a nest box.

Detail of a noctule bat (*Nyctalus noctula*).

The pipistrelle (*Pipistrellus pipistrellus*).

The history of *Pipistrellus pipistrellus* in Britain has been well documented but, as Bell indicates, these observations have not always been accurate. He refers to the species under the scientific name of *Vespertilio pipistrellus* and documents it thus:

WE owe to the Rev. L. Jenyns the elucidation of the synonymes of our Common Bat. In the 16th volume of the Linnæan Transactions, that gentleman has given an elaborate and satisfactory paper on this subject, in which it is investigated with great acumen and judgment; and the conclusion which he draws, and which appears to be completely established, is, that the Common Bat of Britain is the Pipistrelle of the Continental authors.

The careless and implicit manner in which authorities are constantly followed without sufficient investigation, and error thus propagated from error, is as conspicuous in the present case as in most that could be adduced. Because Vespertilio murinus [the mouse-eared bat] *was the Common Bat of the Continental naturalists—their 'Chauve-souris' par* excellence—*it was presumed that our Common Bat must be the same species; and Pennant having once stated such to be the case, every subsequent writer on our British Mammalia has copied the mistake; and V.* murinus, *one of the rarest of our indigenous species, was still to be the Common Bat of Britain. It was left to Mr. Jenyns to correct this long-established error; and it is sufficient to refer to his paper every one who wishes to be satisfied on the matter. I have carefully followed out the comparisons instituted by Mr. Jenyns, as far as my opportunities have enabled me, and can come to no other conclusion than that which he has established. The synonymes, therefore, of all our British Faunists, from Pennant down to Fleming inclusive, are erroneous as regards the present species.*

The pipistrelle shows some variation in size, with the female again tending to be a little larger. An average head and body length is something in the order of 40 mm ($1\frac{1}{2}$ in) with a wing span of between 200 and 250 mm (8 and 10 in). Macgillivray, the eminent Scots naturalist, writing in the middle years of the nineteenth century comments thus on the habits of the 'flittermouse':

...from the middle of spring, but earlier or later according to the warmth of the season, to the middle of October, sometimes commencing as early as March, and continuing till November, this Bat may be seen after sunset in the neighbourhood of towns and villages, over the streets of cities or the roads, in the alleys and lanes, or along the course of brooks and rivers, fluttering with an unsteady motion, and apparently undetermined course. Its flight is not rapid, like that of a bird, but rather resembles that of a large Moth or Butterfly. It turns and winds in all directions, flying at various heights from ten to twenty or more feet, and sometimes as high as the tops of the trees, but more commonly at an elevation of about fifteen feet. It is attracted by a white handkerchief, or any other body, thrown up in the air, for which reason boys are fond of tossing their caps at it. Sometimes it has been caught upon the fly-hooks of a fishing-rod hung over a bridge. It

continues its flight until dark, and probably during the night, as well as in the morning twilight; and reposes through the day in the corners and crevices of old buildings, towers, and steeples. As its food consists entirely of insects, and especially the nocturnal Lepidoptera, it is forced by the increasing cold of winter to relinquish its pursuits, and betake itself to some secure retreat in a ruined building or cavern, where it remains until the returning heat arouses it from its torpor. In this state it is found suspended by its feet in chimneys, crevices, or corners, or jammed into a hole or fissure. A frequent place of retirement is under the roofs of houses, and especially churches; but it presents great variety in its selection, and I have obtained specimens from the hollow of a decayed tree near Duddingston.

The Pipistrelle rises with facility from a flat surface, and is capable of advancing on the ground with considerable celerity, and ascends a vertical plane, provided it be somewhat rough, without much difficulty. In confinement it feeds on flies and raw meat.

The letter columns of popular nature magazines often mention sightings of pipistrelle bats during the winter months and, judging from Lydekker, this seems to have been the case for many years.

From its hardy nature, as indicated by its northern range in Britain, the Pipistrelle is by no means continuous in its winter slumber, any unusually warm day being sufficient to awaken the little creature. During the mild winter of 1893–94, I observed on the evening of January the 20th one of these Bats flying near my own house in Hertfordshire; and in the north of Ireland Thompson states that it may frequently be seen abroad in mid-winter.

As I indicated at the beginning of this chapter, bats may be awakened by especially cold spells of weather and now we find the pipistrelle and probably other species also active during warm spells; thus it seems that hibernation is far less rigid than has often been allowed.

The Barbastelle *Barbastella barbastellus*

The barbastelle was first described by Daubenton in 1759, being named *Vespertilio barbastellus* by Schreber in 1774, but Bell referred to it as *Barbastellus daubentonii* in 1837. Bell also records the first English recognition by Sowerby, whose specimen was obtained from some powder mills near Dartford in Kent. Lydekker refers to the species as *Synotus barbastrellus* and also makes the point that it is a delicate bat which hibernates very early. This may very well account for its absence in northern England and Scotland, but is less convincing if we try to discover the reason for its absence in Ireland. The Rev. H.A. Macpherson recorded a number of individuals from the Carlisle region during the middle years of the nineteenth century but this seems to be the furthest north it has ever ventured.

The barbastelle (*Barbastellus barbastellus*).

OPPOSITE: A grey long-eared bat (*Plecotus austriacus*) clinging to a rock.

Common long-eared bats (*Plecotus auritus*) roosting in a roof.

By the time Sir Harry Johnston's book *British Mammals* was published in 1903, as part of the Woburn Library of Natural History, the scientific name had changed yet again, this time to the one still in use—*Barbastella barbastellus*. Johnston notes:

> . . . *the fur is soft and deep black, with a grayish tinge on the surface caused by the tips of the hairs being that colour. The region round the genital organs is of a whitish-brown colour, and fine hairs of grayish-white grow sparsely on each side of the flying membrane, the skin of which is dusky black in colour. This is also the tint of the naked skin on the face, so that in average aspect the Barbastelle is the blackest of British bats. A perfectly white specimen of the barbastelle, and another in which the body was black, while the head and membrane were pure white, were seen and noted by the late Mr. Bell, who also records an extraordinary specimen that was caught in Warwickshire which had the fur of the under parts strangely tinged with purplish-red.*

He then adds a footnote in an attempt to explain this latter phenomenon:

> *In some other Vespertilionid bats there is a tendency in the breeding season for the males to develop a rich yellow tinge in the lower half of the hair of the under parts. It may be the same tendency which tinged the fur of this example with a purplish tone.*

It is noted in *The Handbook of British Mammals* that males are four times more likely to have signs of albinism than are females and this work also mentions that the black fur of this medium-sized bat (wing span about 250 mm or 10 in) is often flecked with hairs of a lighter colour, giving a sort of frosted appearance.

The Common Long-eared Bat *Plecotus auritus*

For a change, we find that the scientific name used today is the same as that given by Bell in the 1837 edition of *British Quadrupeds*. In this volume, the author provides us with a delightful description of the species:

> *It is one of the most common of our British Bats; and the extraordinary development of the ears, their beautiful transparency, and the elegant curves into which they are thrown at the will of the animal, render it by far the most pleasing: it is also more readily tamed than any other, and may soon be brought to exhibit a considerable degree of familiarity with those who feed and caress it. I have frequently watched them when in confinement, and have observed them to be bold and familiar even from the first . . . .*
> *The large and beautiful ears are usually folded under the arm during sleep, especially if the sleep be profound: and this is also the case during hibernation; the long tragus then hangs down, and gives the animal the appearance of having short and slender ears.*

The distribution of the common long-eared bat is very wide and it is only in the most exposed area of northern Scotland that it is not encountered. *The Handbook of British Mammals* suggests that there may be a tendency towards an increase in size as one moves from south to north. This is probably due to the fact that larger animals have a smaller surface area to volume ratio and thus will lose less heat to the environment which is an important survival factor. This is known as Bergmann's rule. The head and body length averages 50 mm (2 in) with the tail extending a further 45 mm ($1\frac{3}{4}$ in). This means that this species is larger than our other common bat, the pipistrelle, from which it can also be distinguished by its longer ears. This feature alone is sufficient to separate it from all but the grey long-eared bat (*Plecotus austriacus*), which has only recently been added to the British list (in 1963) on the authority of Corbet and, so far, it has been noted only from Dorset, Hampshire and Sussex. The common long-eared bat is smaller than the newcomer, but only by a few millimetres and so this is not an easy distinction to make. As its name implies, *P. austriacus* tends to be more grey, but it is in the thumb structure that we find the best point of distinction, although, as usual in bats, we need to have the specimen in hand to make a positive decision. In long-eared bats, the thumb is long and slender being over 6.2 mm ($\frac{1}{5}$ in), a figure which is never reached by the grey long-eared bat. The tragus of the latter is also broad in contrast to the narrow tapering structure of the common long-eared bat.

There are four additional species of bat which, although placed on the British list, have been recorded so seldom that they have no real part to play in the past or present account of our mammals and it is unlikely that they will figure prominently in the future. I will therefore content myself with merely listing them. They are the pond bat (*Myotis dasyceme*), the notch-eared bat (*Myotis emarginatus*), the parti-coloured bat (*Myotis murinus*) and Nathusius' pipistrelle (*Pipistrellus nathusii*). Anyone wishing to know more about these should consult the relevant literature quoted in *The Handbook of British Mammals*, but would do well to seek more up-to-date information from bodies such as the Mammal Society, the British Naturalists' Association or the Nature Conservancy Council (NCC). Indeed, on the 28th September 1982, the NCC published details of the protection afforded to all bats and a quote from it will ensure that this chapter closes on an optimistic note:

It is now illegal for anyone without a licence intentionally to kill, injure or handle any wild bat in this country. It is also an offence to damage, destroy or obstruct access to any place that a bat uses for shelter or protection, or to disturb a bat while in occupation. However, if a bat—usually a young, inexperienced one—enters the living area of a house it can be carefully removed.

The law is intended to stop the destruction of bats—all of which have been declining severely in recent years—and to encourage anyone with problems caused by bats to seek the help and free advice of the Nature Conservancy Council, or the NCC's specialist adviser, Dr. R.E. Stebbings.

The greater horseshoe bat (which together with the mouse-eared bat was already protected under the Conservation of Wild Creatures and Wild Plants Act 1975) has declined by about 95% in the last hundred years; but even the commoner bats such as the pipistrelle have almost halved in numbers in the last three years.

The decline in bat populations is due mainly to loss of roosts, loss of feeding grounds and food, pollution, and bad weather at critical times. But probably the greatest single threat to bats is remedial timber treatment, with over 100,000 buildings now being treated annually, often using chemicals that are lethal to bats.

People are generally unaware of bats roosting in their houses or property, as they fly mainly at night. Bats do not chew or cause any damage to buildings or paintwork, and they do not build nests but simply hang by their toes. Many people welcome bats, as they are fascinating to watch at dusk. They can each catch as many as 3,000 insects a night, including mosquitoes, moths and beetles.

If bats are unwanted, or if a householder proposes to carry out any work which is likely to disturb bats or their roosts, or when woodworm treatment is necessary, the NCC or Dr Stebbings must be consulted. They are experienced in giving practical advice, for which no charge is made, and it is important that their advice is followed because colonies often contain all the breeding female bats from a wide area.

Let us hope that this heralds a similar sympathy for other species which are also facing problems. At times this also applies to rabbits and hares which are described in the next chapter.

5 Lagomorphs: the Rabbit and Hares

R abbits and hares, at one time, were classified as rodents but were thought to be sufficiently different to warrant being placed in their own sub-order called the Duplicidentata. This signifies the presence of a large pair of incisor teeth on the upper jaw, behind which is a second very much smaller pair. The dental formula is:

$$2 \times \left\{ I\frac{2}{I} \quad C\frac{0}{0} \quad PM\frac{3}{2} \quad M\frac{3}{3} \right\} = 28.$$

These and other differences, such as having all the teeth with open roots so that they can thus grow continually, a short tail and the habit of eating their own faeces (a habit known as refection and which will be discussed at length later) persuaded taxonomists to place them in a separate order. This was named the Lagomorpha and consists of two families; the Ochotonidae, otherwise known as the pikas, and the Leporidae consisting of the rabbits and hares. Britain has no representatives of the former family, but the Leporidae are represented by the introduced rabbit and the native brown and mountain hares.

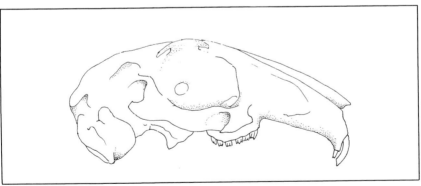

Figure 22. The upper jaw of a rabbit showing the extra incisor tooth which is lacking in rodents.

The Rabbit *Oryctolagus cuniculus*

The adult rabbit, or coney, weighs between 1.5 and 2 kg (3 and $4\frac{1}{2}$ lb) and the buck is heavier than the non-pregnant doe. The head and body together are up to 400 mm ($15\frac{3}{4}$ in) long and the ears are another 70 mm ($2\frac{3}{4}$ in) long. Breeding occurs from January to August and litters of up to seven bunnies, as the young are called, are produced. The gestation period is about 30 days and the female can become pregnant again within days of bearing a litter. Both sexes are sandy brown in colour and the female is usually the smaller with a narrower head. Moulting is annual, usually beginning in March and usually starting on the hind quarters.

Oryctolagus cuniculus is not thought to be a native of these islands, the weight of learned opinion suggesting its introduction by the Normans. The bones of extinct but not identical forms of rabbit have been found among the Pleistocene fossils of Italy and central France and these are between 10 000 and 15 000 years old. In Britain, there are also records dating back to this period, but care must be taken, since the rabbit is a burrowing animal and can therefore reach lower levels; any animal dying at depth would add its bones to those of an older period. It would seem safe to suggest that any rabbits present in Britain prior to the Ice Ages would not have survived these rigorous conditions. The first definite European evidence concerning the rabbit is circumstantial dating to the year 300 BC when Polybius reported the absence of hares from Corsica, but went on to mention the presence of smaller hare-like animals which burrowed in the ground and were called *kunikloi*. From this we can easily derive the Latin name *cuniculus*, which we still retain as the specific half of its scientific name.

The first sign of conflict between man and cuniculus is documented by Strabo in about 30 BC. He refers to a petition presented to the Emperor Augustus by the inhabitants of the Balearic Islands of Majorca and Minorca. They begged for relief from taxes because the rabbits had not only eaten a high proportion of their crops, but also burrowed so industriously under the foundations of their houses that many were in imminent danger of collapse. Pliny the Elder also refers to this Balearic problem and he also mentions the rabbit's great abundance in Spain. Mankind has never usually

The rabbit (*Oryctolagus cuniculus*).

been found slow to make use of food sources and the Romans quickly learned to eat rabbit. In the reign of the Emperor Hadrian, who held power from AD 117 to 138, the rabbit was held in such high esteem that it was engraved on one side of a coin with the emperor's image on the other. These coins were freely circulated in Britain and this has probably been instrumental in persuading many past natural historians to assume that the rabbit is one of our indigenous animals. By AD 200, rabbit flesh was so esteemed in the Roman world that walled enclosures called *leporaria* were specially constructed, either to hold them or to breed them specially for the table. Hares were also kept in this manner.

The fact that the Latin name for the rabbit appears in similar form in many European countries indicates the rabbit's culinary fame in the time of the Roman Empire. In Italy, its vernacular name is still *coniglio* and in Spanish it is *conejo* whilst the German's know it as *Kaninchen*. The literal translation of cuniculus is 'an underground passage' and it is thus a very appropriate name. In 1956 H.V. Thompson and A.N. Worden (see bibliography) suggested that the word rabbit could be an old Walloon word— *rabbet*—which was initially reserved for the young of the cuniculus but this is not recorded prior to the fifteenth century. Before this we find the old English word 'coney' and this is very similar to *connin* which is old French in origin. The same workers are also at pains to point out that the 'coney of the rock' referred to in the Bible is not *Oryctolagus cuniculus* but most probably *Hyrax syranicus*, the Syrian hyrax. A group of rabbits were often called a *coneygarth* or *conigree* signifying an earth full of coneys and the term warren was not used very often in early history.

It is known that cuniculus was one of Julius Caesar's favourite dishes and the fact that it is not mentioned in any of his voluminous writings concerning these Islands is almost certain evidence that it was not present in Britain at this time. What is perhaps even more significant is that no mention is made of the rabbit in the *Domesday Book* and so we are left with the probability of its introduction by the Normans. However, we are still rather short of positive evidence although Sheail (1971) does quote some interesting finds. He mentions the discovery of a number of rabbit bones in a midden associated with Rayleigh Castle in Essex, which was occupied between the eleventh and thirteenth centuries. Household rubbish excavated at the Buttermarket in Ipswich produced rabbit bones actually below pottery dated back to the early twelfth century. The actual layout of the finds and its careful extraction rules out burrowing rabbits from a later century and so the bones must be accepted as contemporary.

Gradually during the thirteenth century, the coney is mentioned more often in the documents and, in the year 1274, over 2000 skins were produced from the Island of Lundy and they are mentioned in such a way that a great deal of money must have changed hands, concerning both the meat and the pelts. At this time the rabbit most certainly was far from common and household accounts dating from the early part of the fourteenth century indicate that a rabbit cost the same as a suckling pig, and it continued thus throughout the fifteenth century. Rabbits regularly appeared on the menu of important banquets such as coronations, weddings and the installation ceremonies of ecclesiastics. When George Neville, Archbishop of York and Chancellor of England, was installed in September 1465 the food offered was as follows:

Wild bulls	6
Swans	400
Geese	2000
Capons	1000
Plovers	400
Quailes	1200
Ruff	2400
Peacocks	104
Mallards and teal	4000
Cranes	204
Rabbits	4000
Bitterns	204
Young herons	400
Pheasants	200
Partridges	500
Woodcocks	400
Curlews	100
Egrets	1000
Stags	500
Pike and bream	608
Porpoises and seals	12

In addition to the above, Redshanks, Stints, Skylarks and Swallows were also provided in some quantity. I wonder who ate at this banquet, how many attended and how they felt the day after. I also wonder who did the cooking and how long the feast lasted!

By Shakespeare's time, towards the end of the sixteenth and the beginning of the seventeenth century, the rabbit was becoming more common and is mentioned in his works:

They will out of their burrows like conies after rain.

Coriolanus IV, 5, 226–7

With your arms crossed on your thin-belly doublet, like a rabbit on a spit.

Loves Labour Lost III, 1, 19

In *King Henry IV Part 1* (II, IV, 480), Falstaff remarks:

Depose me? If thou dost it half so gravely, so majestically, both in word and matter, hang me up by the heels for a rabbit sucker, or a poulters hare.

Doubtlessly, resourceful rabbits had escaped from captivity, where they were looked after by a manorial employee called the Warrener, from which we derive the surname, and doubtlessly because of the varied habits of the animal, country folk erroneously thought that there were three types. These were referred to as 'warreners', which burrowed in open situations, 'parkers', which inhabited parklands around the manors, and 'hedgehogs', which were said to have less furry coats than the others and made their homes in thick undergrowth. This was noted by W.S. Berridge (1934) who also refers to *The Life of Bede* by Dr Brown in which the removal of the body of St Cuthbert from Lindisfarne to Durham is mentioned. A horseman is shown in a copy of an illustration with a hawk on his wrist and a row of rabbits at his feet. This must not be taken as proof that rabbits were present in Britain before Norman times, since the monks who produced the original between 1085 and 1104 were probably Normans exercising some poetic licence.

The 'escapee' rabbits would soon be popular additions to the diet of such predators as stoats and foxes. They would certainly thrive on a diet of rabbit flesh, which is the richest source of animal protein yet measured. It was thus not until the eighteenth century that any significant increase in the rabbit population occurred due to human activity. Agricultural efficiency had improved to such an extent that fodder crops were being produced in vast quantity to help cattle and sheep overwinter. The rabbit has always been an opportunist feeder and this extra food kept more of them alive during the winter, thus resulting in a greatly increased breeding population the following spring. The does would also have been in better condition and able to feed a greater proportion of the litter. It is reasonable to suppose that the increased rabbit population would have supported an equivalent number of additional predators, but, once again, human activities interfered with the balance of nature.

Shooting became a sport rather than a method of feeding a family and large 'bags' were demanded by sportsmen. Gamekeepers were employed to protect pheasants, partridges and grouse from their predators; foxes, stoats and any bird with a hooked bill were ruthlessly hunted down and hung on a grisly-looking gibbet. These were just the animals which would have held the rabbit population in check and, by 1900, the rabbit was numerous enough to be the most destructive mammal in Britain after the mouse and the brown rat.

By 1950, a figure of £50 million pounds was the estimated cost of rabbit damage and many respected authorities think that this figure was very much too low. So the rabbit had changed from the much-sought-after banquet luxury to a pest of the most expensive kind, as reflected in a publication produced by HMSO just after the World War 1, which had this to say about the rabbit:

In agricultural circles the wild rabbit has long been a topic of conversation and, to those who know from experience what it can do, the subject of heartfelt execration. That the latter is justified cannot be denied, for the rabbit is not only one of the greatest mammal pests with which the farmer has to cope, but in this respect it is second only to the rat. It does enormous damage, and there are few cultivated plants that it will not eat. It has been known to eat off large areas of young sprouting corn, to clear whole sowings of turnips, lettuces and radishes, and to make serious inroads on most other kinds of crops grown on British farms.

The rabbit is a prolific breeder. A single doe, beginning to breed at the age of six months, may have four or five litters in a year with five, six or more young to each. Left unchecked, in a few years the progeny of one pair of rabbits will reach an astonishing figure. Moreover, the rabbit has a knack of surviving and even increasing in unexpected places and in circumstances which might be thought anything but favourable.

The rabbit is a gregarious animal, and, as is generally well known, usually lives in underground buries which it digs out for itself. A rabbit bury may house only a single family and have from two to half a dozen entrance and exit holes. On the other hand, a bury may accommodate a number of rabbit families, and some cover a considerable area of land, involving a vast network of tunnels. The writer has particularly in mind one in South Devon that covered over a hundred square yards and in which there were at least fifty holes. Apparently all these holes were connected, and nothing less than half a dozen ferrets worked at the same time would bolt a worthwhile proportion of the rabbits. Again, many large rabbit warrens, such as are seen on parts of Dartmoor, are composed of separate but contiguous buries of various sizes.

In their early days the doe rabbit disposes her young in a 'short' hole, cosily lined with grass, wool and other materials. This hole she carefully stops up with soil when she herself comes out to feed, opening it again on her return. At times this stopping is so well camouflaged that it is very difficult for the untrained eye to detect the hole at all.

The rabbit is an active and wary animal, and stalking a feeding rabbit to within gunshot is a good test for the beginner with a gun. The rabbit's trick of giving warning to its fellows below ground by thumping the earth with its hind feet has been disputed in some quarters, but as the result of personal observation the writer is convinced that not only is the trick a matter of fact, but that it works very well. The signal thus given is clearly received and appreciated by the rabbits below, and once the signaller dives underground one will usually have a long wait before another shows itself.

Strange as it may seem, rabbits are often seen in trees, particularly in hollow pollarded willow inside which the rabbits have regular runs. On several occasions the writer has shot rabbits looking out from holes in such trees.

Occasionally unusually coloured wild rabbits are seen. There are districts in which black ones are not uncommon, and now and then one comes across other abnormally coloured rabbits. Probably most of these colour aberrations are the result of crosses with tame rabbits, either escaped or liberated.

Many observers must have been struck by the fact that periodically rabbits seem to be unusually abundant, and that in other years they are very much less common. From careful observation extending over many years the writer agrees with those naturalists who assert that with the rabbit as with many other wild animals, there is a fairly regular cycle of increase, abundance and decline; the last usually appearing to be due to, or at least to be accompanied by, some epidemic disease such as coccidiosis. It seems probable that this cycle, although its progress may to some extent be hastened or retarded by extremes of weather, is not greatly affected by normal climatic conditions. The full period of the cycle has been assessed variously at from five to ten years, but probably six or seven years is a reasonably accurate estimate. On these assumptions, it is held by some that nature in due time adjusts the balance. That may be so, but it does not take into

Young rabbit (*Oryctolagus cuniculus*) on the alert.

account the years between a cyclical reduction and the next increase peak—years during which the rabbit can do an immense amount of damage to the farmer's crops. If following a drastic cyclical reduction one allows a year, or perhaps two, for a return to what may be a normal basic rabbit population, the rabbits will in the third year start to increase. In the fourth year their numbers will likely be such as to make them a nuisance to the farmer, and in the fifth, sixth or possibly subsequent years they may become a very serious pest. There should be open war on the rabbit every year and in all seasons, but in days gone by the rabbit destruction was often discontinued just at the time when the most intensive efforts should have been made; that is, when the reproduction cycle had reached its lowest level.

Under Section 98 of the Agriculture Act, 1947, farmers and other occupiers of land may be required to keep down rabbits on their premises. The good farmer will do his best to cope with his rabbits without any fear of the law or special incentive, but if he feels that the task is beyond his resources of time and labour, usually he can have his rabbits destroyed at reasonable cost by officers of the County Agricultural Executive Committee.

There are many ways of killing rabbits, the most generally popular of which is shooting, and of all forms of shooting the 'free-for all' which occurs when the last patch of corn is being reaped in a field is the most exciting. Many good shots, however, decline to take part in these affairs on the grounds that they themselves are as likely to become casualties as the rabbits. Certainly these shoots, unless well and carefully organized, can be a very real danger to the participants, and the writer has seen some in which the shooting was high, wide, but anything but handsome. Excitement in such circumstances seems to be contagious, and not infrequently the important fact that if men shoot from opposite sides of a patch of corn they are quite likely to send a few stray pellets in each other's directions, is forgotten in the heat of the moment. More important methods of destroying rabbits are trapping, snaring, ferreting, and, when conditions are right, the use of that valuable old instrument the long-net. But the surest and most economical way, where rabbits are concentrated in large numbers, is gassing. It has been stated by some that killing rabbits by gassing is uneconomic because the animals die in their buries and are not recoverable and so much food is lost to the community. This is surely the wrong way to look at it, since the saving of damage done by a rabbit is of far greater importance than its own potential value as food. A rabbit will make a meal for two or three people: that same rabbit in a year will destroy more food than three people could eat in a week. If rabbits can be put on to the food market, so much the better, but the first objective must be to destroy them as pests. If gassing is the surest way (and there is little doubt that in most cases it is), then that is the method which should be used in the interests of food production and of the community as a whole.

It is little use for one farmer to destroy rabbits on his land if his neighbours leave their rabbits to breed. Concerted action by area schemes of control are the most likely means to successful clearance, and farmers and landowners are urged to get together and plan schemes of this kind. County Committees are always willing to advise and help.

It was obvious by the early 1950s that the rabbit problem could be ignored no longer and government action was essential. In the event, it seemed that the problem had been solved by the introduction of myxomatosis. The virus named *Myxomatosis cuniculus* appeared to 'spread by accident' from France into the south-eastern counties and, from there, to the rest of the country and, by the middle 1950s, a kill of over 99% had resulted in some districts. The important thing about *Myxomatosis cuniculi* is that it is selective in its action and is therefore harmless to other forms of wildlife. In Britain, it was essential that the hare was not adversely affected since this was a valuable game animal. The existence of myxomatosis had been known since a series of experiments carried out in Montevideo by Saherelli in 1897. He successfully destroyed European rabbits with the virus but the problem was how to infect wild populations. R.M. Lockley attempted an introduction to his island of Skokholm in the late 1930s but without success. It was in Australia that the breakthrough occurred when it was found that a vector was needed

Rabbit with myxomatosis.

to transmit the virus and it was discovered that mosquitoes could be the essential agent. In Britain, it was eventually found to be spread via the rabbit flea (*Silopsyllus cuniculi*), and by pure chance this particular flea is not found on Skokholm, which explains Lockley's failure.

By the winter of 1956, the rabbit was almost—but not quite—extinct in Britain, but the manner of death, as the pus-filled swollen eyes of the dying animals flickered and closed, horrified all but a very hard-hearted minority. Public opinion was such that the people's servants in Westminster were forced to legislate against further spread of the disease. The rabbit in many districts was as rare as at any time since the Middle Ages and many prophesied its extinction. But they reckoned without the resilience of the species and old Brer Rabbit was not done yet. A very small number of individuals had some immunity to the disease and either recovered or did not succumb at all. This immune population has gradually increased and the disease has now lost much of its destructive capability and, when outbreaks do occur, the percentage kill is very much lower and falling all the time. There is now no doubt that *Oryctolagus cuniculus* is now well on the road to recovery and will very soon present a threat to agriculture. A similar virus attack will, I hope, not be countenanced by mankind a second time, and yet numbers must be controlled. This could be done by allowing a build-up of the natural predators and by making use of the richest source of animal protein by having a national campaign 'Drink Milk and Eat Rabbit'.

HARES

The Brown Hare *Lepus capensis*

The brown hare is also known as puss, sarah or the grass cat. It is about 500–600 mm ($19\frac{1}{2}$–24 in) long, with ears of another 100 mm (4 in), and weighs about 3.5 kg ($7\frac{3}{4}$ lb). The female is slightly heavier than the male. Pregnant females are found in every month but birth occurs mainly in April and May. The gestation period is 42 days and up to four litters a year are produced. The warm brown summer pelage is moulted out to produce a redder winter coat. There are two moults a year. The long ears are tipped with black and the tail is white except for a black stripe on the dorsal surface.

Thomas Bell (1837) pointed out the great similarity in the European vernacular names for this animal; in Britain we have our hare, the German's have their *Hase*, the Danes recognise the *haze* and the Swedes their *hara*. The Anglo-Saxon root of all these languages is also *hara* and this appears to have derived from their word for 'hair', which was *hoer*, signifying a hairy coat. Bell discounted a second suggested etymology deriving from the word *hergian*, which meant 'to harry'. Man has certainly been harrying the hare for some considerable time, as much of this chapter will show all to clearly.

Easily distinguished from the rabbit by its larger size, longer back legs and black-tipped ears, the hare most certainly warrants a place in the list of our indigenous fauna and remains are frequently found in the caves of prehistoric man. It is not a burrowing animal and therefore its remains can be considered as contemporary with material found at the same level. The fact that it was kept by Britons as pets is mentioned in writings of Julius Caesar dated at about 54 BC. He also reports that the animal was just as important a food item here as it was in Rome. Like rabbits, hares were kept captive in *leporaria* and were reported to be fed by a keeper who was able to call them to him by blowing a special type of horn. Its flesh was, however, forbidden both to Jews and Mohammedans since to them all animals which they thought chewed the cud were considered unclean. To have informed them that the hare did not chew the cud but merely consumed its own faeces would not, I venture to suggest, have persuaded them to change their view. This process of *refection* practiced by lagomorphs is essential to their survival. A purely vegetable diet is extremely difficult to digest and, by the time the meal has passed once through the gut, it is still moist and rich in undigested material and essential nutrients (see Chapter 1). These wet droppings are eaten and passed through the gut a second time when a goodly proportion of the remaining nutrients and water are extracted; the drier faecal pellets are this time ignored.

The hare has been an important creature of the chase for centuries and was listed in the top five beasts of the venery, namely the hart, hind, hare, boar and wolf. At one time, special sanctuaries were set apart to encourage the survival of the hare and Thorburn mentions a Tudor structure near Cheam in Surrey and another of several acres is listed as being near to Guildford; this was enclosed by high walls, complete with holes through which the hares could enter and leave but which could be stopped up.

The brown hare (*Lepus capensis*).

Opinions regarding the morals of hare coursing have been polarised for many years. Bell (1837) leaves us in no doubt as to where his sympathies lie:

Its hearing and sight are most acute; its timidity, if possible, greater, and its course swifter, than in any other. These qualities, combined with its excellence as an article of food, have rendered this poor harmless animal in all ages a favourite object of the chase; and the various doublings, and other ingenious devices, to which it resorts for the purpose of baffling its pursuers, give to Hare-hunting an interest and zest of which the timidity and innocence of the object would otherwise have deprived it. But, after all,
'Poor is the triumph o'er the timid Hare;'
and whatever excuses may be found for the pursuit of the Fox on the score of necessity, as ridding the country of a noxious animal,—an excuse, however, which can scarcely be made by those who forbid its destruction by any other means as an unpardonable offence against the sportsman's arbitrary code,—no such excuse can be made for this sport; whilst, on the other hand, the degree of danger and difficulty is scarcely sufficient to invest it with enough of excitement to conceal its character of cowardice and cruelty. It is true that coursing is in a degree less cruel, as the poor trembler's agony is comparatively short-lived; but it appears to me that mercy and humanity can scarcely consist with the ardent love of either variety of a sport, the whole interest of which depends upon the intense exertion to which a helpless and defenceless creature can be driven by the agonies of fear and desperation.

It was, however, very early an object of the chase. Xenophon, in his Cynegeticus, *enters with considerable minuteness, and no little zeal, into the detail of the sport . . . .*

In our own country it has always been a more general sport than either Stag or Fox hunting, because easily followed, with less expense and more certainty.

At the present time I do not believe we have any excuse for this barbaric practice. In times past, however, hunting the hare had more practical overtones since, apart from the palatable flesh, the skins were also used in the production of felt. Until fairly recent times, an industry based in the town of Stockport used the pelts of hares in the manufacture of bowler hats. The pelt was first treated with acid, which tended to produce a reddish colour in addition to making the felting process easier. The technical term for this was 'carroting'. Hares were also thought, in Britain at least, to be favourite witch 'familiars' and were hunted out of superstition as much as anything else. It must be admitted, however, that the prime object of hunting or coursing is the primitive urge of man the hunter to be in at the kill. The position of the hare in hunting circles is still one of importance as an extract from the *Shooting Times and Country Magazine* by John Buckland for May 29, 1980 clearly shows:

When the Conseil International de la Chasse held their 27th annual general meeting in Rome in early May an extra symposium was added by the Small

Game Commission. The subject was the European brown hare. Earlier in Shooting Times (May 8) I mentioned that there was a certain amount of doubt current in this country about the status of the hare, and since that article was published correspondence has come forward supporting the Game Conservancy's contention that there is a major decline.

In England the hare is not considered to be the most important of the game species (as it is in France), and the way in which it forms a quarry differs also from our European neighbours, but it does feature very largely in our country activities: in shooting, hare hunting and coursing. On many shooting days the hare is merely an incidental to other game, usually to partridges and pheasants: it is only in February and March that there is heavy pressure in the form of hare drives. The choice of these months lies partly because other game shooting has drawn to a close, partly because it is still legal in February to sell or expose for sale this species which has no close season, partly to control an agricultural pest just before its breeding gets under way, and partly, and this is the least of the reasons, it is a chance for a landowner to offer shooting hospitality to those who are not given opportunities at other game, which, as I have said, are more highly regarded than the hare.

A point which should be mentioned is that we in the United Kingdom have no central hunting organisation to which returns must be sent by law. This means that any figures from which study of the hare is made are sent entirely voluntarily and, needless to say, records are not always complete enough to offer the full picture.

The Game Conservancy is, however, extremely grateful to those who do provide them with figures and they certainly receive sufficient information to be quite sure that most of the country is at present undergoing a recognisable decline.

The same article also offers ample proof that there has been some decline in population since 1910 and that more research into the biology of the brown hare is essential. The actual study will never be so simple as that of the rabbit since the hare is a much more solitary animal and, in many cases, its distribution is at best described as local; many areas seem totally lacking in hares while other apparently very similar habitats abound with them. Despite a rather undeserved reputation for stupidity, hares can usually outmanouvre or outrun most predators and can even swim well when the occasion demands. A remarkable account of their swimming ability was recorded by Yarrell in the fifth volume of *Loudon's Magazine*, published in the 1820s:

A harbour of great extent on our southern coast, has an island near the middle of considerable size, the nearest point of which is a mile distant from the main land at high water, and with which point there is frequent communication by ferry. Early one morning in spring, two Hares were observe to come down from the hills of the main land towards the seaside; one of which from time to time, left its companion, and proceeding to the very edge of the water, stopped there a minute or two, and then returned to its mate. The tide was rising; and, after waiting some time, one of them, exactly at high water, took to the sea, and swam rapidly over, in a straight line, to the opposite projecting point of land. The observer on this occasion who was near the spot, but remained unperceived by the Hares, had no doubt that they were different sexes, and that it was the male that swam across the water, as he had probably done many times before. It was remarkable that the hares remained on the shore near half an hour; one of them occasionally examining as it would seem, the state of the current, and ultimately taking to the sea at that precise period of the tide called slack-water when the passage across could be affected without being carried by the force of the stream either above or below the point of landing. The other hare then cantered back to the hills.

If this typical example of poetic licence among natural historians of the period proves nothing else, it does demonstrate the hare's ability to swim well and this must stand it in good stead when being pursued. Hares do, however, seem on occasions to experience difficulty in locating an enemy, due almost certainly to the peculiar positioning of the eyes. These are so placed on either side of the head that the hare can detect an enemy approaching from the side and probably also from behind, but it is often unable to see straight ahead. Old-time poachers as well as modern-day naturalist-photographers and shooters know that to approach a hare head on is a much more reliable method of closing with their quarry. When a predator closes with a hare, it does not always achieve the desired effect because the powerful back legs can often deliver a fatal kick and it can also bite and scratch. There is also a record of a hard-pressed animal jumping a vertical height of some 2.5 m (8 ft)!

Not only does the brown hare differ in appearance from the rabbit, but its breeding behaviour is also significantly different. A favourite saying is to call someone as 'mad as a March Hare'. Although hares have been observed to copulate in all months of the year, it is during late winter and early spring that the full range of boxing antics between rival males and the high-speed chasings and uninhibited gyrations of buck in pursuit of doe reach a peak of frenzy. Young have been produced in every month of the year in Britain and the leverets are all born above ground. They emerge fully furred and with their eyes open and soon become self-sufficient. The young are placed in areas of flattened vegetation called 'forms' but the doe is careful not to deposit all her offspring in one place; instead she spreads them around in ones and twos (up to seven may be produced in one litter), visiting them all at intervals for the purpose of suckling. The instinct of the youngsters is to lie perfectly still to avoid predators. At least two litters a year are produced and, in some areas, quite large and potentially destructive populations can build up. The reproductive powers of the hare have long been a source of controversy and this has continued to the present day. It was once said that, as the animals emerged from Noah's Ark, the doe was drowned and, to compensate for this, God gave the buck the power to give birth. In the seventeenth century, Sir Thomas Browne, a physician from Norwich, tried to marry fact with religious myth and suggested that, although the sexes were separate, the male hare was able, on some occasions, to produce live young.

As usual fact is sometimes stranger that fiction and recent scientific investigation has resulted in the discovery of a fascinating phenomenon in the doe which has been called *superfoetation*. This means that it is possible for an already pregnant female to be fertilised and for the two pregnancies to continue without one hindering the other. In *The Handbook of British Mammals*, however, it is pointed out that this phenomenon is not common.

While the hare does not do as much damage as the rabbit there are times when 'puss' can be a nuisance and the 'barking' of trees, especially apple, pear, plum and damson can result in economic ruin for market gardeners. The animal can also cause problems in areas where wheat and sugar beet are grown. Remedies, often expensive, have been tried, including netting the bases or painting the bark with unpleasant chemicals. At one time, some success was achieved by laying out bunches of green twigs of uneconomic species between the fruit trees, the hares seemingly preferring to feed upon this 'bait' at ground level rather than to chew away at the tough old bark on the fruit trees.

Hares in the wild seem to live for 10 or 12 years, but until recently there has been no reliable method of ascertaining the age of an individual with any degree of certainty. It has now been found that, in most mammals, the dry weight of the eye lens increases with age and so, once a number of lenses have been extracted from experimental animals of known age, a weight scale can be drawn up and individual animals can be aged by reference to this scale.

Apart from what has been discovered with regard to the natural science of the animal there is also considerable folklore attached to it, in addition to its supposed connection with witchcraft mentioned earlier in this chapter. This folklore was summarised in *British Mammals* by Sir Harry Johnston in 1903:

> *The cunning and agility of the hare made a deep impression on early man, especially in Southern Europe and Africa. The hare enters into Grecian and Iranic fables, while in African folklore it is universal, and takes the place of the fox, the European emblem of astuteness and cunning. Elsewhere the hare is really the origin of 'Brer Rabbit.' The negro slaves imported from West Africa into the United States brought with them their beast stories and fables, in which the hare played such a prominent part. In the early days of American colonisation the white settlers called every hare a rabbit. The negroes, therefore, adopted this name for their equivalent to 'Reynard the Fox.'*

The etymology of the Aryan word for hare has a root meaning a 'jumper', which fits perfectly well, but the derivation of the Latin name *lepus* (from the original Greek) still eludes scholars. Thus 'puss', like the rest of our mammals, has secrets yet unfathomed and will continue to fascinate future naturalists just as much as it has their forebears.

The Mountain Hare *Lepus timidus*

The mountain hare is a smaller animal than *Lepus capensis*, only weighing some 2.7 kg (6 lb) at the most, whereas the brown hare can often exceed 4 kg (9 lb), there being occasional specimens of some 5 kg (12 lb). The blue hare, as this species is sometimes called, has shorter ears and legs and is therefore slower over the ground than its brown cousin. In winter, its bluish grey pelage is moulted out to be replaced by white, apart from the ear tips which remain black. In the southerly parts of the range the moult may not be complete and therefore the origin of the 'variable hare' referred to by early British naturalists is satisfactorily explained. The appearance of these animals is almost certainly responsible for the suggestion that interbreeding occurs between blue and brown hares, despite the fact that there is no evidence to support this contention. Like the brown hare, there seem to be two litters of young produced each year, but there are usually only three or four young born on each occasion.

The mountain hare (*Lepus timidus*) in summer (left) and winter (right).

The mountain hare does less damage to agriculture simply because it prefers to live at altitudes where arable farming is less important, although in hard weather it leaves the highlands and descends to the lower arable lands and earns the disfavour of the farmers. The brown hare (*Lepus capensis*) is not found in Ireland, despite attempts to introduce it, and this accounts for the confusion which once existed amongst taxonomists. In Bell's 1837 edition of *British Quadrupeds*, for example, two hares in addition to the brown hare are described, namely the Irish hare (*Lepus hibernicus*)

The mountain hare (*Lepus timidus*).

and the alpine or variable hare (*Lepus variabilis*), to which I have already referred. By the time Sir Harry Johnston had compiled his *British Mammals* (published in 1903), these two were recognised as the same species and described under Linnaeus' name for the species, *Lepus timidus*. Sir Harry fully describes its distribution at the turn of the century, in addition to providing a good field description:

In the summer-time, between April and November, the woolly, soft fur of the mountain hare is fulvous-gray, the under hair being almost bluish-gray, with longer hairs on the surface that are yellowish-brown. The backs of the ears are gray and the tips are black. The belly is dirty white, and the under parts generally range between gray and white in tint. . . . In the northern parts of Scotland the mountain hare assumes the snow-white coat which this animal bears during the winter season in the Alps and the Arctic regions. Only the tips of the ears remain black. But in Ireland (the mountain hare is extinct in England) this change to complete white is never known to occur. . . .

The mountain hare at the present day has its habitat in these islands reduced to Scotland and Ireland, but during the Pleistocene Epoch it equally inhabited England, where, indeed, it seems to have preceded the arrival of the common hare.

Recent work has resulted in the recognition of two subspecies, namely *Lepus timidus scoticus*, the Scottish mountain hare, and its close relative from Ireland, *Lepus scoticus hibernicus*. There have also been partially successful introductions into the outer isles of Scotland, the Isle of Man, near Bangor in North Wales round about 1885, and at several points in the Pennines. The English introductions have been well documented by Coward (1910), Stubbs (1929), Hewson (1956) and, more recently, by Yalden (1971). An unspecified number of animals were introduced into the Penistone district in about 1870, twenty onto Saddleworth Moor in 1876 and, in 1880 a further fifty alpine hares were released at Greenfield near Oldham. Although the signs are that their range is diminishing, these populations still hang on and I have frequently watched them in the latter two areas. In winter, they are easily distinguished from the common hare, but in the summer there can be a problem. Yalden, however, providing a vital pointer to field identification, mentions that the bob-tail of the mountain hare is all white in every season whilst that of the brown hare has some black on the upper surface but is white below.

Work on hares in the Isle of Man was studied by Susan Fargher (1977). She reports on the statement of Garrad (1972), in which it is suggested that there is a considerable overlap in range between the species. From her researches, Fargher compiled a map on which she plotted sightings of both species and this certainly suggests that the ranges of the two seem to be discreet. She also summarises the status of both species in the Isle of Man:

The origin of hares on the Isle of Man is not known, and in the early literature there is confusion regarding the specific names (Kermode 1893; Kermode 1917). Garrad (1972) suggests that the Brown hare is a native to the island, but there is no firm evidence that this is so. Some bones of Mesolithic age have been referred to L. capensis but both the dating and identification are open to doubt. Barret-Hamilton (1910) suspected the introduction of the Brown hare to the island, but knew of no records to support this. However, Kermode (1917) states that the Stanleys who were granted the Lordship of Man in 1405 introduced Brown hares for sporting purposes. The present population is believed to have descended from these animals, augmented by various other unrecorded introductions. It would seem that the presence of Mountain hares is the result of a recent introduction since Barret-Hamilton makes no mention of L. timidus on the island and Garrad (1972) states that the introduction of these animals in the nineteenth century was a failure. A subsequent attempt resulted in successful colonisation of the central hill region (Garrard 1972).

From my own, albeit more superficial, investigation in the Pennines, it would seem that the two species of hare are seldom found in the same habitat and thus one of nature's cardinal rules is obeyed. This postulates that two similar species are unable to survive together in an identical habitat without one or the other becoming extinct. This habitat is termed the 'ecological niche'. This phenomenon can also be seen to apply in the case of our two squirrels, which are discussed in the next chapter.

6 Rodents: Squirrels and Voles

Squirrels belong to the rodent order, but this is so diverse that taxonomists have divided it into three sub-orders. These are the Myomorpha, which includes the rats, mice and voles, the Hystricomorpha, which includes the porcupine and that popular pet the guinea-pig (which, incidentally, is mentioned in scathing terms in Bell's 1837 edition of *A History of British Quadrupeds*) and the Sciuromorpha, which itself includes nearly 1400 species. In Britain, one family, the Sciuridae, occurs and is represented by one native and one introduced species. These two animals and our three native species of vole form the main subjects of this chapter while the other British rodents are described in Chapter 7.

Grey and red squirrels compared. Note the ear tufts on the red squirrel and the rounded ears of the grey species.

OPPOSITE: The red squirrel (*Sciurus vulgaris*).

SQUIRRELS

Most rodents are small and therefore have not often been found as fossils until the more diligent searchings recently proved them to have been a dominant force for at least 20 million years. Squirrels have long been used as food items by man, but have also figured prominently in religion and were kept as pets by society ladies of Ancient Rome. In the old Norse religion, the sacred tree was the ash which was the home of the mighty god Yggdrasil. Keeping watch on the crown of the tree was an eagle and down in the roots of 'hell' was a flesh-eating serpent called Niddhogg. The human race occupied the middle regions and the squirrel's job was to carry messages up and down the tree. In Indo-Germanic religions, the red squirrel was associated with Donar, the god of thunder. Early Christians had a hard task to convert believers in these pagan religions to the true faith and squirrel-hunting rituals evolved with the object of killing the poor beasts just to prove that they were mortal.

The Red Squirrel *Sciurus vulgaris*

As I have just suggested squirrels are an ancient family and were in existence by the Pleistocene period. It is highly probable that they reached Britain via the land bridge from the continent at this time. (In 7000 BC, melting ice raised the sea level and finally made Britain into an island.) Some fossil remains of squirrels, which may well have been red ones, were found, together with some chewed and obviously contemporary fir cones, in caves rich in bones. Identification is most easily based upon dental formula and tooth structure. The formula is:

$$2 \times \left\{ I\,\frac{1}{1} \quad C\,\frac{0}{0} \quad PM\,\frac{2}{1} \quad M\,\frac{3}{3} \right\} = 22.$$

Hinton, on the evidence of the structure of a premolar tooth found in deposits from the Late Pliocene, thought that they were from a distinct species, *Sciurus whitei*, which may mean that Britain was once richer in squirrel species than it is at present. In historical times, there does not appear to be any real record of more than one species of squirrel native to Britain. This is the common European squirrel, *Sciurus vulgaris*, and early naturalists did not consider the British squirrel to be any different from the continental form. Then, in 1761, Thomas Pennant wrote of a 'beautiful variety with milk white tails'. In 1792, Kerr defined *Sciurus vulgaris leucourus*. He gave us no other character except the white tail by which we could separate this subspecies, as we now regard it, from the continental red squirrels and, for the next century, naturalists continued to regard bleached individuals only as a distinct variety among the British red squirrels. In 1897, a paper on the bleaching process was published by Thomas and, since this time, it has become much more common to see the name 'light-tailed squirrel' applied to red squirrels native to Britain. The tail is obviously the animal's most significant feature and, in Greek, the word *sciurus* means 'shade-tail' and our word 'squirrel' has come from the Norman-French derivative of the original Greek via Latin.

Although there is little documentary evidence concerning the red squirrel in the Middle Ages, Harvie-Brown made reference to red squirrels depicted on runic stones at both Ruthwell and Bewcastle, probably relating to the Scandinavian mythology discussed earlier, and some thirteenth-century stained glass at Bowness-in-Cumbria shows a squirrel. Barret-Hamilton also unearthed some interesting information from his study of skins exported from Ireland and finds squirrels listed as early as 1243 but, after the end of the fifteenth century, there is no further mention until about 1815. A Welsh hunting text, dated about 1560, lists what is probably the wild cat as 'the grey-climber', the polecat as 'the black-climber' and the squirrel as 'the red-climber'.

The distribution of the red squirrel in Britain has been extensively researched and the position with regard to Ireland is particularly interesting. There are no accounts of fossils being discovered there, but it is probable that some animals reached Ireland from Scotland before rising sea levels separated the two countries; it does, however, seem to have been extinct from the fifteenth to the begining of the nineteenth century, when re-introductions began. Even in Scotland, the red squirrel seems to have come very close to extinction—the last known record of them in Sutherland is in 1630, according to Harvie-Brown, but Fraser-Darling says that a few persisted in southeast Sutherland in 1793, in Moray 1775, in Ross and Cromarty in 1792 and in Dumbarton in 1776. There are no records of them in Angus in 1813 or in Aberdeenshire in 1843.

It seems probable that the main cause of their demise was the widespread forest destruction; large areas were cleared for cultivation and for sheep pasture, others were burned to rid the area of wolves or for the smelting of iron. Just at the time the Scottish squirrels were feeling the pinch, a series of very severe winters caused a further reduction in their numbers. The year 1740 was, apparently, particularly cold and 1788–89, 1795 and 1797–98 were not much better. There is just a chance that some epidemic may have played its part but Monica Shorten, who searched diligently through the literature of these times, doubts this. In England and Wales, timber demands, especially during the Civil War of the 1640s, must have affected the red squirrel to some extent but it never seems to have approached extinction. Conifer species began to be introduced at the end of the eighteenth and the beginning of the nineteenth century. As this century progressed and the woodlands matured, the squirrel population increased and, by 1890, red squirrels were particularly abundant, reaching pest proportions in some areas. There is some suggestion of abundance in the 1837 edition of White's *Natural History of Selbourne*, in a note made by the Rev. William Herbert who states that not less than 20 000 red squirrels were sold annually in London markets:

I was much surprised at hearing from a man who kept a bird and cage shop in

London, that not less than 20,000 squirrels are sold there for the menus plaisirs of cockneys, part of which come from France, but the greater number are brought into Newgate and Leadenhall markets where any morning during the season four or five hundred may be bought. He said that he himself sold annually about 700 and he added that once every 7 years the breed of squirrels entirely fails, but that in other seasons they are equally prolific . . . the mere manufacture of squirrel cages for Londoners is no small concern.

From this account it seems that a goodly number of continental squirrels were being imported each year, some of which probably found their way from captivity into the local countryside. Harvie-Brown, however, produced a paper in 1880 and, in a footnote, he makes reference to the statistics quoted above, pointing out that:

Mssrs Jamrach and Castang, well known importers of live animals . . . assure him that no such immense sales of squirrels ever took place in London as the quoted account says.

Thus controversy as in all history, natural or otherwise, reigns supreme!

One thing is, however, quite obvious and that is, by 1880, Britain had no need to import red squirrels, but could well have benefited from some movement in the opposite direction! By 1880, control measures were essential, not only in England but also in Scotland. In 1903, the Highland Squirrel Club was formed in an attempt to control the rising populations on the large estates. In the first 30 years, this club destroyed nearly 85 000 red squirrels! At this point, however, nature played her traditional hand in controlling numbers and, by the mid-1920s, the population was decimated. Some recovery was observed by 1930, but there was another sharp decline during World War II, probably due mainly to a reduction in habitat. Although epidemic diseases have been suggested, this is not considered to have been the main cause, although it may well have been a contributory factor. Yet another reason given is direct interference by the introduced grey squirrel, which has been accused of killing and eating the smaller red. This is not now believed to be true, but the grey squirrel does adapt more quickly to a new habitat and, when replanting occurs, it can prevent the red squirrel returning by defending its territory too fiercely for it to gain a pawhold. Before considering the inter-relationships between the red and grey squirrel, it will be best to describe the history of the latter species in Britain since its introduction from North America. Table 6 provides a physical comparison between the two species.

The Grey Squirrel *Sciurus carolinensis*

The specimens I have seen were as large as a polecat, or three quarters of a grown rabbit; the head roundish, the eyes very prominent, the ears shorter than the common red squirrel and not the slightest appearance of tufts on them; the body

The grey squirrel (*Sciurus carolinensis*) descending a tree trunk.

and legs of a fine grey colour, the latter short and muscular and furnished with strong claws; there is a beautiful variegation of red along the side of the ribs, from the elbow to the hind legs; the tail is covered with hair rather longer than in the common sort, and of a mixture of grey and black.

Table 6   COMPARISON OF RED AND GREY SQUIRRELS

Common Name	Scientific Name	Average Weight	Average Body Length	Average Tail Length	Breeding Habits	Appearance
red squirrel	*Sciurus vulgaris*	300 g (10½ oz). No significant sex difference.	210 mm (8¼ in)	180 mm (7 in)	Early in year but influenced by food and weather. Can be 2 litters a year. About 40 days' gestation.	Summer coat: chestnut red. Winter coat: thicker and darker. Tail light in British animals.
grey squirrel	*Sciurus carolinensis*	520 g (18 oz). No significant sex difference.	260 mm (10 in)	210 mm (8¼ in)	Early in year but influenced by food and weather. Usually 2 litters a year (1 in yearling females). 43 days' gestation.	Summer coat: short glossy grey. Winter coat: silver grey with brown on head and flanks.

This reads like a very accurate field description of *Sciurus carolinensis* and yet it appeared in the *Cambrian Quarterly* magazine of 1830 and relates to an animal shot in Denbighshire, and thus pre-dating by some 36 years the records of introductions compiled first by Middleton in the 1930s and then by Shorten in the 1950s. These workers, however, deal only with known and deliberate introductions, which began in 1876 when a Mr Brocklehurst brought a pair from America and set them at liberty in Henbury Park, Cheshire. This seems to have begun a chain reaction, part of which I have documented in Table 7. It can be seen from this that only one of the introductions was a positive failure and clearly shows how easily the grey squirrel adapted to our environment. In scientific terms, we say that the animal had found an ideal ecological niche and it was certainly not slow to exploit it.

Soon the novelty of the 'new grey pet' began to wear off as the 'tree rat' proved a prolific breeder and country folk saw the results of the activities of the beast. The anti-grey squirrel campaign was soon launched, but in 1931 a catastrophic fall in population was noted and autopsies revealed the presence of coccidiosis, an intestinal infection caused by an organism called *Eimeria*. Middleton was of the opinion that it was this disease, plus the failure of the beech mast crop in the winter of 1930–31, which caused the deaths of many animals. The setback was, however, only temporary and the population recovered and the expansion of range and population still continues today. Workers interested in population studies express what has happened here, and also what has happened to other species finding a suitable niche, in the form of graphs (see Fig. 23). In the initial stages, the population builds up slowly and then expands quickly until competition for space and food results in a stable population, which is the maximum which

Table 7   INTRODUCTION OF GREY SQUIRRELS 1876–1930

Date	Place of Introduction	Origin of Stock	Number of Animals Introduced	Result
1876	Henbury, Cheshire by T.V. Brocklehurst	America	4 (1 pair possibly 2)	Increased
1889	Bushey, Middlesex	America	5	Failed to establish
1890	Woburn, Bedfordshire	America	10	Greatly increased as shown below
1892	Benenden, Kent	Canada	3	Increased
1892	Nuneham, Oxfordshire	Woburn	3	Increased
1896	Loch Long, Scotland	Canada	3	Increased
1902	Richmond, Surrey	America	100	Increased
1903	Wrexham, Denbighshire	Woburn	5	Increased
1903–4	Lyme, Cheshire	Unknown	25	Increased
1905–7	Regents Park, London	Woburn	91	Increased
1906	Malton, Yorkshire	Woburn	36	Increased
1906	Clivedon, Bucks.	Woburn	36	Increased
1908	Kew Gardens, London	Woburn	4	Increased
1908	Farnham Royal, Bucks	America	4	Increased
1909	Farnham Royal, Bucks	America	5	Increased
1910	Frimley, Surrey	America	8	Increased
1910	Dunham, Cheshire	America	2	Increased
1910	Sandling, Kent	America	2	Increased
1911–12	Bramhall, Cheshire	Woburn	5	Uncertain
1912	Birmingham	Woburn	5	Increased
1913	Castle Forbes, Ireland	Woburn	8	Increased
1913	Bedale, Yorkshire	Woburn	8	Increased
1914	Bingley, Yorkshire	London	14	Slight increase
1914–15	Darlington	London	14	Increased
1915	Exeter	London	4	Increased
1918	Stanwick, Northants	London	2	Increased
1919	Dunfermline, Scotland	London	2	Increased
1919	Bournemouth, Hampshire	London	6	Increased
1921	Hebden Bridge, Yorkshire	London	8	Slight increase
1921	Edinburgh	London	8	Doubtful, but numerous these days (1980)
1922	Aberdare, Glamorgan	London	8	Slight increase
1929	Needwood Forest	Bournemouth	2	By 1930 still no positive result one way or the other. Almost certainly successful.

After Middleton and Shorten (1938, 1953).

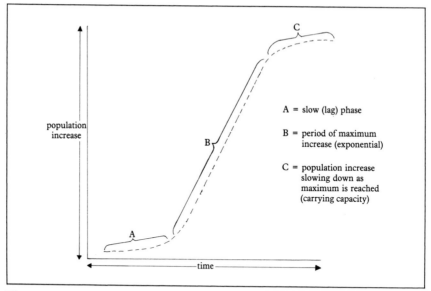

Figure 23. Graph to show the growth of a grey squirrel population.

can be supported by the environment. This is termed its 'carrying capacity'. Because the grey squirrel has found few competitors and man has reduced the numbers of its potential predators and is planting new habitat, it is still in the exponential phase and will continue to be so unless some check is imposed upon it, a fact which was realised in an H.M.S.O. document published for farmers as long ago as the late 1940s:

There seems to be no precise information as to range and population of the grey squirrel during the war years 1939–45, but at the present time it is certainly much too common for the good of agriculture. Whatever may be said of the red squirrel (which admittedly cannot honestly be described as harmless) there is no doubt as to the character of the grey, and not only is the latter one of the worst pests that we have, but in this respect is probably inferior only to the brown rat and the rabbit. Unlike the red squirrel, it prefers deciduous woods, but is also frequently seen in orchards, gardens and open parkland. It spends a good deal of its time on the ground, and many specimens have been bolted from rabbit buries. There is one instance known to the writer where a litter of grey squirrels was actually born in a rabbit bury, although as a rule the young are born in a drey rather like that of the red squirrel and similarly situated.

There are few things that the grey squirrel will not eat, either animal or vegetable. It takes fruits of many kinds, both wild and cultivated, corn, roots, leaves and shoots of plants and trees. In spring it does much harm by stripping the bark from trees. On one estate in Sussex in 1942 nearly two acres of good wheat were ruined by grey squirrels, and on this same estate 300 squirrels were shot in one week and 800 in one summer. A gardener of the Writer's acquaintance had nearly the whole of his stock of spring bulbs uprooted by grey squirrels, and another had some fine espalier pear trees stripped from top to bottom—bark, leaves and all. A host of farmers, market gardeners and others have reported depredations as bad or even worse than these.

Bird-lovers have good cause to dislike the grey squirrel. From a hide the writer once watched a grey squirrel make four successive visits to a hedge-sparrow's nest, each time taking away a young bird. This sort of thing is quite common.

Some time ago, a writer who sought to defend the grey squirrel undeterred by the great mass of reliable evidence against it, stated that this animal's habit of taking eggs and young wild birds and its visits to gardens, etc., had been 'cunningly chosen' to attract the attention of the layman. There is not the slightest need to choose any of the grey squirrel's depredations for special comment, for every experienced field naturalist knows that its harmful activities are not mere aberrations but are common and widespread, and that it well deserves all the hard things that have been said of it.

What chiefly concerns all who know this animal's true character is the question of how to cope with it. Extermination is difficult if not impossible, but much can be done to reduce its numbers by shooting and trapping. Cage traps, suitably baited, seem to be most successful in autumn or winter. Shooting can be carried on all the year round, as the grey squirrel is not a true hibernator and may be seen

The grey squirrel (*Sciurus carolinensis*) drinking.

out and active during mild weather in winter, but the best time for shooting is early spring, before the foliage of the trees becomes too dense. In a Kentish wood, in one afternoon, with a companion the writer once shot 34 grey squirrels. Probably the best weapon is a 'four-ten' or a 28-bore shot-gun. It is a good plan to put a charge or two of shot into any new grey squirrel's drey found in spring, and for this purpose the heavier and much more powerful 12-bore is more suitable.

Since this was written, the expansion has slowed a little but Scotland and Ireland are being gradually colonised and this obviously poses some threat to the red squirrel still holding its own in the developing coniferous forests. The question of direct competition between the two species deserves some consideration.

The grey squirrel is certainly becoming more common whilst the range of the red squirrel has been shrinking. It is obvious that, if the grey squirrel had never been introduced, then the red squirrel would find it easier to recover, but whether the grey actually contributes by direct interference is open to question. There have been frequent mentions in the literature of grey squirrels seeking out and killing juvenile and even adult red squirrels, but the weight of recent scientific opinion is convinced that such isolated behaviour cannot account for the present state of imbalance. Another oft-expressed theory is that the grey squirrel introduced some particularly virulent strain of disease from North America to which it had acquired resistance. The red squirrel of Britain, faced with the disease for the first time, had no such immunity and easily succumbed. This may well have been a contributary factor but it seems that the red squirrel's naturally see-sawing population may have been responsible for its own downfall. In an environment with only one specialised species, a population crash every 7 years or so is quickly corrected by the offspring of subsequent years moving back into depopulated areas, which have thus had a chance to get over the effects of heavy grazing. But what happens if a similar but larger species appears, showing no periodic fluctuations and with a capacity for producing more offspring than the native beast? This effect, although more subtle, can be much more destructive to the red squirrel than downright aggression. The grey squirrel simply moves in to empty habitat and then prevents any red squirrel from returning.

There is, however, a refuge for the red squirrel in the form of the increasing and developing conifer plantations of both private landowners and the Forestry Commission. Grey squirrels have not yet worked out a totally successful survival strategy for life in a coniferous woodland and, provided that this situation continues, then the future of *Sciurus vulgaris* would seem to be assured.

In contrast to this struggle for survival between the squirrel species, our native voles have been together long enough to work out strategies which ensure peaceful co-existence and, as long as no new species is introduced, this is likely to continue.

VOLES

The British voles (see Table 8) can be distinguished from mice by their rounder muzzles which make them a more 'friendly choice' for writers of children's animal stories. They also have more powerful bodies, smaller ears and shorter, stouter tails. The teeth are open-rooted, or almost so. Three species are widespread and common (apart from in Ireland): the bank vole, the short-tailed field vole and the water vole. There is also the Orkney or Guernsey vole (*Microtus arvalis*), which is only distinguishable from *Microtus agrestis* by a terminal inward-facing loop on the second molar teeth. Corbet (1961) suggests that these animals may well have been introduced from Iberia to the islands concerned, perhaps some 5000 years ago by traders.

Table 8 BRITISH VOLES

Common Name	Other Common Names	Scientific Name	Average Head and Body Length	Average Tail Length	Distribution
bank vole	red-backed vole, wood vole, red vole	*Clethrionomys glareolus*	100 mm (4 in)	40 mm ($1\frac{3}{5}$ in)	Throughout mainland Britain. Discovered in S.W. Ireland and is spreading—almost certainly due to un-recorded introduction. Absent from Isle of Man.
field vole	short-tailed field vole, short-tailed field mouse, meadow mouse	*Microtus agrestis*	110 mm ($4\frac{1}{2}$ in)	40 mm ($1\frac{3}{5}$ in)	Throughout British Isles except Ireland and Isle of Man.
water vole	water rat	*Arvicola terrestris*	200 mm (8 in)	120 mm) ($4\frac{4}{5}$ in)	Absent from Ireland, Isle of Man, N.W. Scotland and the isles.

The Bank Vole *Clethrionomys glareolus*

This species, also known as the red vole, has been discovered in fossil deposits from Kent's Cavern near Torquay, Wookey Hole, Glamorgan, Brixham cave in Devon and in the famous 'forest beds' of Norfolk. These date back to the Pleistocene period.

The species was described by Baillon, the French naturalist, under the name of *Arvicola agrestis* but the first British description was given in the *Proceedings of the Zoological Society* for 1832 by Yarrell. He called it *Arvicola riparia*. Bell, in his 1837 edition of *A History of British Quadrupeds*, calls it *Arvicola pratensis*, but in the second edition (1870) this was changed to *Arvicola glareolus* and, in Lydekker's *Mammals* of 1896, the name given was *Microtus glareolus*. It is now included in the genus *Clethrionomys* on the

A pair of bank voles (*Clethrionomys glareolus*).

grounds that it differs from the other voles in having semi-rooted molar teeth; these are less well adapted to the consumption of tough vegetation. Thus they are often found in different habitats from the short-tailed vole which has a 'tougher' dentition. Lydekker's description of the habits of the bank vole reflects the character very well. He says that the habits of the bank vole and short-tailed vole are similar:

. . . but whereas the latter is essentially an inhabitant of the open fields, the former is more partial to sheltered situations, often frequenting gardens, where it does

much damage by devouring the bulbs [sic] *of crocuses and newly-sown peas and beans. Mr. Roper writes that its favourite haunts 'are old rough ivy-covered hedgebanks, especially those from which the soil has been washed away in places, leaving the roots bare, and thus forming hollows behind them; banks adjoining woods and plantations seem particularly attractive to them. In spots like this, pleasingly varied by a sprinkling of mossy old stubs, brambles, and bushes, with the roots of overhanging trees backed by deep cavernous recesses, the Bank-Vole makes its burrow, and forms runs in all directions, partly above and partly below the surface; probably also making use of those of the Mole. I have caught them, too, among artificial rock-work, and in a plantation in which are banks thickly covered with the lesser periwinkle, among the roots and stems of which they had formed numerous runs.'*

Bell states that the Bank-Vole is more omnivorous in its habits than the common Field-Vole, and that it is less addicted to burrowing; while it is even more frequently seen abroad during the daytime. Its food comprises almost all kinds of vegetable substances; and it is probable that insects are also occasionally eaten. In addition to the harm inflicted on roots and bulbs, the Bank-Vole often does much damage to the bark of fruit-and other trees, more especially in the spring and winter. In parts of Scotland these animals have seriously damaged young larch-plantations by their ravages on the bark and buds.

Recent work on the bank vole has shown it to be distributed throughout England, Wales and mainland Scotland, but absent from most of the outer islands, the Isle of Man and apart from the records mentioned in Table 8, absent from Ireland. Work done by Jeffries and French (1972) reveals a significant increase of lead in the bodies of animals captured near main roads compared with those sampled from rural areas and studies similar to this will doubtless become important in future years, if for no other reason than this pattern must also be repeated in the human species.

The Short-tailed Field Vole *Microtus agrestis*

Of all the smaller Rodentia which, by their depredations in the fields or the woods, may be considered as injurious to mankind, there is not one which produces such extensive destruction as this little animal, when its increase, as is sometimes the case, becomes multitudinous. The nature of its food, which, like that of the rest of the genus, is exclusively of a vegetable kind, prevents it from becoming domesticated amongst us, and drives it to the wood, the corn-field, the rick-yard, and the granary; in each of which, but especially in the former two, its ravages are sometimes excessively extensive. Whilst the Field Mouse confines itself principally to drier situations, the present species frequents meadows and damp pastures, but by no means restricting itself to such localities. After having followed the labours of the reaper, and taken their share of the harvest, they attack the newly-sown fields, burrowing beneath the surface, and robbing the husbandman of his next year's crop; and at length, retreating to the woods and plantations, commit such devastations on the young trees as would scarcely be

The short-tailed field vole (*Microtus agrestis*).

credible, were not the evidence too certain to be doubted. In the years 1813 and 1814, these ravages were so great in the New Forest and the Forest of Dean, as to create considerable alarm lest the whole of the young trees in those extensive woods should be destroyed by them.

This account of a vole plague, recorded in 1837 by Bell, reads very much like an account of the hordes of lemmings which build up at regular intervals in northern Europe. This is not surprising, however, since lemmings are related to the voles and their remains have been identified as fossils in

Pleistocene deposits of south-eastern Britain. A similar vole plague to the one described above did enormous damage in Scotland during 1891–92, but regular periods of peak density occur at approximately 4-year intervals. At these times, their teeth can literally gnaw into a farmer's profits. Like the rest of the voles, the dental formula is:

$$2 \times \left\{ I \frac{I}{I} \quad C \frac{O}{O} \quad PM \frac{O}{O} \quad M \frac{3}{3} \right\} = 16.$$

The factors responsible for the population fluctuations have been subject to much research, but so far few tangible results have been produced. One of the most attractive theories, or so it seems to me, is that predators, such as the fox, weasel, stoat and birds of prey, have been drastically reduced in recent centuries and so one natural brake may have been removed. This is not, however, the only factor involved and neither does it account for the sudden crash in the population of this attractive rodent. This may be due to stresses and actual fighting as population levels become intolerable and food and breeding sites become impossible to find. It is certain that some natural restraints are imposed in the form of a build-up in predator populations, particularly those of the short-eared owl (*Asio flammeus*). In his monumental work, *British Birds*, William Yarrell and others note:

... *field mice and especially those of the short-tailed group or voles are their chief objects of prey, and when these animals increase in an extraordinary and unaccountable way, as they sometimes do, so as to become extremely mischievous, Owls, particularly of these species flock to devour them. Thus there are records of a 'sore plague of strange mice' in Kent and Essex in the year 1580 or 1581, and again in the county last mentioned in 1648. In 1754 the same thing is said to have occurred at Hilgay near Downham Market in Norfolk, whilst within the present century the Forest of Dean in Gloucestershire and some parts of Scotland have been similarly infested. In all these cases Owls are mentioned as thronging to the spot, and rendering the greatest service in extirpating the pests.... An additional fact was noticed by Wolley, namely that under such circumstances the Owls seem to become more prolific than usual, and on two occasions it came to his knowledge that as many as seven eggs must have been laid in one nest.*

The breeding of *Microtus agrestis* is not continuous throughout the year, but there are records of young being born in every month of the year; the peak is reached during early summer. From early April until well into November, a female may produce a succession of litters, each consisting of four to six young. The breeding cycle seems to be initiated not by temperature but by the number of hours of daylight; this is technically referred to as the *photoperiod*. The young born during spring in the snug nest at the base of a grass tussock are capable of breeding in autumn, but the life expectancy is very short, seldom longer than a year. Few individuals ever reach the breeding stage because *Microtus agrestis* faces predators on every hand, being a vital link in the food chain between the energy-producing vegetation

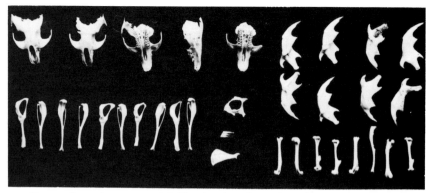

Bones of wood mouse and field vole taken from the pellets of a tawny owl.

and the hungry carnivores. These include weasels, stoats, domestic cats and many birds, including herons, kestrels and all of the five common species of British owl—the tawny, short-eared, long-eared, barn and little owls. An analysis of the pellets which are produced by these species reveals the presence of many small mammals. The owls cannot digest bones or teeth; these are regurgitated and can be assigned to recognisable species.

The short-tailed field vole is a greyish brown animal with a blunt snout, small ears and eyes. Its colouration does show quite considerable variation, but it is never as red as the bank vole. There are also differences in dentition since the molar teeth of the short-tailed field vole are open-rooted and thus can be renewed as fast as they are worn away; these teeth also have angular areas on the grinding surface, a feature lacking in the molars of the bank vole. In Ireland, this bank vole is only present in the southwest but the field vole does not occur at all in this green and pleasant land. The next species to be described, the water vole, is also absent from Ireland.

The Water Vole *Arvicola terrestris*

This is one of our most ancient mammals and recognisable fossils have been found in the Pleistocene brick-earths of the Thames valley as well as in the forest beds of Norfolk and a number of caverns. The scientific name, *Arvicola terrestris*, is in many ways surprising; *Arvicola* derives from the Latin *arvum* which means 'a ploughed field' and *colo* which means 'living in'. Now we come to the word *terrestris* which, again, has a Latin root and means 'of the ground'. Whilst it is true that this is an animal which burrows in the ground, it shows a distinct preference for river and stream, despite the scientific name suggesting the contrary A more attractive name, it seems to me, would be *Arvicola amphibia*, which was in use in the taxonomic circles of 1835. The vernacular name of water rat is likewise incorrect, since the water vole is a harmless herbivore compared to the eat-anything, disease-spreading, introduced brown rat. There are occasional records of water voles eating carrion, particularly fish, but this behaviour is most unusual.

The water vole (*Arvicola terrestris*).

Some controversy has been generated in taxonomic circles regarding how many species make up the genus *Arvicola* but, according to Corbet and other recent workers, there would seem to be only two, namely *Arvicola sapidus*, found in France and Spain, and the widely distributed *Arvicola terrestris*, which is the one British species. At one time it was thought that two species were present here, but even as long ago as 1837, Bell was expressing doubts about this:

A black variety of this species has long been known, and has been described by Pallas, and by several other Continental zoologists. It is probably identical with the animal described by Mr. Macgillivray in the sixth volume of the Transactions of the Wernerian Society of Edinburgh, under the name of Arvicola ater. *According to that gentleman's account, it is exceedingly common in the counties of Banff and Aberdeen; and it is said that the common Water Vole is not found where this one abounds. Its habits are similar to those of the former; but Mr. Macgillivray believes that there exist sufficient differences in the organisation and colour of the two to constitute them distinct species. It is of a deep black colour above, and black with a greyish tinge beneath. It is smaller than the brown one; but the proportions are not conspicuously, if at all different. This author believes the number of caudal vertebræ to be different; and were this constantly the case, it would go far to establish their specific distinction: but an examination of a stuffed specimen belonging to my friend Mr. Yarrell does not, on a comparison with several of the common sort, appear to me to justify this supposition. Mr. Jenyns states that 'the black variety is not uncommon in the fens of Cambridgeshire, and differs in no respect from the other but in colour;'—a testimony which must weigh very heavily against the opinion of its being specifically distinct, when we consider the great accuracy of that gentleman's observation.*

This black variety is still found in both Scotland and parts of Cambridgeshire. The water vole is a very wary animal and approaching the animal closely is not easy. It is well worth the effort, however, for there are few British mammals which are so attractive in their habits. Imagine a stroll along the banks of a meandering river on a balmy summer evening and meeting 'Mr Ratty' of *Wind in the Willows* fame, sitting up on his haunches, chewing stems of water plants like a child sampling celery for the first time. In complete contrast to the other British voles, this species presents few threats to agricultural interests. Just occasionally, their tunnels can cause sections of a river or canal bank to collapse and this may result in minor flooding. They may pay the occasional clandestine visit to vegetable gardens or fields of crops, much to the annoyance of the green-fingered brigade, both amateur and professional. There are also a few isolated records of water voles barking trees but on balance, 'Ratty' is a decorative asset to the country scene and is never found in the plague proportions reached by the bank vole and particularly the short-tailed field vole.

This may be due to the fact that only one (two at the most) litter of four or five young is produced each year. The litter size is difficult to calculate with any certainty because the breeding nest is often situated below ground, except in areas such as fens and marshes where the water table is very high, in which case the nest may be sited beneath tufts of grass or rushes. Breeding seldom begins before April and reaches a peak during the summer months. *Arvicola terrestris* has a longer life expectancy than the short-tailed field vole and can live for up to 5 years, although many are taken by predators during the early days of their independence. When they leave the comfort of their natal nest, they are only about half-grown; some are taken by pike, others by mink and stoats. Experience brings safety but it is often hard-earned. Water voles can, however, defend themselves with great ferocity and Trevor Smith, who has successfully bred the species in captivity, always insists on wearing thick protective gloves when handling his 'pets'. The species was described in detail by Lydekker in 1896:

The Water-Vole has the body full; the neck very short; the head short, broad, rounded, and convex above; the limbs small; and the tail rather long and slender. The short and rounded ears are entirely concealed among the thick fur, and are naked internally, and thinly covered with soft hairs externally; the aperture of the internal ear being capable of being closed by an operculum. On the fore-feet the claws are greatly compressed, but in the hind-limbs are longer; while in

*neither are the toes webbed. The tail is cylindrical and slightly tapering, some-
what compressed towards the tip, and covered with short closely-adherent hairs.
The fur is composed of two kinds of hairs, some being longer and a little thicker
than the others. At the base all the hairs are bluish-black on the upper-parts, and
bluish-grey below. The incisor teeth are brownish-yellow, the eyes black, the nose
dusky, the soles of the feet pale flesh-colour, and the claws, according to Mr. de
Winton, are 'purple, as if dyed with black-currant juice.'*

From the delightful 'Ratty' on his river bank, we must now turn our
attention to the mice and rats, which have a much less savoury reputation,
although some of the family deserve better treatment.

7 Rodents: Mice, Rats, Dormice and the Coypu

Perhaps no family of mammals has had such a Jekyll-and-Hyde relationship with man than the Muridae, which includes what are popularly referred to as rats and mice. The six British species, which range from the delicate and much beloved harvest mouse to the feared and disease-ridden sewer rat, are summarised in Table 9.

MICE

The Harvest Mouse *Micromys minutus*

This, the smallest British rodent, has been discovered fossilised and dated in Pleistocene deposits found in China. The harvest mouse almost certainly evolved in Asia and is the only representative of the genus *Micromys* still existing at the present time. A rather larger fossil species, *Micromys praeminutus*, has been unearthed in Europe and dates back some 3 million years. It is often stated that *Micromys minutus* is less common in Britain than it used to be, but most workers strongly refute this suggestion, pointing out that it is notoriously difficult to take a census of this species. At one time, the animals were often seen scampering for cover as workers in the fields harvested their crops by hand and the sweat of their brows. With the accelerating tendency towards mechanised harvests, fewer people work so close to the land and those who are involved are perched high in vibrating cabs, concentrating their attention on steering a straight course. The modern farmworker is more of a press-button factory hand at this period of the agrarian calender, and the tiny harvest mouse is almost certainly under-recorded.

What is required is a really concentrated effort to investigate its range and it may well be that the harvest mouse will prove to be much more widespread than the present distribution maps indicate; indeed the first Welsh record dates from 1964. All Britain's wildlife is constantly engaged in nature's game of swings and roundabouts and harvest mice have made good use of motorway verges, abandoned railway lines, quiet stretches alongside dis-used canals and derelict factory sites. Any loss in marginal habitat taken up for building will often be more than compensated for by the gains listed above. It must be admitted, however, that Britain is on the northwesterly limit of the harvest mouse's distribution and it does not occur at all in the Isle of Man or Ireland. There are some records from Scotland. Macgillivray for example, mentions specimens from Aberdeenshire, Midlothian and Fifeshire and Evans recorded it near Aberlady. These specimens, however,

The harvest mouse (*Micromys minutus*)—nature's acrobat.

are thought to have been accidentally introduced in loads of hay from southern England. They do, however, give encouragement to Scottish naturalists to keep searching. The harvest mouse probably reached Britain at the conclusion of the Ice Ages, but it was not until the Rev. Gilbert White wrote a series of letters to his friend Thomas Pennant, during 1767 and 1768, that we have the first English description. Pennant, in his first edition of *British Zoology* (1768), describes it under the name of the 'lesser long-tailed field mouse' but, by the 1776 edition, the name 'harvest mouse' was used. By quoting the full text of White's letters (from *Natural History of Selbourne*) it is possible to see what a truly wonderful field naturalist he was:

August 4th 1767.
I have had no opportunity yet of procuring any of those mice which I mentioned to you in town. The person that brought me the last says that there are plenty in harvest, at which time I will take care to get more; and will endeavour to put the matter out of doubt, whether it be a nondescript species or not.
November 4th 1767
I have procured some of the mice mentioned in my former letters a young one and a female with young both of which I have preserved in brandy. From the colour, shape, size and manner of nesting I make no doubt that the species is nondescript. They are much smaller and more slender than the Mus domesticus

medius *of Ray; and have more the squirrel or dormouse colour; their belly is white, a straight line along their sides divides the shades of their back and belly. They never enter into houses; are carried into ricks and barns with the sheaves; abound in harvest; and build their nests amidst the straws of the corn above the ground, and sometimes in thistles. They breed as many as eight in a litter, in a little round nest composed of the blades of grass or wheat. One of these nests I procured this autumn most artistically platted, and composed of blades of wheat, perfectly round, and about the size of a cricket ball; with the aperture so ingeniously closed, that there was no discovering to what part it belonged. It was so compact and well filled that it would roll across the table without being decomposed, though it contained eight little mice that were naked and blind. As the nest was perfectly full how could the dam come to the litter respectively so as to administer a teat to each? Perhaps she opens different places for that purpose adjusting them again when the business is over; but she could not possibly be contained herself within the ball with her young which moreover would be daily increasing in bulk. This wonderful procreant cradle, an elegant instance of the efforts of instinct, was found in a wheat field suspended in the head of a thistle.*

Here we have White at his best and one can imagine this cultured clergyman searching for the truth so often concealed by nature from all but the most patient observer. We find him accepting the need to kill the odd individual in the interests of accurate observation and, on 22 January 1768, he took up his quill and ink once more to acquaint Pennant with the following:

As to the small mice I have further to remark, that though they hang their nests for breeding up amidst the straws of the standing corn, above the ground; yet I find that in winter they burrow deep in the earth and make warm beds of grass: but their grand rendezvous seems to be in cornricks into which they are carried at harvest. A neighbour housed an oat-rick lately under the thatch of which were assembled nearly a hundred, most of which were taken, and some I saw. I measured them; and found that from nose to tail they were just two inches and a quarter, and their tails just two inches long. Two of them, in a scale, weighed down just one copper halfpenny which is just about a third of an ounce avoirdupois.

White was obviously thrilled by his new discovery and, on March 30 1768 he wrote again to Pennant 'I can show you some good specimens of my new mice. Linnaeus perhaps would call the species *Mus minutus.*'

The year 1768 was indeed an important one in the annals of the harvest mouse for it was also in that year that the German naturalist, Peter Simon Pallas, published his account of the species and it is he who is given the credit for its discovery, although many, including myself, continue to support White's claim.

Living as it does in the long grass of fields, or in the reeds of swampy areas, *Micromys minutus* has evolved many adaptations to assist its survival. The most obvious of these is its truly prehensile tail, a feature not possessed to the same degree by any other British mammal. The terminal couple of centimetres can be tightly wrapped around stems and can also be held straight out behind the animal and used as a balancing organ should the need arise. The tip of the tail and the soles of the tiny feet are also thought to be sensitive receptors, enabling the animal to decide whether or not a particular strand of vegetation is able to support its weight. The hind feet have five toes, the outer one being opposable and thus capable of locking around a support. Another important adaptation is the very light skeleton when compared with those of similar-sized ground-based rodents. Many nests are, as White pointed out, in cereal fields but others are sited in reeds above standing water or among sedges in salt marshes and harvest mice are quite powerful swimmers should the need arise. There is a record of a harvest mouse being removed from the water some 3 km (about 2 miles) out to sea and it was observed to be swimming bravely, front limbs tucked under its chin and deriving momentum from its hind limbs.

White also appreciated the problem which the harvest mouse has had to overcome—what to do when the vegetation on which it depends dies down during the numbing cold of winter. Although they cannot actually dig their own burrows as White suggests, they readily take to those made by other species and also make full use of birds' nests, the domed cosy structure built by the wren (*Troglodytes troglodytes*) having a particular attraction. In summertime, there is no housing problem and the harvest mouse is found often in high densities from sea level to 300 m (nearly 1000 ft). The breeding nest is sited in tussocks of grass usually only about 20 cm (8 in) above the ground but there are records of nests at 1.5 m (5 ft). Each breeding nest is only used for one litter and, as the breeding season can last from March to November, or even into a mild December, the female is kept busy. Harvest mice actually live less than a year and sexual maturity can be reached within 2 months following birth.

The actual mating behaviour can be very aggressive, as is often the case with animals which follow a solitary rather than a gregarious life style. After a gestation period of about 18 days, an average of about five (although White's figure of eight is not unheard of) naked, blind, pink young are born. The female is often willing and able to mate on the day following this event and thus will be suckling one litter whilst the next is forming within her. Development is rapid and, in just over a fortnight, the young are independent. Such is the reproductive efficiency of the harvest mouse that populations build up very rapidly indeed during the summer. Considering their 'wish to be alone', the species can thus soon occupy extensive areas, the territory of an individual animal varying from 200 to 1000 m^2 (240 to 1200 yd^2), the males being more inclined to range over larger areas in urgent pursuit of willing females. Thus the short, active life of this delightful animal has proved, surprisingly to many people, to be one of constant struggle and aggression, but its future in Britain is most certainly more secure than many naturalists allow.

The yellow-necked mouse (*Apodemus flavicollis*).

The Yellow-necked Mouse *Apodemus flavicollis*

The scientific name has its origins in the two classical languages; *Apodemus* is derived from the Greek *apo*, meaning 'away from' and *demos* meaning 'country', whilst *flavicollis* is from the Latin *flavus*, meaning 'yellow' and *collum* meaning 'neck'. Thus we have 'a yellow-necked animal living away from open country', i.e. woods—a very good description.

This species differs from the wood mouse by the presence of a conspicuous broad yellow band across the breast and by the fact that it is a larger animal (see Table 9). It is also much more attractively coloured, the rich reddish upper surface being clearly delineated from the white belly region. The species was first described as a British species by De Winton in the *Zoologist* in 1894. The above-mentioned distinctions make separation in the field quite easy, but it is rather a pity that we have no equally certain method of separating their skeletal remains, such as may be forthcoming from an analysis of owl pellets. The dental formulae of both *A. sylvaticus* and *A. flavicollis* are those of a typical murid rodent namely:

$$2 \times \left\{ I \frac{1}{1} \quad C \frac{0}{0} \quad PM \frac{0}{0} \quad M \frac{3}{3} \right\} = 16.$$

Apodemus flavicollis is distributed throughout most of Europe and actually extends further northwards into Scandinavia than *A. sylvaticus*. As far

The wood mouse (*Apodemus sylvaticus*).

as Britain is concerned, the yellow-necked mouse seems pretty well restricted to southern England and parts of Wales and even here the distribution seems patchy. Its favourite habitat is woods, even quite dense coniferous woods seem acceptable, and although they are found in hedges all the evidence at present to hand would suggest that, in Britain at least, it is less of a threat to crops than the wood mouse. In 1967, however, a rather puzzling Yugoslavian newspaper report told of a heaving stream of mice some 15 km (9 miles) long, individuals being some 150 mm long (6 in) and yellowish in colour. The group was so arrogant that all normal predators were totally ignored and it literally ate its way through the countryside. Eventually experts seemed agreed that the offending horde consisted of a mixture of yellow-necked mice and wood mice. Some evidence has been produced to suggest that *A. flavicollis* is a more skilful climber than *A. sylvaticus* and is therefore more prone to enter human habitation and outbuildings. Although they are not able to dig their own burrows, there are many records of wood mice taking over the burrows of other species, such as moles and shrews, and even those of potentially dangerous predators, such as the badger.

The breeding biology of *A. flavicollis* is very similar to *A. sylvaticus* and a normal lifespan would be something in the order of 18 months, although many are taken by predators long before this.

The Wood Mouse *Apodemus sylvaticus*

The wood mouse, or long-tailed field mouse as it is otherwise known, has been present in this country since the Pleistocene period and Lydekker (1896) reports the finding of a fossilised lower jaw in the forest beds of Norfolk. The same writer also gives an account of the habits of the species:

> *Although its name would imply that woods were the favourite resorts of this species, yet, as a matter of fact, it is more commonly found, during the summer, in thickets, hedges, corn-fields, and gardens; while in winter it resorts for shelter to barns or other out-buildings, as well as corn-stacks; and Thompson records an instance where a specimen was taken in an inhabited house in Belfast.*
>
> *Feeding on corn of all kinds, as well as bulbs, nuts, acorns, and various smaller seeds, together with insects and grubs, the Wood-Mouse is an unmitigated nuisance to the farmer and gardener; the amount of good it does by the consumption of such animal food as it devours, going but a small way towards recompensing the damage it inflicts on newly-sown crops of all kinds. Moreover, although this Mouse makes a regular winter retreat, it does not become torpid,—or at all events does so only for very short periods—and consequently needs a large supply of food during the cold season, so that the unfortunate farmer or gardener has to support the creature from one year's end to another. As a rule, the retreat takes the form of a burrow in the ground; but instances are on record where deserted birds' nests have been occupied and fitted up, while regular nests are often made in hedge-banks, or even in standing grass. At other times old Mole-runs are selected as dwelling places. In such safe retreats, of whatever nature they may be, the Wood-Mouse during the summer and autumn accumulates enormous stores of provender for its winter consumption; acorns, beech-mast, nuts, peas, beans,*

Wood mice (*Apodemus sylvaticus*).

and corn, being gathered in by the pint. It is not only the loss of these various seeds that the farmer has to deplore, for, in districts and seasons when Wood-Mice are very abundant, pigs learn to hunt for and root up these hidden stores, and may then do much damage, both to pasture and arable land.

Breeding several times in a season, after a gestation of only three weeks, and producing from five to seven young in a litter, the Wood-Mouse is one of the most prolific of Rodents, famous as are many of these animals for their rapidity of increase. Some idea of the rate at which they propagate may be gathered from some interesting observations published by Mr. R.M. Barrington in the Zoologist for 1881, by whom several of these Mice were kept in captivity. It is probable, however, that the number of young in a litter would not be so large as in the wild state. One of these captive specimens, when about five and a half months old, gave birth to a litter of three on the 7th or 8th of March. Observation was kept on this female (A), and a second one (B), with the following result:—

								Interval since last litter.
March	7 or 8	...	A	...	3 young	...		—
,,	19	...	B	...	5 ,,	...		—
,,	31	...	A	...	3 ,,	...		24 days
April	18	...	B	...	5 ,,	...		29 ,,
,,	24	...	A	...	3 ,,	...		24 ,,
May	11	...	B	...	5 ,,	...		23 ,,
,,	17	...	A	...	4 ,,	...		23 ,,
June	12	...	A (?)	...	4 ,,	...		26 ,,
July	9	...	A (?)	...	4 ,,	...		27 ,,

Had not one of the adult females made its escape in the beginning of June this record of the number of young produced by a couple of Wood-Mice in less than five months would probably have been still larger. 'During April,' writes the narrator, 'we had twelve to twenty Mice, young and old, in the nest; they all slept together, and it was certainly a curious sight to see fathers, mothers, and children of all ages and sizes in the nest, the young of different ages suckling the same mother at the same time, and the mothers appearing to suckle each other's young indiscriminately.'

To counteract this extreme prolificness, it is fortunate that the Wood-Mouse has a large number of enemies. Foremost amongst these are Kestrels, Owls, Stoats, and Weasels; while many of these Mice are killed by Foxes, which seem especially fond of them and their cousins the Voles. Rooks and Crows are also stated to aid in the extermination of these pests by digging up the nests and young with their strong beaks; while several other of the larger birds probably occasionally assist in the destruction.

Mr. Trevor-Battye writes:—'In the dry summer of 1893 the Black-headed Gulls breeding on Scoulton Mere (as I was assured by the keeper), frequently brought "Mice" to their nests, killing them by dropping them from a height. The Mice were probably of this species.'

The Wood-Mouse is as readily tamed as the Dormouse, and will soon learn to

The brown rat (*Rattus norvegicus*).

The coypu (*Myocastor coypus*).

OPPOSITE: The common dormouse (*Muscardinus avellanarius*).

permit itself to be handled without resentment, although it always displays considerable timidity. Specimens have been kept in confinement for upwards of two years.

Lydekker's text is supported by modern work and, while the life expectancy in the wild is only a matter of weeks, many individuals survive into their second year and captive animals do indeed survive for longer than 2 years. The suggestion of 'partial' rather than 'complete' periods of hibernation was supported by Morris (1968) and, in the same year, Brown noted family groupings in the wild which were being controlled by a dominant male.

One of the most fascinating things about the long-tailed field mouse concerns its method of locomotion. When it is not being pressed it uses all four limbs like any other rodent, but when danger threatens it can lift its front limbs and use the rear ones in the manner of a kangaroo to make quite prodigious leaps. To escape predators, it has been observed to make standing jumps through a vertical distance of almost a metre (3 ft). It is an excellent climber and makes full use of its long tail as a semi-prehensile limb, often taking over empty rook's nests over 20 m (about 70 ft) from the ground.

At one time it was thought that there were a great many subspecies of this mouse and, at the turn of the century, the eminent naturalist Barret-Hamilton recognised nineteen subspecies, at least six of which were thought to occur in Britain. Modern opinion, however, suggests that there is a great deal of variation throught the range and far too much overlap to support any idea of subspecies.

House Mouse *Mus musculus*

This animal has been closely associated with our dwellings for many centuries and, although there seems to be little doubt that its origins are Asiatic, it had already spread into Europe by prehistoric times and Vesey-Fitzgerald, in his book *The Vanishing Wildlife of Britain*, suggests its presence in Britain prior to 1000 BC. Its spread throughout the world in the wake of human settlement is quite remarkable; by deliberate domestication many colour varieties have been produced but by far the most familiar is the albino. Looking through the extensive literature concerning the species, two quite remarkable behavioural 'varieties' are listed. These are the waltzing mice and the singing mice. The waltzers were so named because of their habit of chasing their own tails during periods of high activity, only pausing to reverse direction. The individuals showing this trait were either fawn and white or black and white and the waltzing was thought by some to be inherited; others were of the opinion that the behaviour was due to some disease of the brain or ears. Waltzers were said to be smaller and more fragile than 'ordinary' individuals. There does not seem to be any acceptable

The house mouse (*Mus musculus*).

modern-day theory to account for it, which is not the case with the equally bizarre phenomenon of the singing mice. Sir Harry Johnston described their behaviour in 1903:

The common mouse is the reverse of a silent animal except when suspicious of danger. Its squeaks are varied in tone, and individuals actually develop singing powers. The present writer was incredulous at one time as to this fact, but several years ago had his attention drawn to mice that had been captured in Tunis and kept for a time in confinement, and to similar instances in England. The singing of these mice resembled the chirping, quavering notes of a young cock canary who is beginning to experiment with his voice. Mr. Lydekker states that an example of these singing mice has been heard to 'run up an octave and end with a decided attempt at a trill.... An octave seemed to be about its range ... and one could distinctly see the expansion of its throat and chest. Its favourite position when singing was an erect one, standing on its hind feet.'

Modern workers have suggested that the singing noise is produced by mice suffering from inflammation of the lungs and is therefore a sign of illness rather than an expression of well-being.

Bell, in his *History of British Quadrupeds* (1837), gives an excellent account of the animal itself and of the relationship between man and mouse:

It is an elegant little animal, timid, but easily tamed. Its astonishing multiplication may be well imagined from the following experiment of the great father of natural history:—Having, says Aristotle, placed a pregnant female of the Common Mouse in a closed vessel filled with grain, I found after a short period no less than a hundred and twenty Mice, all sprung from that single parent. This astonishing increase is easily accounted for. The Mouse breeds indifferently at all seasons, and several times in the course of the year, producing ordinarily five or six young ones. In a fortnight the young are able to leave the mother, and assume an independent existence; and at a very early age they also reproduce.

In addition to the usual means employed for their extermination, such as traps of various kinds, and the carnivorous instinct of the Cat, the Ferret, and the Weasel, there still exists in Wales a custom so disgustingly cruel, that the very mention of it would be scarcely pardonable but for the possibility of thus producing some degree of shame in the perpetrators of it, and consequently saving some poor little Mice from being the victims of such barbarity. It is customary in some parts of Wales to roast a Mouse alive, hanging it before the fire by its tail tied to a string, that its screams may scare the rest from house.

This practice of cruelty to mice was also part of Eskimo culture, but, even in Victorian Britain, mice were cooked in pies and fed to children in an attempt to cure a variety of illnesses. Unless these complaints were due to a lack of fresh meat then the remedy must be considered to be of dubious value, apart perhaps from making the patient sick and clearing out the stomach. Although there is little doubt that the house mouse is responsible for the spread of some diseases it is quite a spruce little beast and makes an interesting subject for study. There are few accounts to surpass that given by Macgillivray in the middle of the nineteenth century:

It is pleasant to sit quietly at midnight watching one which has ventured from its retreat and stolen to the hearth in quest of crumbs. It glides along, now slowly, now by sudden starts, and on finding some fragment of food, sits on its haunches, lays hold of it in its fore-feet, and raising it up, nibbles it, or if apprehensive of danger, runs off with it to its hole. Although extremely timid, Mice sometimes exhibit considerable boldness, and venture quite close to a person who does not molest them. Their agility is astonishing, and to escape when pursued they perform extraordinary feats. I have seen one leap from the top of a stair-case upon a table, a distance of twelve feet, apparently without receiving any injury. If seized in the hand they bite severely, but if caught by the tail and thus suspended, are unable to turn upon their persecutor. Although when in small numbers they are scarcely injurious to a house, yet, owing to their fecundity, they soon become very destructive, devouring meal, flour, bread, cheese, butter, tallow, in short, almost every article of food that comes in their way, and often gnawing clothes, leather, and furniture. Their great enemy, the Cat, is not always able to extirpate them, so that the additional aid of traps and poison is

An immature house mouse (*Mus musculus*). The tail is used as a balancing organ.

required. The ravages of this species are not confined to houses, for it often betakes itself to the fields, and nestles in the corn-stacks, which are found towards the base traversed by its tortuous runs. The ground beneath is also filled with them, and on removing a stack numbers almost incredible are often met with.

In addition to man, the mouse has many enemies, including birds, especially the barn owl (*Tyto alba*) and predatory mustelids, such as weasels, stoats and man-directed ferrets. The brown rat is also thought to have some effect and eats a great many mice; indeed it may well be a more effective brake on the mouse population in some areas than the cat. The breeding efficiency, however, is such that populations are bound to remain high. In suitable situations, up to ten litters can be produced in a year by a single female, the gestation period being only about 20 days and up to eight young can be produced in a litter—such is the enormous breeding potential of *Mus musculus*.

As you would expect, the species occurs throughout Britain and Ireland; there are even records of successful breeding in deep-freeze systems. Their survival in such inhospitable spots seems to depend upon their ability to lay down stores of brown fat which, as mentioned in the discussion of hibernating hedgehogs, generates a great deal of energy when utilised. The rodent's teeth can gnaw away through frozen food and so there is plenty of food available. One thing is certain—if *Mus musculus* can survive in these conditions its future is very secure indeed.

Table 9 BRITISH RATS AND MICE

Common Name	Other Common Names	Scientific Name	Size	Distribution & Notes
wood mouse	long-tailed field mouse	*Apodemus sylvaticus*	Head and body about 100 mm (4 in). Tail 80 mm ($3\frac{1}{5}$ in).	Throughout Britain and Ireland. Probably introduced to Ireland from Scandinavia.
yellow-necked mouse	De Winton's mouse	*Apodemus flavicollis*	Similar to above but tail usually longer than head and body (115 mm or $4\frac{1}{2}$ in). Weight 30 g (1 oz) is $1\frac{1}{2} \times$ that of wood mouse.	Restricted to southern England and Wales but distribution patchy.
harvest mouse	dwarf mouse, ranny	*Micromys minutus*	Head and body 60 mm ($2\frac{2}{5}$ in). Tail 40 mm ($1\frac{3}{5}$ in). Smallest British rodent weighing 6 g. ($\frac{1}{2}$ oz).	Some restriction in range this century; absent from N. England, Scotland, Isle of Man and Ireland.
house mouse	—	*Mus musculus*	Body length 80 mm ($3\frac{1}{5}$ in).	Introduced but now found throughout Britain and Ireland.
black rat	ship rat, Alexandrine rat, roof rat, old English rat	*Rattus rattus*	Head and body 240 mm ($9\frac{3}{5}$ in). Tail longer than this (up to $1\frac{1}{4} \times$).	Range is now shrinking.
brown rat	common rat, sewer rat, Norway rat, Hanoverian rat, house rat	*Rattus norvegicus*	Head and body 280 mm ($11\frac{1}{5}$ in). Tail up to but not exceeding this length.	Introduced and very common.

RATS

The Black Rat *Rattus rattus*

Now called the ship rat, this is yet another rodent which is thought to have its origins in central Asia and has extended its range as human trade links were permanently forged. The rat is not mentioned by the classical writers of either Greece or Rome and, if folks of this period knew them at all, they called them 'big mice'. The fur of *Rattus rattus* is typically fine and soft, the colour varying a great deal over its range. At one time, when the species was more common than it is now, the shiny black dorsal fur with the contrasting paler areas of the belly made it a valuable item of commerce. Just when the species reached Britain is not certain but it may well have been during the eleventh and twelfth centuries at the time of the Crusades. It seems reasonable to assume that it came by way of France and, indeed, its Welsh name was the 'French mouse'. The earliest reference to the species in Britain is given by Giraldus Cambrensis, who was Archdeacon of Brecon and lived between 1146 and 1220. His *Itinerary Through Wales*, written of course in Latin, when translated obviously refers to *Rattus rattus* as 'the larger kind of mice, commonly called rats'. One fact is established beyond question and that is that bubonic plague was transmitted via the agency of a flea shared by both *Rattus rattus* and *Homo sapiens*. Cases of plague are now very rare in the British Isles but the occasional rat is still found to be infected with the virus and even now the authorities controlling the sea ports keep a wary eye open, despite the fact that the range of the species has been shrinking dramatically in the last few centuries due to its failure to compete successfully with the larger (see Table 9) and more aggressive brown rat.

The reduction of areas supporting the black rat was clearly stated by Bell in 1837 and, by 1896, Lydekker summarised the position regarding the species thus:

It would seem, however, that subsequently to its introduction it became pretty generally distributed in England and Wales until routed out by the Brown Rat, and was known even in the Orkneys. There, however, it is now completely exterminated, as it is in most districts.... In Argyllshire and Caithness it is unknown, but one specimen was taken in Sutherland in 1879; while a small colony was observed near Pitlochry in 1860, and specimens are occasionally taken in old houses in Edinburgh. Unknown in Northumberland, a colony existed in 1879 at Stockton-on-Tees, in Durham; and in 1883 it was stated still to linger among the farms of Westmoreland. It would be tedious to mention the isolated occurrences of specimens of this Rat which have been recorded from various English counties from time to time during the last few years, more especially as many of these—and notably such as have been taken in or near sea-port towns—have in all probability been imported by vessels. It may be mentioned, however, that it still survived in Norfolk up to about 1834, while occasional specimens were met with for twenty years later. In Warwickshire, where it is now extinct, it was not uncommon even so late as 1850.

In Ireland, remarks Mr. Harting, the Black Rat has been met with in various counties, and in localities widely distant from each other; but there is no evidence to show that it was ever plentiful, and it must now be regarded as very rare.

The latest edition of *The Handbook of British Mammals* points out that the species is just hanging on, in and around the sea-ports of Britain, perhaps still assisted by the odd import. The occasional occurrence in inland spots is no doubt due to animals being transported with imported goods. *Rattus rattus* only thrives within the confines of buildings in Britain because our winters are too severe for the species to breed in the open. This has made the black rat more vulnerable to extermination measures than the more wide-ranging brown rat. Although its breeding potential is enormous, it only fulfils this threat in warmer climates. With a gestation period of only 21 days and a litter size of up to ten (averaging about seven) it is easy to see how an unchecked population can increase.

Not all stories of rats are designed to send the shivers up the spine, however, and there are many records of rats demonstrating an impressive degree of altruistic behaviour. One particularly charming example is quoted by Bell (1837) in *A History of British Quadrupeds*:

> ... *there are instances on record of its evincing considerable attachment, not only to each other, but to man-kind. Mr. Jesse, in his usual amusing and pleasant style, gives us an anecdote, which the respectable authority from which he derived it would forbid us to doubt, exhibiting a degree of tenderness and care towards the disabled and aged members of their community, which, were it imitated by Christian men, would either render our poor laws unnecessary, or remove the disgrace and opprobrium which their maladministration too often causes to attach to them. His informant, the Rev. Mr. Ferryman, walking out in some meadows one evening, 'observed a great number of Rats in the act of migrating from one place to another, which it is known they are in the habit of doing occasionally.* [The origin of the Pied Piper of Hamelin?] *He stood perfectly*

The black rat (*Rattus rattus*) is confined to sea-ports.

still, and the whole assemblage passed close to him. His astonishment, however, was great, when he saw an old blind Rat, which held a piece of stick at one end in its mouth, while another Rat had hold of the other end of it, and thus conducted his blind companion.' It appears also from several instances that this animal is not insensible of kindness, and that it may be powerfully attached to those who feed and caress it.

The Brown Rat *Rattus norvegicus*

Sometimes called the common rat, this is yet another animal which is now very much part of our environment but had its origins in the days prior to our own civilisation and the establishment of trading routes leading out of its home in central Asia. It is often suggested, perhaps with some element of truth that, following an earthquake on the Asiatic side of the Volga river in 1727, the brown rat swam the river and entered eastern Europe. Russia was very quickly colonised and Paris was reached by the middle 1750s. England's first specimens are thought to have arrived by 1730, possibly carried by ships trading out of the Baltic, but there have been suggestions that the species had already arrived here at about the time the first Hanoverian claimed the throne in 1715. *Rattus norvegicus* still carries the vernacular name of 'Hanoverian rat' because of this belief. The animal has proved notoriously difficult if not impossible to contain and an official was appointed by George II and called by the exalted title of 'Rat killer to the Crown'. He was dressed in a most impressive livery of scarlet and gold with his very own emblem depicting rats munching away at sheaves of corn. Here then was not a lowly rat-catcher but a splendid rodent disposal officer commanding the impressive salary of £100 per annum. One variety of *Rattus norvegicus*, however, is actually essential to the life of modern human societies and that is the albino laboratory rat which is so much a feature of schools and universities and, indeed, can also make a charming pet. Its habits, unlike those of the wild brown rat are clean, even fastidious, and its manners are usually exemplary. It is only when it is confined in crowded conditions that stress factors lead to aggression and cannibalism, especially of the young. Before we condemn the animal we should not overlook the connection between poor living conditions and violence in our own society.

A most wily adversary, the agile rat has a semi-prehensile tail and Cuvier estimated that there are more muscles in a rat's tail than there are in a human hand. The scales which cover this organ of balance overlap to such an extent that, if a rat is held off the ground by means of its tail, it can slip off the skin as easily as we peel off a glove, and so make good its escape.

When I was discussing the rabbit (Chapter 5), I pointed out that one way of ridding ourselves of surplus populations of this troublesome beast was to eat them. This method has also, perhaps surprisingly, been tried in the case of *Rattus norvegicus* and a book called *Wild Foods of Great Britain*, still in print in the 1920s, stated that a delicious dish, not unlike snipe in flavour, could be prepared from rats. The Rev. J.G. Wood is reported to have enjoyed the meal 'especially' when stuffed with breadcrumbs with a sprink-ling of sweet herbs and garnished with appropriate amounts of pepper and salt. In China, its original home, the rat was used in the preparation of soup. Bearing these 'treats' in mind, the appearance of rat on the menu of the fashionable restaurants of siege-bound Paris during the Franco-Prussian War of the 1870s is not quite so horrific as historians would have us believe.

The flesh may well have had its flood in the tide of history, but so has the rather fragile fur which, unlike that of *Rattus rattus*, has never been possessed of any commercial value. However, during the cold experienced by troops during the Russo-Japanese War of 1905, the Japanese caught rats and used their skins to make ear caps—a case of any fur being better than none as the agonies of frostbitten extremities stimulated invention.

To return to the reproductive facility of the rat, which is the main reason for its unpopularity in human eyes, the phenomenon was investigated by J.G. Millais in the late nineteenth century. He wrote:

If we take it for granted that a rat has a litter 8 times a year; that she gives birth to her first litter on January 1; that each litter is composed of 7 males and 6 females; that each female born within the year has a litter when she is three months old and subsequently a litter at the end of every six weeks; By the end of December one rat will have been responsible for the birth of the enormous total of 35,004 rats.

Even allowing for a degree of exaggeration in Millais' figures, it is easy to see the problem. The diet of the brown rat in the wild is very catholic and they even gobble up human excrement way down below ground in the clammy steaming heat of a city's sewers. No wonder that a bite from a sewer rat can occasionally result in severe illness, the cure for which even modern medical science has had difficulty in finding. We will never succeed in wiping out *Rattus norvegicus* from either the surface or the bowels of our land, but we must never relax our vigilance in attempting to control the danger it threatens. I would not go so far as to provide our rodent operatives with scarlet and gold apparel, but they must be rated as vital and respected members of our society; neither must our chemists become complacent for there is already evidence to show that some rats have developed such an immunity to rat poison (warfarin) that they can actually eat the stuff and not only survive the dose but carry on breeding afterwards! We must fight hard to deserve even a draw against such a formidable adversary as *Rattus norvegicus*.

DORMICE AND THE COYPU

This section concludes the chapter of this volume devoted to rodents and, although the coypu is not related to the dormice, it is, like the edible dormouse, an introduction and, like both these 'sleepy heads', has a very restricted distribution. It is convenient therefore to discuss them together.

Dormice belong to the family Gliridae and, compared with most rodents in this country, they have a lower breeding rate. Neither do they cope well with low temperatures and consequently have a long period of hibernation with all its attendant physiological complications already discussed in Chapters 3 and 4. In Britain, we have only two species, the common dormouse (*Muscardinus avellanarius*), which is native to Britain although quite restricted in its distribution, and the edible dormouse (*Glis glis*) which was introduced to Britain very early in the twentieth century. The introduction has proved modestly successful (if introductions of 'foreign' beasts can ever be regarded as 'successful') but, apart from surviving, there is no evidence of wide extensions of the range, doubtless due to periods of hibernation and low fecundity. The coypu, although also an introduction, has proved to be more formidable, although its range is still restricted.

The Common Dormouse *Muscardinus avellanarius*

Other names for this attractive little creature include sleeper, sleep mouse, dory mouse and hazel dormouse.

The last name mentioned relates to the animal's liking for hazel nuts. In opening these nutritious fruits, the dormouse gnaws a smooth round hole with its incisor teeth whereas the holes made by bank voles and wood mice, for the same purpose, show characteristic teeth marks. (This subject has been intelligently studied by Elaine Hurrel.) The dental formula of the dormouse is:

$$2 \times \left\{ I\frac{1}{1} \quad C\frac{0}{0} \quad PM.\frac{1}{1} \quad M\frac{3}{3} \right\} = 20.$$

Although other fruits are taken, this preference for hazel nuts is reflected in the specific half of the scientific name. *Muscardinus* is derived from the French *muscardin*, which literally means 'dormouse' but this in turn was derived from 'muscardin', which is a lozenge with a musky smell; the dormouse had a similar odour. *Avellanarius* comes from the Latin *avellana* meaning 'a hazel nut'.

A fluffy little beast with large bright eyes and a body measuring about 80 mm ($3\frac{1}{3}$ in), with a slightly bushy tail measuring just over 60 mm ($2\frac{1}{2}$ in), the dormouse is one of our most attractive mammals. It lives happily enough, doing little damage and building or appropriating a summer nest where it raises from two to seven young but the average litter size is usually about four. In Britain's climate, it is only usually possible for one litter to be produced in a year. The lifespan probably does not exceed 6 years and is frequently much less and so populations are never likely to show dramatic increases. Furthermore there is plenty of evidence to show a steady contraction in the range of the common dormouse. It is now almost confined to southern England, with a few sporadic sightings from as far apart as the Midlands and Lancashire, but we must always wonder whether the sightings are accurate and, if they are, can we rule out escapes from captivity? There are no recent records from Scotland and it is absent from Ireland.

The dormouse always hibernates in winter, often constructing a more substantial nest for the purpose, frequently amongst the roots of trees or in a hole in the ground. There are occasions when the summer nest is used as a hibernaculum; this was suggested as long ago as 1885, by Rope, writing in the *Zoologist*. Rope listed three factors which he thought contributed to the dormouse's decline, which was very obvious even a century ago. These factors were actual food shortages and the presence of the recently introduced grey squirrels, which were taking the food out of the mouth of the dormouse but he also laid some stress on a series of milder winters which allowed the dormice to attempt to remain active for too long, thus using up available fat stores. He considered that a seasonal pattern of hot weather followed by a sudden plunge into cold weather was more suited to the physiology of the dormouse and I think that he may well have been right. By inference, hibernating in the old breeding nests, perhaps exposed to the rigours of winter, might also be a contributory factor. It would seem that, although the dormouse at present is rather restricted in its British range, it is in no danger of extinction, nor is it very likely to expand its range in any dramatic manner.

The Edible Dormouse *Glis glis*

This creature is also known as the fat dormouse, squirrel-tailed dormouse or seven sleeper (probably in reference to its hibernation period of October to April which is seven months' duration). The English name comes from the Latin *dormio* meaning 'I sleep'. This species is much larger than the common dormouse, being up to 180 mm ($7\frac{1}{5}$ in) long, to which must be added a squirrel-like tail of up to 150 mm (6 in). A prominent dark ring around the ocular orbit serves to emphasise both the size and the beauty of the animal's eyes.

Glis glis is not native to Britain, but was introduced in about 1902, by Lord Rothschild to his estate near Tring from whence it has spread. Its real home is in south central Europe and it was especially favoured by gourmets of Ancient Rome. It was fattened, especially just prior to hibernation, in special jars filled with grain and appropriately called *gliraria*.

The preferred natural habitat of *Glis glis* is mature woodland rather than developing scrub or open areas, but it is often found in orchards and houses, where it breeds and often hibernates in the roof spaces. In the recent past, naturalists have not reached agreement as to whether the species is able to construct its own nest or whether it simply takes over suitable structures. Since it is almost completely nocturnal, careful observations can present technical problems. There seems no doubt that it can build a nest if it has to, but being a resourceful type of beast it prefers to save energy where it can and is more than willing to take up squatter's rights in old nests and among the rafters of buildings sufficiently dilapidated to allow it access. The summer nest is often high in a tree and close to the trunk rather than out on a limb. Hollow trees and eroded spaces between tree roots are favourite places

The edible dormouse (*Glis glis*) in its typical habitat.

for the winter sleep. The edible dormouse has its fair quota of predators, including tawny owls, cats, stoats and weasels, but if it survives all these hungry beasts it can live into its sixth year; it does not breed until 2 years of age. In its turn, the edible dormouse can turn predator and eat the eggs and nestlings of birds, although the diet is mainly vegetable matter, such as fruit and fungi. With only one litter a year, of five young, born around the month of July, the population can hardly ever reach the plague proportions so typical of other rodents, but there are occasions when it is a nuisance, especially when it produces disturbing nocturnal noises in the rafters of houses in which folk are attempting to sleep; it can also do a great deal of damage to valuable stores of apples.

There is certainly no question of either of our dormice becoming a pest of the same proportions as the last of our British rodents, the coypu.

The Coypu *Myocastor coypus*

The genus *Myocastor* is represented by this single species only, which was introduced to Britain by fur farmers in the 1920s; the pelt, and sometimes the animal, is referred to as nutria. The dental formula of:

$$2 \times \left\{ I \frac{1}{1} \quad C \frac{0}{0} \quad PM \frac{1}{1} \quad M \frac{3}{3} \right\} = 20$$

is typical of rodents and with teeth such as this it proved impossible to keep all the animals in close confinement. Escapees, breeding in the wild, resulted in viable and expanding populations in the 1930s and 1940s, especially in Norfolk where it became a real threat. The winter of 1962–63, combined with intensive trapping programmes, brought them under control—almost; the threat is still there. There are occasional sightings in other counties, including a few in an area along the Lancaster canal, but these are isolated, sometimes vague, and difficult to prove beyond doubt. During the autumn of 1981, positive sightings were made at Samlesbury near Preston between the River Ribble and the M6 motorway, but this seems to have been a deliberately released animal.

In its natural habitat in its native land, the coypu is a 'good natured', gentle vegetarian, looking superficially like a beaver with large, bright orange, incisor teeth, but in Britain it has proved unpopular on two counts. Firstly, it has developed a liking for sugar beet, a most essential item in the East Anglian economy and, for once, the farmer and the wandering sportsman are in complete accord in their hatred of *Myocastor coypus* because its diggings into river banks cause erosion which can be dangerous to anglers as well as wasteful of land. Reeds, which give shelter to wild fowl and other game, are eaten down, thus destroying the shooters' sport. All hands are therefore against this large rodent which grows to a length of about 1 m (just over 3 ft) and can reach the impressive weight of 6.75 kg (14 lb 14 oz)—it can take an awful lot of reeds to satisfy the appetite of a family of these giants! Being so large, it is easy to spot and its tracks are likewise quite distinctive; the hind-foot print often reaches a length of 150 mm (6 in) and shows quite clearly five claw marks and the webbing. Despite these signs, the coypu has not, however, been eradicated from this land, probably due to its semi-aquatic habits and perhaps also due to its ability to breed throughout the year; litters of about five young are produced at the end of a gestation period of 18 weeks. A series of mild winters following the severe weather of 1962–63 meant that the survivors could breed without their offspring having to fight for space; thus more survived and populations climbed once more, but the carrying capacity of the Norfolk Broads has still not been reached. Trapping of coypus can often lead to the accidental death of otters which share the same habitat and, as we shall see in Chapter 10, this must be a source of worry for all who love the indigenous wildlife of this country.

8 Carnivores: the Fox and Cat

U sually, it is the large carnivores which spring most immediately to mind in any discussion of mammals, doubtless because of the threat which they have always posed to either human life or livestock. Gone are the slinking wolf and swift striking lynx, but we still have both the red fox and the wild cat. Neither of these predators is welcome in our environment (the human species is arrogant enough to demand *all* the environment!), but it is the purpose of this chapter to present as balanced a view as possible of both species in the context of the late twentieth century as well as to trace their history.

The Red Fox *Vulpes vulpes*

The red fox, or reynard, is the largest British carnivore, weighing between 6 and 10 kg ($13\frac{1}{4}$ and 22 lb); the female on average is 1 kg ($2\frac{1}{4}$ lb) lighter. The length of the body is 580–770 mm (23–30 in) and the tail is 320–480 mm ($12\frac{1}{2}$–19 in) long. The dental formula is:

$$2 \times \left\{ I\frac{3}{3} \quad C\frac{1}{1} \quad PM\frac{4}{4} \quad M\frac{2}{3} \right\} = 42.$$

It is reddish in colour with a pale underside and black on the ears and the front of the legs, which may assist in camouflaging it. The tail is bushy and tipped with white, although there is considerable variation. Moult occurs from April onwards but the full breeding coat is obvious from October. As far as breeding is concerned, there seems to be a bond between the sexes and, after a period of aggression, the female accepts the male. Mating occurs in January or February and four to six cubs are born after a gestation period of 52 days. The cubs are independent at 4 months of age.

Deschambre made a study of the fossil history of carnivores and published his results in 1951; he suggests that they may have followed not one, but possibly two lines of evolution, a situation technically referred to as *diphyletic*. Wolves and dogs probably evolved from a creature called *Amphicyon*, while the foxes, accompanied so far along the route by the jackals, developed from a fossil beast called *Cynodictis*. Providing another possible link on the way to the modern fox, a fossil named *Vulpes alopecoides* has been dated back some 400 000 to 650 000 years, but it is not until the middle of the Pleistocene that remains which can be assigned to *Vulpes vulpes* occur. Early Man certainly used fox pelts for making garments and there can be no doubt that its flesh was frequently eaten; there is also just a suggestion that, in parts of what is now Switzerland, the animal was at least

The red fox (*Vulpes vulpes*).

partially domesticated. Before the end of the last Ice Age, Britain was physically part of the continent and three species of fox co-existed here: the arctic fox (*Alopex lagopus*), the corsac fox (*Vulpes corsac*) and, of course, the red fox (*Vulpes vulpes*). As the ice melted, the resultant rise in sea level created our islands and the arctic fox was driven into the northlands, while the corsac fox become confined to the Russian steppes. Britain now had one fox and, furthermore, it was an isolated population; nineteenth- and twentieth-century scientists, detonated by the work of Darwin, exploded into the task of identifying new species. Many workers believed that any isolated population, of whatever size, was quite likely to evolve at least into a subspecies and, perhaps, even into a totally separate species. There seemed to be a distinct possibility of there being a British fox to those biologists who have become known as *splitters*. These biologists are distinct from those known as *lumpers*, who keep their classification simple and think that, as long as fertile offspring can be produced from a mating between individuals of geographically discreet populations, then they must be considered as belonging to the same species. Some insight into the thinking concerning these matters at the turn of the twentieth century can be gained by a consideration of Lydekker's book, *Mammals*, published as part of *Lloyd's Natural History* in 1896:

OPPOSITE: A female (vixen) red fox.

There are, however, certain racial or individual variations in the colour even of the British Fox. Macgillivray, for instance, observes that the largest race, 'or that which occurs in the Highland districts, has the fur of a stronger texture and of a greyer tint, there being a greater proportion of whitish hairs on the back and hind-quarters, while two or more inches of the end of the tail are white. The Fox of the lower districts is considerably smaller, more slender, of a lighter red, with the tail also white at the end. Individuals of a smaller size, having the head proportionately larger, the fur of a darker red, the lower parts dusky or dull brownish-white, and the tip of the tail either with little white or none, occur in the hilly parts of the southern division of Scotland. The skull of the Highland Fox appears remarkably large and strong beside that of the ordinary kind, and the breadth is much greater in proportion. Occasionally Foxes are killed in England with the tip of the tail grey or black; and a pure white Fox was killed in 1887 by the Taunton Vale Hounds, in the West Somerset country. Of more interest is the circumstance that some time previous to 1864, a young Fox was killed in Warwickshire in which the whole of the under parts were of a greyish-black hue. The coloration of this individual resembled that obtaining in the Foxes of Southern Europe; and assuming it to have been a native-bred animal, the occurrence of an individual of this southern race in England is a matter of some importance from a distributional point of view. In Wales, as Mr. W.E. de Winton tells me, a blackish-brown form of Fox sometimes occurs.

Regarding the Warwickshire specimen, Mr. Trevor-Battye remarks:—'I

agree about the interest of this specimen, but it raises a question. By this time the native blood must be pretty well diluted, and I suspect that we should find, had we proper means of enquiry, that our Foxes are now larger than they were, say, thirty years ago. The Swedish Fox, imported of late years into this country, is a decidedly larger animal than the native English Fox—larger even, I believe, and I have seen many examples of both forms, than the "Greyhound" Fox, as the gillies call the inhabitant of the Scottish hills.'

Present-day thinking does not allow us to accept the existence of a highland fox since any animal will vary in colour, size and behaviour, depending upon the time of year, diet, habitat and state of health of the individual; thus we have only *Vulpes vulpes* on our list and we can also rule out the existence of hybrids resulting from mating with other species. These variants may well be due to imports made in the early days of fox hunting or arrival from North America, Alaska, Russia and Europe. These animals, which are all subspecies of the red fox, may well be the ancestors of the 'Brent fox' (*brent* meaning 'burnt') which has black underparts and of those with longer legs than usual which may be the origin of the so-called 'hill fox'. In the course of history, there have been many suggested matings between foxes, wolves and domestic dogs and, in 1607, Topsell mentions a beast called 'simi-vulpa', the result of a cross between an ape and fox. None of these however are backed up by scientific observations.

A young fox cub outside the badger sett where it was born.

THE FOX IN FOLKLORE AND HISTORY

It seems that the reputation of the fox as a sly beast, slinking around and upsetting the plans of Man, has been established for centuries and it is accused of damaging the vine in the Song of Solomon, also proving that its diet tends to be more catholic than its enemies allow. In the thirteenth chapter and the fourth verse of the book of the pessimistic prophet Ezekiel, we find another insult, both to Israel and to the fox; 'Oh Israel thy prophets are like foxes of the desert'. Many of our present-day tales regarding foxes, which often find their way into children's stories and, occasionally, even decorate the pages of natural history magazines, have their origins way back in classical times, when considerable poetic licence was acceptable.

Aristotle in 500 BC, Herodotus in 300 BC and Aelian in 200 BC reported many details regarding the wiles of the crafty fox, often involving the intelligent use of its most obvious physical feature—the brush. The fox was said to wade into water and then lower its brush under the surface, fascinating the fish to such an extent that they became entangled in the fur. A quick muscular flip threw the fish onto dry land where they could be consumed at leisure. The fox's diet, according to these ancients was nothing if not varied and the animal was also reputed to proceed backwards until the brush touched a nest of wasps. The angry animals flew into the fluffy tail and the fox then beat them to death against a tree trunk. This behaviour was continued until all the wasps were dead and the nest full of grubs could be eaten in peace.

It was also the Greeks who first made reference to two other aspects of fox folklore—feigning death and the unique method of de-lousing. The fox has often been credited with pretending to be dead, either to attract inquisitive prey to approach close enough to be captured, or, on occasion, to avoid capture itself. I am sure that this 'freezing' is instinctive and much more common than we often suppose. I once actually tripped over a young fox lying 'doggo' and it was only when I made physical contact with it that the cub took flight. In my wanderings through woodland, field and fell, I wonder how many foxes I have almost trodden on without knowing they were there! With regard to the second point, I am a little more sceptical, but letters still appear in the popular press from time to time regarding the fox's method of ridding itself of external body parasites: wool, leaves, flowers, a twig or feathers are held in the mouth and the crafty beast is reputed to wade slowly into water, gradually immersing its body until only the foreign bodies remain above the water level. The parasites seek this last refuge and once they are all gathered the material is dropped and the fox emerges clean and fresh. It is doubtful whether this method would work because parasites are not all that active and some residual air is always trapped under the fur; this would be quite adequate to provide oxygen for their respiratory needs. It is also doubtful whether the fox is all that particular about hygiene, but it was also reputed to look after its health by eating the resin of pine trees and to go in search of a mythical plant called 'the sea onion', which was supposed to protect it from its arch enemy the wolf.

So much then for the fox's own medicine, but especially in the Middle Ages and Tudor times, various parts of its body were used in the treatment of human disease, some of which seem quite horrific to our more sensitive modern tastes. Fox extract literally looked after human health from head to foot; the fat was used to cure the gout and blood rubbed onto thinning hair was thought to be a sure cure for baldness. Even more bizarre was the use made of a dog fox's genitalia; his testicles were tied around a child's neck as a cure for toothache whilst the fretful infant's parents, fed up with its crying, were encouraged to tie the penis around their aching heads to relieve the throbbing. Topsell, writing in 1607, adds to this grisly list by recommending a mixture of fox faeces and vinegar as a cure for leprosy (I think I'd prefer to carry the bell!), a fox tongue hung on a chain around the neck defended the wearer from blindness, the bile cured ear-ache, and powdered liver and lungs, when added to wine, guaranteed relief from breathing problems; gall stones were cured by drinking reynard's blood and epileptic children were treated by being fed fox brains. Finally, the fat of a fox, and also that of other animals, including the otter and badger, was rubbed upon rheumatic limbs to make them more supple and less painful. It is quite obvious from this impressive, if unattractive, list that foxes were being killed on quite a large scale and we could be forgiven for thinking that the organised fox hunt had long been a part of our country scene. This is not so, as a summary of the well documented history of fox hunting will very clearly show.

FOX HUNTING

Hunting is as old as man himself but ritualised hunting purely for sport, as opposed to a combination of food, fun and proof of manhood, came relatively late in Man's history and, in Britain, reached a peak in Saxon culture, maintaining its position until Elizabethan times, when shortage of suitable game strangled the 'sport'. Fox hunting did not figure highly on the sportsman's list and, although it was practised by the Greeks and the Romans, it gave no pleasure, being seen as a boring job necessary to keep the vermin down. In Thrace, however, fox skins were used to make caps for use in the winter months, a tradition which has continued into modern times.

It was the French nobility who took the lead in mediaeval hunting and as early as 1387, Gaston de Foix produced an impressive treatise on hunting in which he listed, in order of merit, the beasts of the chase; the top ten were the hare (rather surprising this), hart (red deer) buck (fallow deer), roe, wild boar, wolf, fox, badger, wild cat and the marten. This work was adapted for the English in 1420 by Edward, Duke of York, under the impressive title *The Master of Game*. On the continent, hunting continued unabated well into the seventeenth century but, in England, problems had arisen and, by the sixteenth century, demand had long outstripped supply. The wolf and boar were to all intents and purposes extinct and hart and buck were in such short supply that the deer park had taken the place of the forest. The park

consisted of an escape-proof enclosure, often of very substantial proportions, in which were constructed a number of vantage points towards which
imported deer could be literally driven to the slaughter. The deer thus
retained their prominent position in the hunters' popularity league and fox
hunting still received few mentions in the contemporary literature, none of
which were complimentary. Three new factors now reduced the deer stocks
still more and may be said to have played their part in the origins of our fox
hunt; these were the evolution of accurate easy-to-load firearms, the destruction of the deer parks during the period of the Civil War and
Cromwell's period in office and, of even greater significance, the felling of
the forests to fuel the greed of the industrial revolution. By the time of
Charles II, deer were being imported from the Continent on a large scale to
satisfy the demands of the hunt, the focus of attention was turned upon the
hare (see Chapter 5) and harriers began to replace the packs of deerhounds
in the eighteen-century gentleman's entourage. The hare is, however, very
small and the lusty chaps began to turn their attention to hunting fox. This
shift in emphasis had already gained some momentum when, in 1793, the
Prince of Wales began to convert his pack of deerhounds into foxhounds.
The fox was now a popular beast conserved for the pleasure of gentlemen
rather than an item of vermin to be destroyed and presented to the churchwardens in order to collect the bounty on its head.

It would seem that, in the north country, this tradition had already begun
early in the seventeenth century, as reference to the diaries of Squire
Nicholas Assherton of Downham written in 1617 shows:

*June 24th: To Worston Brook. Tryed for a fox; found nothing. Towler lay at a
rabbit and we stayed and wrought and took hime.*
*June 25th: I hounded and killed a bitche foxe. After that to Salthill. There we
had a bowson [a badger]. We wrought him out and killed him.*

This exploit of Squire Assherton is mentioned in Harrison Ainsworth's *The
Lancashire Witches* and some details of his character, typical of many hunting men of the time, are most enlightening:

*... Nicholas Assherton of Downham, who, except as regards his Puritanism,
might be considered a type of the Lancashire squire of the day.*

*A precisian in religious notions, and constant in attendance at church and
lecture, he put no sort of restraint upon himself, but mixed fox-hunting, otter
hunting, shooting at the mark, and perhaps shooting with the long bow, foot-
racing, horse racing, and, in fact, every other kind of country diversion, not
forgetting tippling, cards, and dicing with daily devotion, discourses and psalm-
singing in the oddest way imaginable.*

Assherton may have been just a little ahead of his time but, from the
beginning of the nineteenth century, the practice of fox hunting has become
an established part of English country life, despite gathering objections to

its continuance. This is not the place to discuss a detailed history of the sport or the relative pros and cons of the hunt, but let it be said that there will always be a need to control foxes, especially in the possible event of rabies reaching these islands. Table 10 shows that, in France, the fox is the most important vector in the spread of this horrific disease.

Table 10 RECORDED CASES OF RABIES IN FRENCH WILD AND DOMESTIC ANIMALS FROM 26 JUNE 1968 TO 1 FEBRUARY 1979

Species	Number of Cases
Fox	12,038
Cattle	1,519
Cat	558
Dog	360
Sheep and goats	335

After Lloyd, 1980.

These figures, and the fact that foxes are now living and thriving in urban situations, including London, Birmingham, Nottingham, Manchester, Glasgow and Edinburgh, means that a variety of control methods must be available and shooting, snaring, trapping and gassing all play their part as upwards of 50 000 foxes are destroyed annually without any apparent diminution of population trends. A significant and extremely useful contribution to fox control has been the setting up of fox destruction societies, which, according to Lloyd (1980), numbered about 230 in 1979, by far the largest number being in Wales. Many of these are highly organised and play an important part in protecting the farming and small-holding communities against the ravages of a minority of foxes, which supplement their 'natural diet' by regular raids on poultry, lambs and other domestic livestock. However efficient these methods may be, the future of *Vulpes vulpes* in Britain is secure for many years. The ability of the fox to survive close to increasing human populations is a measure of its powers of adaptation, a feature which is not shared by the wild cat.

The Wild Cat *Felis silvestris*

The male wild cat has an average weight of 5 kg (11 lb), the female being 1 kg ($2\frac{1}{4}$ lb) lighter. The cat is 550 mm ($21\frac{1}{2}$ in) long with a tail of a further 300 mm (12 in). The dental formula is:

$$2 \times \left\{ I\,\frac{3}{3} \quad C\,\frac{1}{1} \quad PM\,\frac{3}{2} \quad M\,\frac{1}{1} \right\} = 30.$$

A breeding pair occupies a territory of about 60 hectares (150 acres). There are two breeding periods: one in early March and another in early July. The gestation period is 63 days and the litter size is between four and five. The

The wild cat (*Felis sylvestris*)—Britain's fiercest beast of prey.

kittens are weaned at 4 months and are independent by 5 months of age. Occasionally a third litter may be conceived in November or December. (These figures are based upon European statistics.) The wild cat is generally yellowish grey with much variation in the dark bands and spots which are a feature of its dorsal markings. The tail is thick and bushy.

There can be little doubt that the true wild cat was once common throughout Britain but, apparently, it has always been absent from Ireland, where any sightings previously made are thought to have referred to large feral specimens.

In 1127, the species must have been fairly common because Archbishop Corbyl decreed that abbesses and nuns were in future not to be allowed to wear or use, for any purpose whatever, fur of greater worth than lamb or wild cat. *Felis silvestris* was, however, a favourite beast of the chase; Richard II (1377 to 1399) granted a charter to the Abbot of Peterborough enabling him to kill fox and wild cat. There is no argument about the wild cat's ability to give a good account of itself and the title of British tiger, given to it in later years by Pennant, was probably well deserved. There are many recorded instances, most suitably embellished, of angry individuals attacking people, often without warning; one which is of particular note is narrated by Mr H.W. Shepherd-Walwyn:

There exists at Bambrough an ancient record commemorating the ferocity of the wild cat. The story is that Percival Cresacre, a youth of distinguished family, was returning to his home from a fair in Doncaster when, as he was passing though a plantation known as Melton wood a wild cat suddenly leapt from the trees and attacked him. This man sought with his gauntletted hands to gripple with his foe, but the latter's sharp teeth were too much for him. Badly mauled Cresacre endeavoured to escape towards Bambrough but the cat pursued him and compelled him to seek shelter in the porch of the Church at Bambrough. Even here the creature did not relinquish the fight but inflicted such terrible wounds as to cause the death of young Percival who in his last struggle seems to have crushed the cat with his foot against the wall. In the morning man and cat were found dead in the porch of the Church where the weird contest had ended.

My worry about this story is that we have almost a blow-by-blow account of a fight in which both combatants perished and where there were no other human witnesses. I have no doubt that many a foul murder was committed under the blanket of night and blamed upon carnivorous beasts. A dead cat plus a human corpse might well have provided enough circumstantial evidence for a verdict of misadventure to be easily accepted. There is no doubt that wild cats will occasionally attack people but this must be the exception rather than the rule. Professor J.J. Simpson in *Chats on British Mammals* describes the hunting technique of the wild cat:

When it has stalked its prey within reasonable distance it finishes up with a series of tremendously quick bounds: it utters a heartrending shriek which strikes terror into its intended victim; the latter becomes paralysed, its muscles benumbed and it falls easy prey.

This sounds a bit like a domestic moggy plus a scream for embellishment. I have been lucky enough on several occasions to watch wild cats prowling and have never heard the blood-curdling scream referred to, but they do invariably carry their prey back to the seclusion of a lair where it is eaten. They also show a distinct liking for trees with branches spreading parallel to the ground; they lie along a branch perfectly screened from below.

As with the ferret and the polecat, it is difficult to decide upon the precise origins of the domestic cat from a wild ancestor(or ancestors), the answer being concealed behind the curtain of time. The Ancient Egyptians certainly used the cat, and it reached Europe via the Greeks, but is this rat-catching usurper of the marten the only ancestor of our domestic tabby? Sir Harry Johnston is quite certain that the European wild cat has had some influence on its development, despite the frequently voiced opinion that *Felis silvestris* is our only wild mammal which can never be tamed. In Ancient Egypt, it was known that rats carried plague, as well as causing catastrophe by eating food urgently needed by the human population in times of famine, and it was therefore no wonder that rat-catching cats were sacred beasts. The goddess Pasht is depicted in ancient carvings with human body and cat's head and it may well be from this deity that our word 'puss' is derived. But, to return to the wild cat in Britain, we find that its distribution has been well documented as befits a fierce beast which frightened folk. The situation up to about 1896 was documented by Lydekker:

... the Wild Cat was formerly widely distributed in Britain, although it appears never to have been a native of Ireland. At the present day it is restricted only to the northern districts of our islands, and is there becoming year by year more rare. This sole British representative of the feline family is proved, both by tradition and by the discovery of its fossilised remains in cavern and superficial deposits, to have originally ranged over the whole of such parts of England as were suited to its habits. Such remains have been discovered in the Pleistocene brick-earths of Grays, in Essex, in company with the remains of Mammoths, Hippopotami, Rhinoceroses, and other Mammals now either totally extinct, or long since banished from Britain to warmer climates. They also occur, in association with similar creatures, in the caves of Bleadon (in the Mendips), Cresswell Crags (Derbyshire), Kent's Hole (near Torquay), Ravenscliff (Glamorganshire), Uphill (in the Mendips), and the Vale of Clywd, while quite recently they have been discovered in a fissure in the Wealden rocks near Ightham, in Kent.

When the Wild Cat disappeared from the south and midland counties of England, appears to be quite unknown; but there is evidence that it lingered till a comparatively late date in the wooded parts of the Lake district, although it does not seem ever to have been numerous there during the historical period. According to the Rev. H.A. Macpherson, there is historical evidence of the existence of this animal in the Lake district in the year 1629, and again as late as 1754; while in the intervening period there are to be found in the parish records numerous entries of the sums disbursed for the destruction of these marauders. At a still later date, Gilpin, when describing a tour made through the district in 1772, says that the mountains around Helvellyn, 'and indeed many other parts of the country are frequented by the Wild Cat, which Mr. Pennant calls the British Tiger, and says it is the fiercest and most destructive beast we have. He speaks of it as being three or four times as large as a common Cat. We saw one dead, which had been hunted on the day we saw it; and it seemed very little inferior, if at all, to the size he mentions.' By 1795 Wild Cats seem to have become very scarce in the mountains of Cumberland and Westmoreland; and the last authentic occurrence of one of these animals in the district appears to have been in 1843, when a fine specimen is stated to have been killed near Loweswater. It is true that the occurrence of the Wild Cat has been recorded in these districts in quite recent years—even as late as 1871—but all such records appear to have been based on large feral specimens of the Domestic Cat.

This large domestic cat versus true *Felis silvestris* controversy arose again in the publication of the 11th Annual Report of the Lancashire and Cheshire Fauna Committee for the year 1924, with an article entitled 'Wild Cats on Lancashire-Westmorland Border' by H.W. Robinson:

Macpherson, in his 'Fauna of Lakeland,' gives no definite records of genuine Wild Cats in Lakeland, except that Wm. Pearson, writing in 1839, believes that one he saw caught in a snare at Cartmel Fell was genuine. The famous hunter, John Elleray, who died some years previous to the publication of the Fauna in

1892, aged well over 90, said that he had been in at the death of more than one wild cat. Mr. Hope informs me that in the archives of the Carlisle Museum there is a statement made by one W. Hodgson, writing in 1885, that Squire Taylor's pack of hounds killed one on Great Mell Fell (in Mid-Cumberland) over forty years before. As there is no description of this animal, it was probably only one of the many feral cats which are continually being killed all over the country.

There seems, therefore, to be no definite record of true wild cats in Lakeland at all. Recent writers state that the true wild cat only survives north of the Caledonian Canal. This is rather a sweeping statement to make, for I can vouch that twenty years ago it still survived in Argyllshire, and also less than twenty years ago, one pair, at least, as far south as North Perthshire. I had never in my most sanguine moments expected to meet the genuine British wild cat in Lakeland, as I have worked the district well for thirty years, both in front of and behind hounds, without seeing or hearing of any trace of such creatures.

In October, 1922, reports came from the shooting tenant of a wild tract of country on the Westmorland and Lancashire border (Dr. Fred Hogarth, of Morecambe) of an enormous pair of cats, of which glimpses had been caught at rare intervals. The male had been shot at, but was thought to have escaped. He probably died of his wounds, as he was not seen again.

On October 29th the female attacked the Doctor's three dogs, and he had to shoot her to save them from a bad mauling. Dr. Hogarth fortunately preserved the animal, which he now has set up. There is no possible doubt but that the animal is a genuine wild cat (Felis silvestris), and not a feral specimen.

About two years previous to this a man named Wildman shot two enormous cats in the same district, which he hung up in a tree. He has seen the Doctor's specimen, and states that, as far as he remembers, the cats were identical.

The place where these cats were shot was Hutton Roof, between Carnforth and Burton on the Lancashire and Westmorland border.

About ten years previously, a well-known landowner turned down a pair of wild cats from Argyllshire on the Lancashire side of Windermere Lake, but as both were trapped not far away too soon afterwards for them to have left any progeny, there can be no connection between them and this pair.

Thus died what is probably the only authentic pair of wild cats recorded in England for nearly a hundred years.

So the record rested in the archives until, in 1959, the 31st Report of the same organisation began to express doubts and published a further report 'Scottish Wild Cat (*Felis silvestris grampia* Miller)':

A pair of Wild Cats near Carnforth in October 1922 was recorded by H. W. Robinson. The ♀ was shot and killed, the ♂ wounded by Dr. F. W. Hogarth, who writes (in litt., 18.2.57), 'It is a genuine Wild Cat such as may now be seen in Inverness or the Highlands. It has the bob-tail, the black dorsal stripe and the bigger dental measurement. It is in my waiting room for anyone to see; indeed many authorities have been to see it.'

Accurate measurements of the skull before the specimen was mounted would have confirmed the identification, but as this cannot now be done, the possibility that it is a large specimen of the Domestic Cat gone feral, must not be overlooked.

In his account Robinson stated 'There seems to be no definite record of true wild cats in Lakeland at all', yet he was prepared to champion this most unusual record.

By now I was determined, urged on by an eminent natural historian, K.G. Spencer, to follow the specimen to its last resting place. I succeeded in tracing Dr Hogarth's daughter, who still resides in Morecambe, and she informed me that, on her father's death, his collection of specimens, including the wild cat, had been donated to the City Museum and Art Gallery at Lancaster. I visited and measured the specimen and the measurements are summarised and compared to positively identified specimens of *Felis silvestris* (see Table 11); we still have no positive proof that we are dealing with

Table 11 COMPARISON OF BODY MEASUREMENTS OF DR HOGARTH'S SPECIMEN WITH THE WILD CAT (*Felis silvestris*)

Specimen	Length of Head and Body	Length of Tail	Diameter of Hind Feet
Dr Hogarth's female	350 mm ($13\frac{3}{4}$ in)	290 mm ($11\frac{1}{2}$ in)	110 mm ($4\frac{1}{4}$ in)
Felis sylvestris: male	370–590 mm ($14\frac{1}{2}$–$23\frac{1}{4}$ in)	310 mm ($12\frac{1}{4}$ in)	140 mm ($5\frac{1}{2}$ in)
female	350–540 mm ($13\frac{3}{4}$–$21\frac{1}{4}$ in)	290 mm ($11\frac{1}{2}$ in)	130 mm (5 in)

England's last wild cat, but the possibility cannot be ruled out. Roebuck and Clarke (1881) suggests 1840 as the last reliable date for the presence of the wild cat in that county. In Scotland, the present situation is certainly more healthy than the pessimism of Lydekker in 1896 would give us any right to expect:

In Scotland, though still lingering, the Wild Cat is rapidly decreasing in numbers. According to Messrs. Harvie-Brown and Buckley, while it has become extremely rare in Assynt during the last few years, it is still not uncommon in the Reay Forest, where it is preserved by the Duke of Westminster. These authors write that 'one keeper in Assynt killed no less than twenty-six Wild Cats between 1869 and 1880, but of these only three during the last six years. Another keeper killed ten between 1870 and 1873, but no more until the winter of 1879–80, when he killed four, one of which is described as a monster.' In Caithness the Wild Cat is still more rare, only four having been recorded as being killed during some ten years before 1880. Writing in 1882 of its present limits in Scotland, the former of the two authors just quoted said that the Wild Cat is 'extinct all south and east of a line commencing, roughly speaking, at Oban, in Argyllshire, passing up the Brander Pass to Dalmally, following the boundary of Perthshire, and including Rannoch Moor. Thence continued north-eastward to the junction of the three counties of Perth, Forfar, and Aberdeen; thence across the sources of the Dee northward to Tomintoul in Banffshire; and lastly from Tomintoul to the city of Inverness. Northwards and westwards of this line the animal still keeps a footing.' In Argyll at this date it had receded to the more mountainous districts, where, however, it was not very uncommon. In the Hebrides the Wild Cat is unknown.

By 1979, however, the wild cat was not only holding its own, but actually making an impressive come-back, expanding its range in Britain perhaps for the first time for many centuries. Most of the highland areas of Scotland now have breeding wild cats and it is interesting to speculate why this should be so. Several reasons have been suggested, including the onset of myxomatosis, which made rabbits sluggish and more easily caught, especially in the winter months when the going can be really tough in these exposed regions. Add to this the increase in tree cover resulting from the extensive plantings, mainly by the Forestry Commission from 1919 onwards but also by private landowners, and a final but not inconsiderable factor of a reduction in hunting pressure and the increase appears almost predictable.

Some interbreeding between feral and wild cats cannot be overlooked but breeding sites are certainly not at a premium. There seems to be some evidence that Scottish wild cats may breed twice a year (March and June) following an aggressive courtship; the gestation period is about 9 to 10 weeks and an average of three kittens are born. The sites favoured by the female, who often has to defend her young against marauding males who would kill them if given chance, are in hollow trees or in clefts in rocky terrain. The young are fed by the female for about a month and can hunt for themselves in 4 months. Most are living on their own and fending for themselves by 6 months of age. They are able to breed when only 1 year old and may live for up to 15 years; thus the reproductive potential is there once restraints are removed and, for the first time in centuries, the future of *Felis silvestris* in Britain seems fairly secure.

9 Carnivores: the Marten, Stoat, Weasel, Polecat, Ferret and Badger

The weasel family, or Mustelidae (see Table 12), is a bit like the oft-mentioned curate's egg—good in parts—when we consider its effects, for good or evil, on the enterprises of mankind. Two chapters will be devoted to its members. The first begins with the rare pine marten and goes on to consider the common stoat and weasel, the uncommon wild polecat and its common domesticated relative the ferret. Finally the badger is described. Chapter 10 will describe the brief history of the newly established mink and the long saga of the indigenous otter.

Table 12 A SUMMARY OF THE BRITISH MUSTELIDAE

Common Name	Scientific Name	Dimensions	Notes
pine marten	*Martes martes*	Males over 10% larger than females: head and body 500 mm (20 in), tail 220 mm (8⅘ in).	Some increase in recent years after centuries of decline.
stoat	*Mustela erminea*	Males 50% larger than females: head and body 300 mm (12 in), tail 110 mm (4⅖ in).	Black tip to tail always present. Found in Ireland where the locals call it a weasel.
weasel	*Mustela nivalis*	Head and body averages 200 mm (8 in) in males and 180 mm ($7\frac{1}{5}$ in) in females; tail 50–60 mm ($2\frac{1}{3}$–$2\frac{2}{5}$ in).	No black tip to tail. Absent from Ireland.
polecat (ferret)	*Mustela putorius* (*Mustela furo*)	Head and body averages 400 mm (16 in) in males and 320 mm ($12\frac{4}{5}$ in) in females; tail 140 mm ($5\frac{3}{5}$ in) in males, 120 mm ($4\frac{4}{5}$ in) in females.	Polecats and ferrets are similar in size and will interbreed if given the opportunity.
mink	*Mustela vison*	Males twice as heavy and about 30% larger than females: head and body 400 mm (16 in), tail 240 mm ($9\frac{3}{5}$ in).	Introduced from North America. The European mink (*Mustela lutreola*) is absent from Britain.
otter	*Lutra lutra*	Head and body averages 800 mm (32 in) in males and 650 mm (26 in) in females; tail 240 mm ($9\frac{3}{5}$ in) in males and 300 mm (12 in) in females.	Numbers diminishing alarmingly in recent years.
badger	*Meles meles*	Head and body 750 mm (30 in) in males and 700 mm (28 in) in females; tail 150 mm (6 in).	Has suffered centuries of persecution which continues despite recent attempts to protect it by law.

The Pine Marten *Martes martes*

This delightful looking mammal, also known as the marten cat, sweet-mart and marteron, is a rich and uniform brown in colour, apart from a creamy yellow bib across the throat. For this reason, it has been referred to as the yellow-throated marten to distinguish it from the closely related white-throated marten, or beech marten, which was once thought to exist in these islands; indeed the beech marten is listed as British in the 1837 edition of Bell's *History of British Quadrupeds*, which also included such beasts as the common marten and stone marten. This taxonomic and geographical confusion has now been satisfactorily resolved and we now have only the pine marten on the British list. In 1879, Alston collected sufficient data to prove that the beech marten is not indigenous to Britain; there is no doubt, however, about the true status of the pine marten because fossil remains have been discovered in Norfolk, Bleadon and at Shandon in Ireland. Although formerly widespread throughout these islands, its range has been contracting, a trend which seems to have gathered momentum from 1830 onwards. By 1870, it had disappeared from most of England with the exception of the Lake District. In the 1903 edition of *British Mammals*, Sir Harry Johnston mentions a recent killing of a pine marten in Herefordshire.

The fur of the animal was of aesthetic value until the seventeenth century, doubtless due to its availability and because it lacked the offensive smell associated with the pelts of the other species described in this chapter; this accounts for its complimentary name of sweet-mart. The hunting pressure certainly contributed to its decline but the pine marten also suffered from loss of habitat as woodlands were destroyed and human settlements proliferated and expanded. Frances Pitt (1938) suggested yet another reason for the decline, pointing out that the marten was so inquisitive that it was easy to

The pine marten (*Martes martes*).

shoot and trap. The fact that only one small litter (three or four young born in April) is produced in a year means that, in areas where persecution of the species is pronounced, the population can decline very rapidly. In her evidence she quotes a story from the 1930s:

A native of the Fell District said he attributed the virtual disappearance of the Pine Marten from Westmorland and Cumberland to the increase of the rabbit. In his young days rabbits were very few and 'marts' were comparatively common, but rabbits gradually increased and spread from the low ground to the fellsides until at the present time they are exceedingly numerous and intensive rabbit catching is a necessity—with fatal results for the [inquisitive] martens.

At one time, the hunting of the marten cat with hounds specially trained for the job was very popular and the aim was to 'tree' the terrified quarry. A huntsman would then shin up the tree and his henchmen would pass up to him a bale of smoking straw or other convenient damp vegetation. This was tied to the end of a long pole and poked at the marten which was dealt with as it fell, blinded by smoke and panic. I expect that its shriekings and growlings earned it the reputation of being a fierce adversary worthy of chase by intrepid heroes and belies the fact that it was at one time kept as a pet. The early Greeks kept martens as such before domestic cats were introduced from Egypt and they proved to be both more friendly and more efficient at ridding dwellings of troublesome rodents. The carnivorous diet of the marten is reflected in its dental formula which is:

$$2 \times \left\{ I \frac{3}{3} \quad C \frac{1}{1} \quad PM \frac{4}{4} \quad M \frac{1}{2} \right\} = 38.$$

Although it will pursue its prey through trees, showing great dexterity, economy of movement and a fearless sense of balance, it is not quite so arboreal as previously thought. Its very varied diet includes birds, squirrels, field voles, eggs, beetles, carrion and even frogs and fish. An ability to function as a predator below, at, or above ground level typifies all the species described in this chapter, not least the stoat.

The Stoat *Mustela erminea*

The stoat is known by a variety of other names, including ermine weasel, stout, greater weasel, club-tail, white weasel, stot, whittret, hob and royal hunter. The word stoat actually means 'bold' and this is certainly a true description of this attractive predator. The word 'cunning' would also fit the species and it has been credited by country folk with the most remarkable methods of obtaining its food. W.S. Berridge (1934), in *Wild Animals of Our Country*, writes:

The most effective method practiced by the stoat for obtaining its prey, however, is to eject an evil smelling fluid that is secreted by two glands situated at the

A stoat (*Mustela erminea*) with a dead rabbit. Note how the stoat is able to kill prey much larger than itself.

roof of its tail. The scent of this secretion which is almost as malodourous as that emitted by a skunk has a terrifying, or even hypnotic effect upon the stoat's victims. Hares and rabbits will scream in a most pitiful manner when they recognise the scent of their foe and long before the stoat comes into view the unfortunate rodents [hares and rabbits are now classified as lagomorphs, not rodents] *become so paralysed with fear that they are rendered incapable of making the least effort to escape. With eyes closed and with rapidly beating heart they remain fixed to one spot. Their limbs become useless and their victims await their doom.*

While admitting a certain measure of anthropomorphic and poetic licence in the countryman's awestruck view of the almost supernatural powers of the blood-thirsty stoat, which is clearly demonstrated in the above quotation, we must not under-rate the beast either. In a letter to *The Field* in the late 1920s, Mr H. Mortimer Batten gives an equally respectful view of the stoat's hypnotic effect on potential prey:

Fishing on the Wharfe near Burnsall I watched a stoat hunting and killing young rabbits. One after the other they appeared at the burrow mouth and sat there shivering till the stoat dispatched them. For some time he did not see me, but the smell of acetylene gas and onions came clearly down the breeze.

Another opinion frequently voiced during gatherings of those fascinated by events occurring in the natural world is that the black tail-tip of the stoat serves the purpose of keeping a group of them together. I must admit that I do not find the argument very convincing, but I cannot deny that stoats are often seen in co-ordinated groups, apparently hell-bent on finding food and have even been accused of attacking sheep, dogs and also people alone in the country. Again Berridge reports:

A few months ago a highland shepherd came across a company of stoats which immediately attacked him. They clambered up his body and endeavoured to reach his throat and it was with the greatest difficulty that the man managed to beat them off.

This was, however, only an isolated incident and may have been due to some unseen phenomenon as well as being subject to a little exaggeration. Any group encountered will more than likely be a jill, as the female is called (the male is called a hob), accompanied by her young, of which she produces between four and seven in a litter. Only one litter is produced each year, some 5 weeks after mating. Copulation occasionally occurs in spring, in which case the young are born in summer and, after a period of some 7 weeks suckling, gradually learn to fend for themselves and are pretty well independent by the onset of winter. They are occasionally sexually mature after 1 year but it is usually the second year before they breed successfully. Usually, however, copulation does not occur until high summer, in which case the development of the embryo is delayed for 7 months (see Chapter 2) before the 2-month gestation period is entered upon. Some workers have suggested that the male may assist in the bringing up of his offspring, so the marauding bands referred to may be made up of nine or perhaps ten individuals.

Arguably, the most discussed aspect of stoat biology is the white pelage (ermine) which develops in some stoats in winter over part of the range occupied by the species. Most individuals in northern and mountainous areas assume the ermine but, further south and at sea level, this change may only be partial or may not occur at all. How the change into white is controlled has long troubled naturalists and one early suggestion was that stoats could bring about the change almost at will simply by eating snow! A curious fact has emerged from recent researches, namely that a greater proportion of females assume the ermine condition, the change being brought about by a complex of factors, prominent among them being a decrease in day length as autumn gives way to winter and a reduction in sex hormone levels following the mating season. Although it often tends to be discounted, I feel that significant falls in temperature must play some part, even if only a small one. It is perhaps significant that, in the Pendleside district of Lancashire where I live, I observed five stoats in ermine during the bad winter of 1982 compared with only one white individual in 1981. At one time, the pursuit of stoats in ermine was a lucrative business and its wearing was at first regarded as the prerogative of Royalty, a fact fully legalised by an Act passed in the reign of Edward III (1327–77). This law was eventually relaxed slightly and the robes and capes of peers of the realm and their consorts, as well as those of learned judges, were allowed to be edged with the white fur. Ermine capes were invariably spotted with black which were not, as has frequently been asserted, obtained from the black tip at the end of the stoat's tail, but from the tails of astrakhan lambs. Any garment with symmetrical spotting all over it was referred to as a 'minerva'.

The stoat is a comparatively long-lived beast, often surviving up to 10 years in the wild, and it is also very adaptable. This was proved in the days when myxomatosis was at its most lethal, when the stoat simply intensified its search for rodents, birds, earthworms and even the odd scraps of vegetable matter. I once sat watching a stoat scrambling and balancing on a riverside elder, swaying over a river in spate due to the combined weight of the heavy berries and the agile stoat. Periodically, the royal hunter found a steady bough, taking with it a bunch of juicy fruit which it munched, licking its chops now and again, but not often enough to prevent its fur becoming matted with thick purple juice. Although the mustelids are not regular eaters of fruit, they do enjoy the occasional dessert, the weasel for example, being quite partial to the occasional blackberry.

The Weasel *Mustela nivalis*

Frances Pitt, writing in the 1940s about the weasel makes, at least in the eyes of gamekeepers, a controversial statement, which incidentally applies equally well to the stoat. She wrote:

The weasel is a valuable visitor to the farmstead and a most useful creature in field and wood where it does much good by keeping down the number of injurous small rodents—a good which far exceeds such occasional mis-deeds as the looting of tiny game chicks.

I share Miss Pitt's view but this 'whitewashing of the weasel' of which I am often accused, does not impress the gamekeeping fraternity, and the maimed, shrivelled pathetic little bodies of the 'vermin' still dangle from their grisly gibbets. That both the stoat and weasel can actually be used to control vermin was known, or should we say admitted, at least from the beginning of the nineteenth century when they were introduced into New Zealand in an effort to control rabbits. In the first edition of the *Naturalist's Library*, Macgillivray (1830) described the weasel as chasing mice into:

... barns, granaries and corn-stacks, despatching them generally by a single bite which perforates the brain. In the fields and pastures it has been seen following its prey by scent, turning and doubling on the track, and pursuing it even into the water.

This service to farmers was also referred to by Bell in 1837:

Above all, it should not be molested in barns, ricks or granaries, in which situations it is of great service in destroying the great colonies of Mice which infest them.

And yet we still kill them! Perhaps some of us enjoy it!

Like the stoat, the weasel has a circumpolar distribution and is still common throughout England, Wales and Scotland. It is known variously as the common weasel, mouse-hunter, kine and, in Wales, *bronwen*. It is not known to exist in Ireland, however, and in that green and pleasant land so short of mammals, the stoat is actually referred to as the weasel. In the 1877 issue of the *Zoologist*, a weasel was reported from County Mayo *but* some doubt was expressed regarding the identification and, even if it was a weasel, one occurrence can only suggest a deliberate introduction. Lydekker, writing in 1896, also notes its absence from the Outer Hebrides and indicates some decline in population levels as a result of trapping and keepering. Weasels certainly vary a great deal in size (see Table 12), but there is no evidence to support the view, once held, that a smaller species existed and was called a 'miniver' or 'finger weasel'. Some errors have also occurred concerning the feeding habits of weasels and also of stoats. It is still widely believed that they only suck the blood of their victims and never eat the flesh; this is just not true, as even the most casual observations of the animal will amply demonstrate.

Like the stoat, the weasel has the light coloured 'shirt front' and also similar under-belly shades but, in addition to the lack of a black tip to its shorter tail, its dorsal colouration is of a much richer and more glistening brown. Furthermore, it would seem that individual weasels can be recognised by the unique shape of the white patch on the breast. I have spoken to naturalists whose views I greatly respect, who are able to recognise each member of a weasel family by its own particular patch pattern. Outside the breeding season, the jill and hob remain separated, each having their own territory, which varies in size according to the availability of prey in the area, but on average the territory of the male is larger and a figure of between 1 and 6 hectares ($2\frac{1}{2}$ and 15 acres) would seem to be the norm. During a year, one or perhaps two, litters, each of five young are produced. Unlike the stoat, there is no evidence of delayed implantation and a jill born in early spring can breed in her first autumn. Very few individuals live beyond their second year and, as with other mammals, it is possible to work out the age by the degree of wear and tear on the teeth. These are very sharp and can inflict a nasty bite on anyone rash enough to try to handle a wild weasel but, despite their understandable reputation as pugnacious little creatures, they have been kept as friendly, even affectionate, pets. This domesticity typical of the whole family is nowhere better exemplified than in the study of the polecat and its close relative the ferret.

The Polecat *Mustela putorius*

Bell, in *A History of British Quadrupeds*, labels the polecat, fitchet weasel,

The weasel (*Mustela nivalis*)

A weasel (*Mustela nivalis*) on the alert for prey.

fitchen, foulmart or fulimart as a menace to farming and sporting enterprises, but he notes that its fur:

> ... *though far less beautiful and of inferior value to that of the Sable, or even of the Marten, is still much esteemed, and numbers are annually imported here from the North of Europe, under the name of* Fitch.
> *The common name of this species,* Polecat, *is probably nothing more than* Polish cat.

These introductions were probably made necessary because of centuries of persecution which brought it to the brink of extinction. In 1896, Lydekker continues the depressing story of the decline of the polecat:

> *The geographical range of the Polecat includes the greater portion of Europe, its northern limits extending to the south of Sweden, and in Russia to the White Sea; it is, however, unknown in the extreme south, and its predilection for a cool climate is indicated by the circumstance that during the summer it ascends in the Alps far above the forest limit. In England, owing to the relentless persecution of*

The European polecat (*Mustela putorius*).

gamekeepers, it is one of those species fast approaching extinction, being now but rarely met with in most of the southern and midland counties. Mr. Montagu Browne, for instance, writes that in Leicestershire and Rutlandshire it is becoming increasingly rare, and will soon be exterminated. In the Lake district, where these animals were once so abundant that in one unusually good season as many as thirty-nine were killed, we are told by the Rev. H.A. Macpherson that within the last thirty years, mainly owing to the employment of steel traps, they have become very scarce. The narrow strip of marshy and heavily-timbered country extending from Bowness is, however, still a stronghold for this much-persecuted creature, and one from which it will with difficulty be completely exterminated. Although to southern ears the idea of hunting such an insignificant animal with hounds appears absurd, yet Foumart-hunting was at one time a favourite sport of the Westmoreland dalesmen; the hunts generally taking place during the night in midwinter. Much the same story is told with regard to Scotland, in many parts of which it has become well-nigh exterminated.

In addition to hunting pressures, it would seem certain that the inbred mustelid curiosity caused many polecats to perish in traps set for the increasing populations of rabbits. Since the turn of this century, their range has diminished still further and many records of their presence these days is often due to confusion with escaped ferrets, which are able to live off the land with little difficulty. *The Handbook of British Mammals* (1977) indicates the polecat's continued presence in all the Welsh counties except Anglesey, but the last Scottish record seems to be dated 1907. A few English counties, such as Shropshire, Herefordshire and Gloucestershire, have recent populations, but their presence is not recorded in Ireland.

Little is known of the breeding of wild polecats in Britain but with such small and restricted populations this is hardly surprising. It is known, however, that one litter of about eight young are produced each year, following a gestation period of approximately 6 weeks; the offspring become sexually mature during their first or, more often, their second year. Captive individuals have been known to survive longer than 10 years but it is highly unlikely that a life in the wild would be longer than half this period. This means that any improvement in the precarious status of the polecat is likely to be slow and the species requires an urgent, thorough and detached survey of both its habitat and dietary requirements. With regard to habitat, the choice open to the polecat is obviously varied these days; woodlands certainly still hold an attraction but so do sand dunes, river banks and even small-holdings and quiet farms. The latter choice is doubtless one, if not the main, reason for their present plight, since no farmer can be expected to welcome such an efficient predator close to his stock. Lydekker comments:

A dreaded enemy to all game-preservers, the Polecat possesses, for its size, a remarkable combination of strength and agility. Dwelling generally in woods and copses, or thicket-clad hills, it selects as a retreat and hiding-place either an empty Rabbit-burrow, a crevice among the rocks, or even the cavities in a heap of stones.... Remaining quiet during the day, and issuing forth towards evening, the Polecat, writes Macgillivray, when settled in the neighbourhood of a farmyard, will, at times, commit 'great depredations among the poultry, sucking the eggs, and killing the chickens, grown-up fowls, and even turkeys and geese. Not satisfied with obtaining enough to allay its hunger, it does not intermit its ravages until it has destroyed all within its reach, so that the havoc it makes is not less subject of surprise than of indignation to those on whom it has inflicted its unwelcome visit.... If undisturbed it sometimes satisfies its hunger on the spot, and in the midst of its slaughtered victims, but in general it carries its prey to some safe retreat. Its ferocity, cunning, and extreme agility, render it a great enemy to game of all kinds; and it destroys the eggs of Pheasants, Grouse, and Partridges, seizes the birds on their nests, pursues Rabbits into their burrows, and frequently seizes on young Hares. Besides birds and mammals, it also feeds on fishes and frogs, which have, in some instances, been found in its nest.'

This well known ability to pursue burrowing rabbits into their dark and tortuous underground retreats must long ago have been the envy of hungry hunting men. Here we have the origins of the domesticated ferrets.

The Ferret *Mustela furo*

There will always be controversy regarding the true origins of the ferret, a sure sign that so much interbreeding and backcrossing has gone on over the centuries that many ancestral types have been involved. The favourite choice of ancestor in the eyes of many sporting naturalists would probably be Evermann's polecat (*Mustela evermanni*) from western and northern Asia, but it should also be remembered that the ferret is still completely interfertile with the wild polecat and it would not, I think, be a sin to classify the two together as a ferret-polecat, a sort of superspecies. The dental formula of the two is identical:

$$2 \times \left\{ I\frac{3}{3} \quad C\frac{1}{1} \quad PM\frac{3}{3} \quad M\frac{1}{2} \right\} = 34.$$

The use of ferrets in the hunting of rabbits and other game can be traced back to, and beyond, classical Rome, and is mentioned in the writings of Pliny but, prior to this authority, mention is also found in the writings of Strabo.

During World War I, large numbers of ferrets were bred on both sides involved in the conflict and released into the trenches in an attempt to keep down rats. In the days before we understood the word inflation, the price of a ferret rocketed by over 500% between 1913 and 1916. After the peace treaty was signed in 1918, the demand evaporated and speculators had to think fast or go bankrupt. People like this do not go bankrupt and the excess albinos were killed and sold off as ermine fur.

The sport of ferreting is still popular and the future for these 'tame polecats' is much more secure than that of their wild relatives. A study of domesticated animals is not part of the objective of this book and for those who wish to read further about this sport, there are many books available. The badger is another animal which has not fared well at the hand of mankind, as the concluding section of this chapter will demonstrate all too well.

The Badger *Meles meles*

The badger has been variously known as bawsin, brock, greypate and baget. An old dictionary defines it thus:

Badger (also called bawsin): a wild four footed beast, somewhat resembling a fox and resembling a hound and a dog. It dwells in burrows, lives on meat carrion and fruit, stinks very much, fattens by sleeping, and shows its age by the number of holes in its tail, one being added each year.

It can be seen from this fanciful description that a great deal of poetic licence was exercised before more scientific attitudes became apparent, which was from the middle of the nineteenth century onwards. Another accepted notion was that the legs of a badger were shorter on one side than

The ferret-polecat—the result of interbreeding between the ferret (*Mustela furo*) and the wild polecat (*Mustela putorius*).

the other, to enable it to walk on sloping hillsides. What seems to have been tactfully ignored is that any advantage gained on the outward journey might very well be lost on the return trip.

Many folk regarded the badger as a lucky animal and parts of it were used as medicines or charms. Badger's blood was a recommended cure for leprosy and poor old brock was often rendered down to produce what was known as 'badger's grease'. This was used in the treatment of rheumatism and sore throats. Witches were said to use the fat of a newborn baby or, if this supply was not available, of a badger, as the basis of their flying

The ferret (*Mustela furo*) is perfectly at home with man.

ointments. Into the fat, they blended extracts from deadly nightshade (*Atropa belladonna*) and henbane (*Hyoscyamus niger*), both of which are very powerful and, if used carelessly, dangerous drugs. Modern research has found their active ingredients to be scopolamine and atropine which, when absorbed through the skin, cause a sensation of flying (the witch on her broom-stick?) and also of growing hair all over the body (the origin of the werewolf?) Thus badger fat was often surrounded by a very special mystique, but it also had more practical uses, one of which was as cooking fat, another as a polish for gaiters. In Ireland, badgers were eaten and cured in much the same way as we now cure bacon. Gamblers also had a love for the badger and they thought that they could improve their fortunes at the card tables by carrying a badger's tooth in their pocket. Farmers in Northumberland used to carry a part or the whole of a badger's tongue as a lucky charm.

If we now turn to the scientific facts concerning the animal we now know as *Meles meles*, we find that it has been present in Britain since Pleistocene times (over 14 million years ago) and fossils have been found in the caves of Kent as well as in other counties; in Ireland, its remains have been found at Shandon Cave. A look at old maps often reveals the presence of badgers incorporated into place names. The ancient name of brock was in use long before the present word 'badger', which derives from *becheur*, the French word for 'a digger'. Names such as Brockholes, Brockley, Brockleby, Brockmoor, Brockbank, Brockenhurst, Brockenborough and many others all indicate the one-time presence of badger setts. Even the word 'sett' itself is of historical importance since *cete* was the collective name for a family of badgers. In Wales, it is often called *mochyn bychan*, which means 'earth-pig'.

Badgers have been generally distributed around Britain but they have had their share of problems. The Rev. H.A. Macpherson, writing during the last 30 years of the nineteenth century, reported that, in the Lake District, the badger had become all but extinct, although a few were surviving in parts of the county of Westmorland and on Cartmel Fell (both now in Cumbria). Lydekker mentions that some were introduced towards the end of the nineteenth century and that they appeared to be settling down. The present distribution of badgers in these areas appears to be more healthy than was the case a century ago, although, as we shall see later, they still face some problems. One of the greatest of these, and certainly the most disturbing, is badger baiting. This practice has been illegal for many years, even before the 1973 Badger Protection Act, which became law on 25 January 1974. It was also in 1974 that the Frodsham (Cheshire) Natural History Society published some very significant figures. In a relatively small area of Cheshire, sixty-eight teams of badger diggers were turned off land, one team boasting that they had captured forty Cheshire badgers in 3 months. In the West Riding of Yorkshire, twenty-four out of thirty-two setts were damaged by diggers in 2 years and I know that, by 1979, the situation was, if anything, even worse. The position in Lakeland, while showing an improvement on the situation reported by Macpherson, is that diggers are preventing any further progress, especially in the Winster Valley and Long Sleddale areas. There is also a lot of evidence to show that working terrier clubs are very well organised and a menace to the future of the badger in many areas.

The 'sport' of badger baiting involves the placing of a live animal in a barrel which is laid on its side. The dogs are then encouraged to draw the badger from its refuge and many of the game little terriers are badly maimed in the process by the powerful jaws and teeth of their equally courageous adversary. To even up the contest, the badger is often beaten with iron bars or sticks in order to break its teeth and jaws before being put into the barrel. 'Sport' is certainly not the correct name for this barbarous practice. On a one to one basis, a terrier would have no chance of survival in a battle with a badger. The weight of a full grown badger varies a lot with the season; it is heavy with fat prior to the onset of winter, even though it does not hibernate. The average weight is something in the order of 10 kg (22 lb), although the heavier males can reach well over twice this figure in autumn. With regard to size, an average badger will stand about 300 mm (12 in) at the shoulder and have a length of 650 mm (26 in).

The teeth of a badger and its jaw structure, as well as its strong claws, make it a fiercesome adversary. The teeth indicate that it is capable of dealing with an omnivorous diet, but a study of its fossil remains from Tertiary times onwards shows its ancestors to have been carnivores, as would be expected of a member of the Mustelidae. The dental formula is:

$$2 \times \left\{ I\frac{3}{3} \quad C\frac{1}{1} \quad PM\frac{3}{4} \quad M\frac{1}{2} \right\} = 36.$$

An interesting point about this dentition is the occasional presence of an extra premolar on the upper jaw, bringing the number of teeth up to thirty-eight.

The incisors, canines and the first couple of premolars are all typical of carnivores, but the back teeth are more like those of herbivores, thus allowing the badger great gastronomic versatility; its diet includes literally anything edible, although it prefers easy pickings rather than the chase-and-kill so typical of other members of its family.

The jaw structure itself is quite typical of the species, the dentary fitting so snugly into a groove on the upper jaw that the jaw will not dislocate. This and the powerful jaw muscles mean that, once a badger really has a grip, it is very difficult to shake off without completely fracturing its skull. The cranium is also very sturdy and this is obviously of great assistance during burrowing. It certainly takes a heavy blow to kill a badger unless the more delicate snout takes the brunt.

If, during a fight, brock fails to get in a telling blow he is still capable of inflicting severe lacerations with his powerful front limbs. These have five digits with very strong, sharp, non-retractile claws. On the front limbs, the claws are extra long and sharp and can be used as weapons of offence as well as for digging and grooming. All of these features mean that badger baiting is bound to be a very bloody spectacle indeed.

Many other animals besides badgers were baited in special enclosures and, sometimes, badgers were baited in conditions designed for other beasts, especially bears and rats. There was, in the first decade of the nineteenth century, a bear baiting pit near Smithfield in London which was occasionally used for badgers; these were nailed by the tail and baited by terriers, bets being laid on how many times a game terrier drew the foe. Alken mentions the record to be seventy-two times in 10 minutes. The poor

The badger (*Meles meles*).

badger either died from injuries received in the fray or as a result of a gangrenous tail. In 1878, when badger baiting had long been illegal, a publican from Birkenhead was found guilty of allowing a badger to be baited on his premises. The fine of £5, a large sum of money in those days, shows some improvement in the attitude towards man's inhumanity to beast. This commendable shift in emphasis towards the badger had been apparent in some areas even towards the end of the eighteenth century. The badger, once regarded as both vermin and as a carnivorous beast causing great damage to the countryside, had been hunted without let or hindrance,

especially by the fox-hunting community, who viewed it as excellent training for their fox terriers. As it became realised that it was omnivorous, taking
as much vegetable as animal matter, but more importantly that it was a
digger of holes in which foxes could also be found, the pressure was taken off
the badger. It does, however, occasionally annoy fox hunters by digging out
the stops made prior to the start of the hunt and allowing the fleeing reynard
to go to earth.

Deliberate cruelty is only half the badger's problem in its struggle for
survival; the other is loss of habitat. Like most of our indigenous fauna, the
badger was originally a woodland dweller, living among the trees, the
dominant species of which were oak, ash and, in the southeast, perhaps
beech. With the disappearance of our once huge forests, the badger adapted

Badger cubs feeding beneath a flowering elder.

to changing conditions, but, even today, the majority of setts are found in
woodland, as a survey of 7992 setts by the Mammal Society in 1963 clearly
shows (see Table 13).

Thus we can see that the badger now has some measure of legal protection
and is also evolving differing patterns of behaviour to enable it to cope with
the destruction of its favoured habitat. The fact that trees are now being
planted in Britain in greater numbers than ever before is good news for the
badger; so good that I was almost able to conclude this chapter on a note of
optimism and to note that the long and distinguished history of the badger

Table 13   DISTRIBUTION OF BADGER SETTS

Habitat	% setts
Deciduous and mixed woods	53.5
Coniferous woods	7.9
Hedge	12.2
Scrub	6.1
Open field	8.9
Quarry	4.5
Sea cliff	0.5
Moor	2.0
Built-up areas	00.7
Other	3.7

Over 85% of these setts were situated on sloping ground.

in Britain would certainly continue into the foreseeable future. There is, however, another black cloud on the horizon; this is the part played by the badger in the spread of bovine tuberculosis. Badgers found dead throughout the country have been analysed and there is no doubt that some individuals, especially from the southwest of England, have been proved to carry the disease and many badger communities were gassed to extinction because of this. Naturalists, however, expressed great concern that there may have been some over-reaction on the part of the authorities and, at the time of writing (August 1982), the exterminations have been halted, pending more thorough research. It appears that the future for Britain's badgers may be more secure in consequence. The report prepared by Lord Zuckerman, however, still finds the badger guilty of spreading disease. After reading the statistics presented in this lengthy document, I find the arguments against the badger far from convincing. Let us examine these statistics, on which the death warrant of thousands of badgers and *no other creature* have been based (see Table 14). Surely the basic laws of statistics demand more equal sampling than this? Badgers were also accused of being a possible vector for human tuberculosis. Not only naturalists but also veterinary and medical experts have cast doubts on conclusions drawn from these figures and an excellent survey of these opinions, by Elizabeth Grice, was published by the *Sunday Times* on 28 December 1980:

According to Norman Littler, a consultant TB and chest physician, the human health hazard from tuberculous badgers is negligible. Bovine TB and human TB are different diseases he stresses. 'Zuckerman tries to give the impression that all human TB comes indirectly from badgers. This is absolute nonsense' Littler told the Sunday Times. 'Bovine TB as a cause of human disease is now almost non-existent. Of all tubercle bacilli isolated from human patients 99.7 per cent were of human types. There were only 21 cases of bovine TB in the whole of the country of which a mere two were in the south-west.'

Other serious criticisms levelled at Zuckerman are that: He grossly overestimated the badger population in Britain—putting it at 38,110 setts compared

Table 14 WILDLIFE EXAMINED IN MAFF VETERINARY LABORATORIES
IN CONNECTION WITH OFFICIAL INVESTIGATIONS, 1971–1979

Species Examined (Faeces Shown Separately)	Number Examined	Number Positive for M. bovis
	1 January 1971 to 31 December 1979	
badger	4,011	576
—faeces	5,704	142
cat	5	—
deer (fallow, sika and roe)	16	—
—faeces	42	—
ferret	1	—
fox	339	3
—faeces	42	—
grey squirrel	141	—
hare	8	—
hedgehog	14	—
mouse (other than wood mouse)	159	—
mink	15	—
mole	80	2
polecat	1	—
rabbit	108	—
rat	291	5
shrew	69	—
stoat	26	—
vole (field and bank)	752	—
weasel	12	—
wood mouse	540	—

From *Bovine Tuberculosis in Badgers* 4th Report by the Ministry of Agriculture,
Fisheries and Food.

with an estimate of 9,381 from Dr Ernest Neal, zoologist and author of a monograph on the badger. This over-estimate could lead to indiscriminate killing by farmers, it is feared, and a threat to survival of the species. His conclusion that TB increased in badgers during the moratorium on gassing in 1979 is based on selective evidence. There was an increase in TB in badgers in Avon and Gloucester at this time, the Mammal Society says, but the Zuckerman report ignored a decline in Cornwall. According to the Mammal Society he failed to produce scientific evidence to justify his description of the south-west as having a 'highly-infected population' spreading TB to badgers in other areas. His report ignores the fact that, in many counties with a high density of both cattle and badgers, there is very little TB in badgers. He too easily dismisses rats, moles and foxes as carriers of bovine TB. [A look at Table 14 will show this from the number of individuals of the various species actually examined.] *His figures are misleading because they relate chiefly to badgers taken in the vicinity of outbreaks of TB in cattle. The Mammal Society's challenge to the accuracy of some of Zuckerman's statements is made in a letter to the journal Nature* [Nature, Lond. 11 Dec. 1980]. *The World Wildlife fund has criticised the report as 'simply a review of inconclusive evidence already available.'*

David Coffey, a practising vet who worked at the Central Veterinary Laboratory when the Ministry's tests were taking place says the experimental work was never published and therefore invalidated. 'It is a fundamental rule of science that you must expose your work to public scrutiny.' The main questions he would like answered Coffey continues are these. 'If badgers caught TB from cattle in the first place how the devil didn't they catch it before 1960 when 30 per cent of the national dairy herd was infected?

'If they had the disease already, how was it possible virtually to eradicate bovine TB from cattle at all? Why didn't the badgers reinfect the herd, as it is claimed they are doing in the West Country now?'

Obviously all is far from well at the time of writing and Phil Drabble also weighed in on the side of the badger in a splendid article in *The Field* of 19 November 1981, in which he mentions the possibility of a programme of immunisation but, as he points out:

The Ministry rejects the idea of immunisation because it has been tried, in the past, elsewhere without 100 per cent success, and because our masters in the Common Market do not like the idea. Nevertheless mass gassing is obviously ineffective and would be an expensive practice to continue indefinitely so it seems sensible to explore more attractive alternatives.

How much better to find the real answer to the cause of infection of both cattle and wildlife and perhaps to call in medical specialists for advice on producing herds with a higher factor of immunity.

So then where stands the badger at this period in the history of British mammals? As a late nineteenth-century historian remarked drily when asked to assess the effect of the French Revolution on British politics: 'It's too soon to tell'. From Britain's most controversial land mammal we can now turn to our two other mustelids.

10 Carnivores: The Mink and the Otter

oth these mustelids occupy an aquatic habitat but whereas we fear for the future of the otter, with its rapidly declining numbers, we need have no qualms about the aggressive mink which is currently enjoying a population explosion.

The Mink *Mustela vison*

What a Rolls Royce is to the automobile industry so is the mink to the world of the furrier. In fact, there are two species of mink now found in Europe, the European mink (*Mustela lutreola*) and the American mink (*Mustela vison*), both of which have been introduced and are now replacing many native species. In Britain, the European mink has never been present and so

The mink (*Mustela vison*).

all the wild mink now ravaging wildlife along our rivers originated from North America. Escapes began as soon as fur farms were set up in 1929 and, as we have already seen in the case of the grey squirrel, a newly introduced animal may well find itself free of the natural restraints in its homeland and so multiplies rapidly and becomes a pest. Mink can be a real threat to valuable fish stocks but they also take rodents and frogs. Delacour, in *Wildfowl of the World*, made the point that:

> *Only a few mammals are in a position to take adult ducks. In North America, the mink* (Mustela vison) *is the major mammal ecologically associated with ducks. Much predation by mink is of crippled or sick birds, but where the mink has been introduced to Europe its effects have been more severe (Errington 1961).*

In Iceland, the damage has been greater still and, in Sweden, the effect upon stocks of game fish and crayfish have been ruinous to many whose livelihood depends upon them. With the proliferation of trout farms in Britain, the mink is likely to become even more of a threat and a measure of control is therefore essential. Planned trapping has proved only partially effective and attempted shooting is useless. Greater efforts will therefore have to be made to render fish farms and poultry runs 'mink-proof'—no easy task. Since 1929, escaped mink have spread from the southern counties over large areas of the British Isles and Ireland, although not yet to the Isle of Man (which also lacks otters, although this is not surprising since the island has no real river system). One can well understand the fuss made by naturalists when it was proposed, in 1978, to set up a mink farm on the Island of Westray in the Orkneys, which is home to vast hordes of sea birds already threatened from other directions. Mink are already causing problems at bird reserves such as the RSPB's Leighton Moss reserve and the Wildfowl Trust's refuges at Martin Mere near Southport and Caerlaverock on the Solway. Indeed, few areas where water birds are found in hundreds can be considered safe from mink.

Mink produce four to six young in April or May and these are able to breed in the following year. This is a much more rapid rate of increase than the otter (*Lutra lutra*) is able to accomplish and has enabled the mink to move into areas once occupied by the otter, which is much more easily disturbed by pollution and Man's everyday activities.

The above comments represent the majority opinion, but it is only fair to point out that there are some knowledgeable folk who are willing to leap to the defence of the mink and feel some sense of outrage when a trapped animal is held up for inspection and a smell of ammonia is generated by the glands at the base of the tail, registering the last defiant flush of anger. In a paper written for the *New Scientist* (2 March 1978) by Ian Linn and Paul Chanin two pertinent questions are posed. Firstly are minks really pests and secondly do mink and otter species compete with each other?

Are mink pests?

*Mink have certainly been known to kill chickens, ornamental ducks, domes-
ticated rabbits, and the like. There is firm evidence that they take young salmon
and trout, and suggestions that they compete with otters. Yet is this enough to
condemn them out of hand? What do they eat when they are not feasting off
salmon and chicken? Is it possible that mink have fallen victim to the
countryman's need to hate his competitors, which leads otherwise charming and
reasonable people to turn livid with rage when contemplating such creatures as
the fox, the stoat and the weasel?*

*Five years ago, in collaboration with Dr M. G. Day, one of us (IL) began to
attempt to answer these questions in an article in the* Journal of Zoology *(vol.
167, p. 463). This detailed results obtained from examining the alimentary
tracts of 1165 mink killed in England and Wales. Unfortunately many guts
were empty, only 273 having identifiable contents. Of these a further 69 had to be
discarded because of possible confusion with bait eaten by the animals after they
had been caught. The remaining 204 items revealed some interesting trends,
however. About one third of the mink's diet, as revealed by this study, was
composed of mammals (67 items). Of these 67, 26 were lagomorphs (almost
certainly rabbits), 20 were mice and voles, and 12 were rats. The remaining nine
were squirrels and various insectivores, plus one unidentified. Here, right away,
was something on the credit side. The majority of the mammals eaten are
properly regarded as pests by farmers.*

*A further third of the mink's diet, according to this study, was bird items—67
of them. Of these, 24 were coots and moorhens. Here there is no direct competition
with man. The mink could be regarded as a pest only if the water birds were
considered desirable and if its predation were depressing populations to an
unacceptably low level. Of the remaining bird items, seven were pigeons (which
would be on the credit side) but 15 were poultry, ducks and game birds. On the
whole, therefore, the mink's effect on bird populations seems to be undesirable.*

A variable fish diet

*Only 26 fish items turned up in this investigation, but, as fish items were
discounted in animals from traps where fish had been used as bait, it seems very
likely that this study underestimated the importance of fish. Moreover, the
proportions of kinds of fish were surprising. The sample was composed almost
entirely of coarse fish, with virtually no game fish. This seems very unlikely on
general principles, so these findings should be regarded as unreliable. This
presumption is supported by the works of Mrs Modupe Akande, who found that
in Scotland the mink's diet was about one quarter mammals, one quarter birds,
and one half fish. The kinds of mammals and birds eaten were pretty well the
same, though the proportions differed somewhat. The fish items were 69 per cent
salmon and trout—but we should not assume that this applies also in England
and Wales, where the availability of prey differs markedly from that in
Scotland.*

*The most reliable estimates of fish prey yet available are probably those made
by one of us (P.C.) in a 1976 PhD thesis. These indicate considerable variability*

in the fish prey taken. In an oligotrophic river (River Teign, Devon) and a pair of eutrophic lakes (Slapton Ley, Devon) about half the prey items were fish. But in a eutrophic calcareous stream (River Frome, Dorset) only a third of the prey items were fish. In the River Teign, some 70 per cent of the fish taken were salmon and trout, while most of the rest were eels. A few loach were taken. This seems (at first sight) a pattern which is deleterious to man's interest: although eels are considered to be pests, the predation of salmonids appears substantial. However, the Teign is very oligotrophic, coming off the granite of Dartmoor, and fish food is scarce. The brown trout in the stream are too numerous for the available food, and as a result too small, on the whole. If—as seems likely—cropping by the mink is mainly on the resident brown trout, and relatively little on the migratory sea trout and salmon, then a thinning of the brown trout population might well be considered an advantage. It could mean more food for each individual fish, and an eventual increase in the number of good sized fish available to anglers....

Do mink affect otters?

One of the criticisms levelled at the mink is that its presence depresses local populations of otters. One of the ways in which this is thought to happen is by competition for food. What evidence is there for this? The otter is very dependent on fish, nearly 90 per cent of its prey items being fish—compared with a maximum of about 50 per cent for mink. Some research workers have reported that mink and otters take different sizes and species of fish, so presumably do not compete. But there is ample evidence that, at least at some times and places, mink and otters do take the same sizes and species of fish prey. Let us examine carefully the implications of this.

In one of the study areas, Slapton Ley, mink and otter seemed to be competing for eels, but much less so for other kinds of fish. Bearing in mind that fish of all kinds are plentiful in Slapton Ley, it seems that mink and otter were not in serious competition in the two lakes which make up the Ley.

On the Teign the picture was different. Fish of any kind are scarce in this oligotrophic river, and both carnivores are reliant on eels and salmonids as major components of their diets. However, otters are much more dependent than mink, as they cannot tap the resources of mammals and bird food to the same extent as mink when fish prey is scarce. The straightforward interpretation might be that otters are suffering from the presence of mink. Possibly the otters on the river are not true residents—only transients, passers-through, which do not make a permanent home there. But an alternative explanation is possible, one which does not assume that mink is the villain. The mink on the river are much scarcer than the available space seems to warrant. Is competition with otters preventing the mink from establishing itself properly on the river? The otter is probably better adapted to fishing than the mink, and in a straightforward competition for fish food it might well come off better.

This reasoned argument is a far cry from the sensational treatment of matters pertaining to the mink in the popular press. Here we find *Mustela vison* treated as if it had Attila the Hun, Old Nick and a fire-breathing dragon lurking in its genetic make-up. An idea of how much heat is generated and how little light is focussed on the problem can be seen by reference to an article in the *Cumberland News* dated 5 November 1976, which I quote in full:

A furry menace with needle-sharp teeth and a licence to kill is spreading through Cumbria and the Borders. And the explosion in the population of wild mink is putting both poultry and fish stocks at risk.

The Dumfrieshire Otterhounds are already hunting down the pests. And the Kendal Otterhounds may follow suit.

But even their combined assault can do little to dent the numbers of the most dangerous vermin in Britain.

Mink are now swarming up Cumbrian rivers and into streams and becks.

They are finding their way into poultry houses, where they kill for the sake of killing, and have been seen taking fish from garden ponds.

National Farmers Union county branch secretary Mr Ken McKeen said yesterday: "If they get among the hens, they are 10 times worse than foxes."

Campaign

And Capt. John Bell-Irving, master of the Dumfrieshire Otterhounds said: 'I do not think people have woken up to the damage these vermin can do in a poultry run or what they can do to fish stocks.'

He believed mink were reducing the British otter population—by eating their young. And, with no natural enemies in Britain, it seemed likely they would continue to expand.

An N.F.U. official in Kendal said the damage mink were doing to Cumbrian fish stocks was tremendous. They were even going into gardens to take fish from ornamental pools.

Retired farmer Mr Jim Bell of Crosthwaite, secretary of a rabbit clearance society, said wild mink had even killed sheep.

The mink now raging through Cumbria are the descendents of escaped Canadian mink, imported for their fur years ago.

Mr Bell would like to see a campaign to rid Cumbria of the pests. This would bring in anglers, Otterhounds, water bailiffs and Ministry of Agriculture pest control officers, with traps.

'But the Ministry do not want to know,' he said. 'They say we will give you traps. But then it turns out that the people in Carlisle do not have any to give.'

Help

But a Ministry official in Carlisle said that since 1971 it had been up to landowners to exterminate pests on their land.

The Ministry was always ready to give help and advice, particularly concerning mink.

He added: 'We have loaned about 100 traps to farmers and landowners all over Cumbria. There are still a few traps available for loan and we can obtain more, if people want them.'

A similar story was reported by Andrew Chapman in the *Sunday Express* of 25 July 1982:

As Mrs. Allison Brown groomed her Yorkshire terrier, Cindy, she suddenly noticed a painful-looking lump on its neck.

Next day she took the dog to the vet. That lump, he told her, had been caused by a bite which would soon heal.

Mrs. Brown, a widow, thought no more of it—until 10 days later when Cindy gave an anguished whimper as she hopped down the back door steps. The terrier's coat was matted with blood and covered with clawmarks and bites.

For days Mrs. Brown never let Cindy out of her sight—until one evening she slipped out to visit a friend.

Lifeless

Three hours later she returned to a scene which horrified her. The mauled body of Cindy lay lifeless under the television set.

Mrs. Brown searched the room for clues. The door had been securely locked, as always, but the window was slightly ajar leaving a two-inch gap.

What ferocious animal so desperate to kill yet small enough to slip through that narrow gap, could have got into the house after its terrified quarry?

It was then that Mrs. Brown noticed something small, white and shiny, rather like a sliver of fine china, on top of the television set.

It looked remarkably like a torn-out tooth. And it was not one of Cindy's.

That tooth, she was to learn, came from a wild mink.

Now, two wire traps have been set on the banks of a small stream which runs past Mrs. Brown's home in Wynlass Beck, Windermere, Cumbria, to snare the mink which killed Cindy, returned to attack Mrs. Brown's other dog, and slaughters an average of one chicken a day.

Mrs. Brown, 51, said: 'I am told they killed out of sheer blood lust and fear nothing. The day after Cindy died the mink had a go at Mandy, my Border terrier.

'It sneaked in through my bedroom window. The place looked as if a burglar had been through it. Photographs and ornaments were strewn about.

'I've been very frightened by all this and now don't leave windows open at night. I'm told mink, if cornered, will attack humans.'

Mrs. Winifred Oakden who runs a riding school, said: 'So far this mink has killed nine of my chickens. It must be caught. Cindy was a lovely dog.'

The vet who treated the terrier said: 'Minks are extremely ferocious and the killing of the dog and chickens is the sort of destructiveness that is their trade mark.'

Menace

Mink, a menace to farmers and poultry breeders, are members of the family which includes ferrets, weasels and badgers. Adults grow up to two feet from head to tail.

A Ministry of Agriculture spokesman said: 'They have grown in large numbers by breeding after escaping from mink farms.

'People should keep well away as they will attack in broad daylight. Parents should warn children to beware of odd-looking animals.'

Thus we have the two diametrically opposed viewpoints of the scientific and popular press but, on balance, I am sure that the mink is an animal which we could well do without. There is also little doubt that, as the otter attempts to re-establish itself in former haunts, the presence of the mink will be anything but an advantage and it is to the otter that we now turn our attention.

The Otter *Lutra lutra*

> *'As through the wild country I rambled,*
> *And lived at extravagant rate,*
> *On eels, chubs and gudgeons I feasted,*
> *And the fishermen all did me hate;*
> *Yet still up the river I went*
> *Where the fishes me stomach did cheer,*
> *Till a challenge from Radcliffe they sen' me,*
> *That the' quickly would stop me career'.*

The above quotation from a song of the Lancashire folk singer, Harry Boardman, shows how widespread the otter once was. Radcliffe is now part of the congested conurbation of Greater Manchester and the river which, in the nineteenth century provided such a good living for the otter, is the Irwell.

The history of the otter in this country is a long one, fossil deposits being found in Norfolk, the brick-earths of the Thames Valley and in several caves and dating back to the Pliocene period (see Table 1).

During Cuthbert's stay on the Farne Islands off the coast of Northumberland, his love for wild things was very evident and he kept a couple of tame otters which used to swim with him in the sea.

In colour, the otter, or water weasel, is normally brown but, especially in Scotland, the odd individual is found with white spots on the breast and flanks. These were regarded at one time as kings of the otters. It was considered unlucky to kill them and anyone rash enough to do so would be sure to die themselves. The skin of one of these beasts was thought to cure many infectious diseases and also to protect the wearer against shipwreck. The pelt of either 'king' or 'peasant' otter is made up of two types of hair. There are stiff guard hairs overlying a waterproof layer of finer texture, an arrangement which serves to trap air; as the otter dives beneath the surface of the water this air escapes as a chain of bubbles. Watchers have long known that the 'otter's chain' can be used to follow the passage of Britain's largest mustelid in the same way that commanders of destroyers once tracked enemy submarines. Sufficient air remains, however, to insulate the otter against the cold and the closely-lying underfur prevents the skin surface getting cold.

A question which surprisingly was asked by folk in the Middle Ages was 'Is the otter a mammal or a fish?' The reason for this dilemma can be seen if one considers a country whose diet was dictated by monastic orders, which, on certain days, forbade the eating of meat but allowed fish to be consumed. Otter often figured on the menu of the monks and therefore, if it were regarded as a fish, it could be consumed without transgressing the laws of their order. Thus the otter hunt, long popular in Britain, may well have originated as much as a search for food as for the protection of fish stocks. A full account of otter hunting is given in Bell's *History of British Quadrupeds*, so often referred to in this present work:

Otter-hunting, formerly one of the most interesting and exciting amusements of which the English sportsman could boast, has of late years dwindled into the mere chase of extirpation. It was in other days pursued with much of the pomp and circumstance of regular sport: the Dogs were chosen for their perseverance and resolution; 'good Otterhounds ... will come chaunting and trailing along by the river-side, and will beat every tree-root, every osier-bed, and every tuft of bulrushes;—nay, sometimes they will take the water, and beat it like a Spaniel.'

An otter (*Lutra lutra*) emerging from a river.

OPPOSITE: An otter (*Lutra lutra*) posing.

The huntsmen and others of the party carried Otter spears, to strike the Otter when driven within their reach . . . and the whole company formed a cavalcade of no inconsiderable extent and importance. . . .

In beating for an Otter, it is necessary to mark the character and direction of his 'seal,' or footmark in the mud or soil, as well as the recent or older appearance of his 'spraints,' or dung. These signs of his having been either remotely or more recently on the spot will afford a tolerably certain indication whether the animal be still in the neighbourhood, or whether a further search must be made for later marks of his presence.

Although Bell, in 1837, was discussing the decreasing importance of otter hunting, I can well remember following the hunt as a fascinated 11-year-old in the 1940s. Spraints were found near Haverthwaite on the River Leven which runs from Lake Windermere on its short journey to the sea at Greenodd. Fascinated, I watched the dogs working, encouraged by their owners who were, in turn, controlled by a red-faced man in a scarlet coat, obviously the squire. My excitement rose as the otter was flushed and headed downstream, submerged, but betrayed by its chain of air bubbles. I was by now a hunting man. The otter came out of the water, was stabbed by a local lad with a long metal pole—the otter screamed and dived again—its blood stained the bank; I felt sick. The bubbles again betrayed the desperate otter. I wanted it to escape. It failed. I not only felt ill but was physically sick. My sporting life had been short and died a heaving vomiting death. A naturalist was born!

The history of otter hunting can be traced back to King John, who had a pack of hounds, and most parts of England could probably trace its continuance up to fairly recent times.

I well remember otter hunting being carried on as late as 1972 at Gisburn near Clitheroe, but the otter is now protected by law. Let us hope that it is not too late to save the species from extinction in England. Many people are working for its salvation, no-one harder than the Otter Trust, following the tradition of otter lovers Henry Williamson and Gavin Maxwell. Williamson would be fairly happy with the fact that the otter is protected in England; Maxwell would turn in his grave if he knew that protection was not extended to Scotland, where the otter is not considered rare enough to merit protection and is therefore still hunted. A body calling itself the Joint Otter Group (JOG), with members from the Mammal Society, the Institute of Terrestrial Ecology, the Nature Conservancy Council, the Otter Haven Project and the Society for the Promotion of Nature Conservation, is working hard to save the otter. This impressive-sounding body reported the otter in England to be in dire straights and in 1978 'JOGGED' the Government's memory with the following suggestions:

1. Protection should be extended to the otter in Scotland.

2. The maximum fine for contravening the Conservation of Wild Creatures and Wild Plants Act 1975 should be increased. (Live otters now change hands for £1000 each.)

3. The British Government should carry through legislation on European protection for the otter as proposed by the Council for Europe.

4. Further protection should be given to areas where otters still breed, and further conservation measures are required to prevent deterioration of habitats where otters still occur.

5. Financial assistance should be made available to the conservation organisations to extend and continue the work being done on otters.

6. Conservation activities should be co-ordinated through existing conservation organisations to prevent duplication of effort and to maximise the benefit to otters of the limited financial resources available.

Thus we have traced the history of man's cruelty to otters, but the species also has a history of domestication, a trend so skilfully depicted in the works of Gavin Maxwell, especially in his *Ring of Bright Water*. If we turn once more to Bell, we find mention that 'the Otter may not only be readily and easily tamed and domesticated, but taught to catch and bring home fish'.

This engaging habit of otters is also mentioned by none other than Izaak Walton who wrote:

. . . I pray, sir, save me one [a young otter] *and I'll try if I can make her tame, as I know an ingenious gentleman in Leicestershire (Mr Nicholas Seagrave) has done; who hath not only made her tame, but to catch fish, and do many other things of much pleasure.*

An otter with fish.

Albertus Magnus goes even further by reporting that otters were kept in Sweden as house pets and their function was to go fishing when told by their master and return with a fish. They certainly must have been treated with kindness and a great deal of patience to become such reliable associates. Bell gives us details of the training method employed:

They should be procured as young as possible, and they are at first fed with small fish and water. Then bread and milk is to be alternated with the fish, and the proportion of the former gradually increased till they are led to live entirely on bread and milk. They are then taught to fetch and carry, exactly as Dogs are trained to the same trick; and when they are brought to do this with ease and docility, a leather fish stuffed with wool is employed for the purpose. They are afterwards exercised with a dead fish, and chastised if they disobey or attempt to tear it; and finally, they are sent into the water after living ones.

Otters are still frequently found in south-western England, Wales, northwest Scotland and the Isle of Man. In the latter two areas, the otter functions as well in the sea as it does in river systems on the mainland. It is also found throughout Ireland and many workers consider the Irish otter to be a distinct subspecies (*Lutra lutra roensis*), which is a great deal darker in colour than the mainland otter (*Lutra lutra lutra*).

As already discussed with reference to the mink, otters are often accused of making severe inroads into the populations of game fish. This is occasionally true, especially in fast-flowing streams only supporting trout (*Salmo trutta*) but, in slow meandering rivers and lakes, otters will take whatever is easiest to catch, which is always likely to be unhealthy individuals. Such fish ought to be weeded out, as should coarse fish which may adversely affect the growth of game fish. The otter also shows a great preference for the eel, which does much damage in game fisheries by eating both eggs and fry. Thus, on balance, the presence of an otter in a river system may well be a distinct advantage. However you view it, the otter must be regarded as ideally adapted for hunting in water; the long, flat, graceful body, webbed feet, oar-like tail and presence of a full set of carnivore's teeth all ensure successful hunting. The dental formula is:

$$2 \times \left\{ I\frac{3}{3} \quad C\frac{1}{1} \quad PM\frac{4}{4} \quad M\frac{1}{2} \right\} = 38.$$

In addition to these features, the hearing on land is acute but special muscles allow both the nostrils and the ears to be closed while the animal is submerged. The eyes function well both above and below the water but, should the water become murky when rivers are in spate, then the whiskers (*vibrissae*) are sufficently sensitive to vibrations to enable the prey to be located. Otters normally live solitary lives, apart from during the breeding period, which can be at almost any time, although late winter and early spring seem to be the times when copulation is most likely to occur. After a gestation period of about 9 weeks (there is no evidence of delayed implan-

An otter resting in its holt.

tation in otters), two to five young are born. For 2 or 3 months until the cubs are able to swim, the bitch otter is at her most vulnerable, being firmly tied to the land by the bond of motherhood. Breeding can occur in the second year of life and, although life in the wild is tough, an otter can possibly live until it is 20 years old.

Now that it has been given protection, at least in England, and that environmental improvements are gaining momentum, the future for the otter is a little brighter now than was the case a decade ago. This last member of the British mustelids to be discussed still faces great problems in the immediate future and all caring naturalists must do all in their power to preserve this magnificent animal. What is required urgently is the extension of the English law to protect Scottish otters. One of my greatest thrills is to sit by a loch in the Western Isles or by an English river and listen to the whistling call of a bitch otter desperate for a mate. Some Scottish otters are equally at home in the sea, where they will occasionally meet those even more fully aquatic carnivores—the seals. These controversial animals form the subject of the next chapter.

11 Carnivores: Seals

Seals belong to an order of mammals technically referred to as the Pinnipedia and are grouped into hair, or true, seals (called the Phocidae), the sea lions and fur seals (Otariidae) and the walruses (Odobenidae). All live something of a wandering life and many species turn up around our coast as vagrants. Included on our list is the harp seal (*Phoca groenlandica*), the bearded seal (*Erignathus barbatus*) and the hooded seal (*Cystophora cristata*); there are also many recordings of the walrus (*Odobenus rosmarus*), including one sighted in the reaches of the Thames as long ago as 1456. None of these species, however, haul out of the water onto the shores of Britain to breed and thus I have excluded them from this brief history of our mammals and will consider only the two species of seal which mate and give birth to their young around our coastline. These are the common seal and the grey or Atlantic seal.

The Common Seal *Phoca vitulina*

This seal is also known as the harbour, black or spotted seal, and also as the ranger or silkie. In the water, the two British species may be difficult to distinguish, but reference to Table 15 may make the distinction easier; this will certainly be the case if the beasts are observed out of water, when the greater bulk of the grey seal will be obvious. There can, however, still be problems to the inexperienced eye since the two species are highly unlikely to be hauled out on the same sandbank side by side for comparison.

There are many stories associating the seal with a profound love of music and this is doubtless the origin of the old tales of mermaids and the like. It is

TABLE 15 COMPARISON OF COMMON AND GREY SEALS

Common Name	Scientific Name	Average Length (nose to tail)		Average Weight		Nostrils	Spots
		Male	Female	Male	Female		
common seal	*Phoca vitulina*	1.7 m (5½ ft)	1.5 m (5 ft)	70 kg (154 lb)	60 kg (132 lb)	V-shaped and joined below.	Many small spots.
grey seal	*Halichoerus grypus*	2.3 m (7 ft)	2 m (6 ft)	230 kg (506 lb)	150 kg (330 lb)	Parallel and not joined at any point.	Fewer spots but larger, forming blotches.

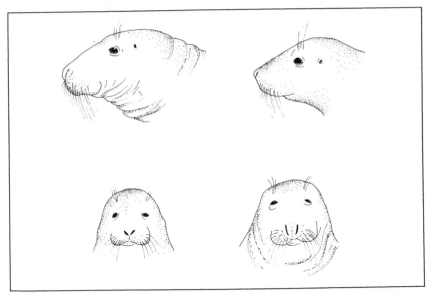

Figure 24. Comparison of the heads of the two seal species commonly found on British coasts. Above: the grey seal (*Halichoerus grypus*)—bull (left), cow (right). Below: the common seal (*Phoca vitulina*)—cow (left), bull (right).

more likely that the slimmer shape of the common seal would lead to this illusion than the less attractive dimensions of the grey seal, however long those ancient mariners had been at sea. I think that this apparent love of music stems from the fact that seals, especially the common seal, have a highly developed brain and an inquisitive nature. Sound travels more easily through water, a denser medium than air, and sea-dwellers must be well aware of the presence of human travellers on the surface (and, in these advanced times, below it) and the intelligent ones often want to take a closer look at the intruders. Until the last few centuries, they were able to do this without fear but, with the invention of accurate guns and then lethal explosively propelled harpoons, the seals have not surprisingly lost their trust in us and mermaid stories have become a part of our folklore which we have lost for ever. Laing, writing of a voyage to the island complex of Spitzbergen, reports that the playing of a violin or other musical instrument would be sure to result in an assemblage of seals, heads popping eagerly above the waves in an effort to investigate this strange 'floating animal' with the peculiar mating call.

In the early 1930s, an observer calling himself Scotus tells of a trip along a Scottish sea loch in a motor boat. During a period when the engine was stilled one of the party sang a Hebridean song called 'The Seal Woman Sea Joy'. Seals not only approached the boat but barked their own response. Only when the human observers tired of the duet and switched on the engine did the seals appear to recall that the presence of humans often brought danger and so quitted the scene. There are any number of references in the histories of mammals due to the fact that, whenever the church bells of Hoy were pealing, seals approached close to the shore as if to listen. Macgillivray, the celebrated naturalist and zoologist (note I stress these two descriptions in the correct order) of the early nineteenth century, reported an account of the common seal given to him by a Hebridean.

In walking along the shore in districts where Seals were abundant in the calm of a summer afternoon, a few notes of my flute would bring half-a-score of them within thirty or forty yards of me; and there they would swim about, with their heads above water, like so many black dogs, evidently delighted with the sounds. For half-an-hour, or, indeed, for any length of time I chose, I could fix them to the spot, and when I moved along the water's edge they would follow me with eagerness, like the Dolphins, which, it is said, attended Arion, as if anxious to prolong the enjoyment. . . .

Other occasions occurred during my residence in these islands of witnessing the habits of these creatures. While my pupils and I were bathing, which we often did in the bosom of a beautiful bay in the island, named, from the circumstance of its being the favourite haunt of the animal, Seal-Bay, numbers of them invariably made their appearance, especially if the weather was calm and sunny, and the sea smooth, crowding around us at the distance of a few yards, and looking as if they had some kind of notion that we were of the same species, or at least genus, with themselves. The gambols in the water of my playful companions, and their noise and merriment, seemed, to our imagination, to excite them, and to make them course round us with greater rapidity and animation. At the same time, the slightest attempt on our part to act on the offensive, by throwing at them a stone or a shell, was the signal for their instantaneous disappearance, each, as it vanished, leaving the surface of the water beautifully figured with a wavy succession of concentric circles. . . .

The fishermen on the island used to assert that, like many other animals both of the land and the water, they never repose without stationing a sentinel on the watch. [Macgillivray is here describing the species basking on deserted beaches] *I cannot positively confirm this, but I have often observed that during the general slumber one of the number, but not always the same individual, would raise its head for a second or two, turning it half round, and again stretch itself in repose. Ever and anon, too, we would hear from some one of the group a melancholy moan coming slowly over the surface of the deep, wild and savage in the sound.*

The common seal is found around the northern regions of both the Pacific and Atlantic Oceans and in Europe is present in Iceland, Norway and Britain with the populations thinning out as you move south; only occasionally do individuals wander as far as Portugal. In Britain, the common seal is not such a commercial nuisance as the grey seal but there is a substantial colony of over 5000 around The Wash with other less numerous aggregations in northeastern England, Scotland, the Western Isles and eastern

OPPOSITE: The common seal (*Phoca vitulina*).

A common seal surfing.

Ireland. It is mainly a shallow-water species and tends not to move very far away from the feeding grounds. Newborn pups tagged in The Wash in 1971 (figures from the *Mammal Society Report* No. 29) showed that 22 animals out of 197 marked were recovered away from the natal area and, of 111 similarly tagged in 1972, only 16 were recovered out of their home range. One of these was observed in a healthy state off Cape Griz Nez on the French coast.

In stark contrast to the grey seal, there is no social organisation during the breeding season—and the great lumbering bull with his associated harem is not a part of the common seal's life. The breeding cycle is imperfectly known; copulation occurs in July and August but there is certainly some degree of delayed implantation. One pup is usually born in June but there is a lot of variation, depending to some extent upon geographical location. Birth is a quick process, taking place on an exposed sandbank and the pup can swim from birth. Suckling may occur on land or in the water and the milk is very rich so that growth occurs very quickly. It seems that females can live for 30 years but males do not live for as long, individuals seldom surviving beyond their twentieth year. At one period, seals must have been abundant all around the British Isles, but with the advent of sealskin garments and uses for the oils, the sealing industry decimated the populations. Some degree of protection was, and still is given (see p. 211) and the problem is to satisfy the fishing industries' demand for total destruction with the naturalists' demands for absolute protection. Nowhere is this polarity of opinion more obvious than in the grey seal controversy, which still rages on and, no doubt, will continue into the foreseeable future.

The Grey Seal *Halichoerus grypus*

Haaf-fish, the old Shetlanders' name for this species, is now no longer used but it is still referred to as the horse-head and the Atlantic or great seal. Such was the greed of the sealing industry, that Lydekker's account of the species reveals a distinct shortage in some areas and the present situation is a great improvement on the status of a century ago.

Its chief haunts appear to be the British and Scandinavian coasts; its northern limits being seemingly marked by the Baltic, the Gulf of Bothnia, and Iceland. This Seal was first recognised as an inhabitant of the British seas in the year 1836; and while rare on the southern coasts of England, it is exceedingly abundant on the western and southern shores of Ireland, as well as in the Hebrides and Shetlands. The specimens taken on our southern coasts must be regarded in the light of stragglers from more northern regions; one of these having been taken many years ago in the Severn, while a second was captured on the Isle of Wight in 1857. It has likewise been recorded from the Welsh coast. On the more southern coasts of Scotland this Seal is likewise rare, but it becomes more numerous as we proceed north. Thus, although now diminished in numbers, a

A bull grey seal (*Halichoerus grypus*) in the Farne Islands.

An adult grey seal (*Halichoerus grypus*).

few are still to be found in suitable localities on the coast of Caithness, where they have been said to breed in the rocky caverns. According to Messrs. Harvie-Brown and Buckley, they 'also occur in some numbers on Eilean-nan-roan, off the Kyle of Tongue, where specimens have been seen over eight feet long. They are most numerous on the outer island. At Souliskeir, to the north of Cape Wrath, they were once abundant, and parties of fishermen used to go from Orkney and the north Sutherland coast to kill them in October.' The same authors state that, although restricted and rare in the Inner Hebrides, it still frequents the more remote Outer Hebrides in some numbers, although, for obvious reasons, they refrain from mentioning its favourite haunts. They add

A colony of grey seals in the Orkney Islands.

that there are 'few localities, even among the Isles, where they could be observed with any degree of regularity. . . .'

A look at Table 16 indicates the low ebb reached in the affairs of grey seals at the start of World War I and it was in that year that the very first Grey Seal Protection Act was issued; this was confirmed each subsequent year until 1932 and remained in force until the passing of the Conservation of Seals Act in 1970. All that the 1914 Act did was to provide the species with a close season, stretching from the 1 October to the 15 December and, even though it was so limited, it resulted in vociferous complaints during the

1920s regarding the damage done by seals to the salmon fisheries. The Government, however, remained deaf to these pleas for 7 years before agreeing to investigate the population, which resulted in the 1928 popu-

---

Table 16   THE GREY SEAL POPULATION AROUND THE UK AND IRELAND

1914	(Accepted by Parliament, although an under-estimate)	500
1928	(Caldwell and Ritchie)	4,000–5,000
1954	(Loxley)	20,000
1963	(First Consultative Committee)	29,500
1970	(Bonner)	53,000–55,000
1973	(ICES Working Group)	61,000

From *The Field* 18 June, 1980.

---

lation figure listed in Table 16. Debate upon these statistics eventually resulted in a very peculiar Act in 1932 which tried to do two opposite things at once. It provided for an extension of the close season to 31 December but, on the other hand, allowed for total suspension of protection for periods of a year at the discretion of the Minister of Agriculture and Fisheries in England and the Secretary of State for Scotland. Thus we had a 'culling when necessary policy'. These powers, however, must have been used with some restraint and sympathy for the seals because a report prepared for the Nature Conservancy, published in 1963, showed populations approaching 30 000. Culling was then deemed to be essential, a view supported by acknowledged experts on seals, including Hewer (1974). During the 1960s, however, the man in the street (whoever he or she might be) was well-tuned in to conservation and the fact that young grey seals left, unlike the more aquatically-active common seal pups, on rocky shores and therefore so vulnerable to slaughter, look so lovely was not designed to generate sympathy for the cull. Add to this the fact that seals excrete excess salt via a gland in the corner of the eye, which glistens like a tear, making the pup appear to be weeping at its misfortune, and culling became a difficult thing to do, despite the passing of the 1970 Act permitting control of escalating grey seal populations. With the pressures imposed by Greenpeace and similar-minded conservation bodies, the grey seal population is now in excess of 70 000 and is rising by over 6% per annum.

Why do fishermen demand that seals be culled at all? Is it greed or do they face ruin? They accuse seals of damaging nets and consuming huge numbers of fish of significant commercial value, some quoting potential annual losses in the order of £20 million! I must perhaps confess at this stage that my own leaning is towards the dewy-eyed seals which have roamed the colder seas of the world since before Noah built his Ark and are therefore just as entitled to a good juicy fish as we are, if not more so. An historian, even one dealing with the affairs of the natural world, must beware of his almost inevitable bias and examine the facts of the situation as dispassionately as possible. I think that damage to nets by grey seals must be discounted, but the consumption of valued fish and thus the threat to the welfare of inshore fishermen means that they and their families must be given a more sympathetic hearing. The positions of some of the largest colonies of grey seals show them strategically straddled across the migration routes of salmonid species and we do nature a great injustice if we think that this is pure chance. We must accept that the function of a seal is to catch fish and it can do this more efficiently in the middle of a migration stream than anywhere else. The fishermen also know these piscean seaways and here is the problem; as the seal population rises and our own essential fishing industry becomes more efficient and more demanding, feelings are bound to intensify. However much I regret it, I fear that some culling must always be inevitable, but should be kept to an absolute minimum. One thing is certainly beyond dispute; the grey seal's gregariousness in the breeding season makes it much more easy to cull than the more pelagic but less destructive common seal.

What is urgently required is a detailed investigation of seal biology and this has already begun and is rapidly gaining pace. It is accepted that the mammalian way of life evolved on land and the respiratory system of lungs and associated vascular and musculature systems is adapted for air-breathing. Imagine the problems encountered by mankind in his desire to penetrate the depths of the seas. Consider the great oxygen demands to be overcome when working beneath the waves. What about the tremendous and unrelenting pressure found in the cold deep dark waters? Seals have had to evolve an answer to all these problems and many more besides. Some of the solutions have proved surprising to say the least.

RESPIRATION IN SEALS

The lungs do not seem to be particularly large and, in any case, seals exhale before diving; fancy that, diving with empty lungs. The thoracic cavity, however, is so constructed that it is flattened by high pressure rather than injured by it. If there is no oxygen available in the lungs, then there is little point in the blood circulating to the lungs to collect it, so seals enter into a physiological state known as *bradycardia*. The heart beat is drastically slowed and the strength of the beat is reduced to an absolute minimum, just sufficient for the blood to be pushed along the carotid artery and keep the brain supplied with sufficient oxygen in order to function. A huge circular muscle (the sphincter muscle) contracts and shuts off the huge veins leading to the heart. All that now remains to be done is for the seal to find an alternative supply of oxygen while it is under water. It was assumed at one time that having a high red blood cell count might be the answer but research has shown that this is not significantly higher in the seal than in ourselves, and much less than some people living at high altitudes.

The solution actually seems to be two-fold. Seal muscle contains a substance called *myoglobin*, which is similar to our red pigment, haemoglobin.

Although a molecule of myoglobin cannot carry as much oxygen as a molecule of haemoglobin, the myoglobin is present in such quantities that considerable amounts of oxygen can be stored. Thus, while the seal is on the surface and breathing normally, these 'reserve tanks' of myoglobin can be charged, to be drawn upon when the animal is submerged. The second adaptation of seals is their ability to run up what is known as an 'oxygen debt'. What happens normally is that, using oxygen, stores of carbohydrate are 'burned' to release energy and carbon dioxide and water as waste products. In times of oxygen shortage, e.g. when the seal is under pressure from predators and must stay submerged, the carbohydrate (glycogen) in the muscle is broken down, but incompletely, releasing energy and lactic acid. This makes considerably less inroad into the available oxygen. The waste lactic acid is oxidised to carbon dioxide and water when the seal has the leisure to lie on the surface of the sea and draw air into its 'landlubber' lungs.

Although the seals are the largest of our British mammals, the distinction of being the largest land mammal belongs to the red deer, which is described in the next chapter.

12 Artiodactyls: Deer

Deer belong to the order Artiodactyla and the family Cervidae. They are herbivorous, cud-chewing animals, related to cattle and sheep. They need to eat large volumes of vegetation in order to build up body tissues from what is not a particularly rich source of food. While spending time feeding, the animals are vulnerable to predators so the habit has evolved of eating quickly and then retiring to the safety of thick cover, where the food is regurgitated and chewed at leisure.

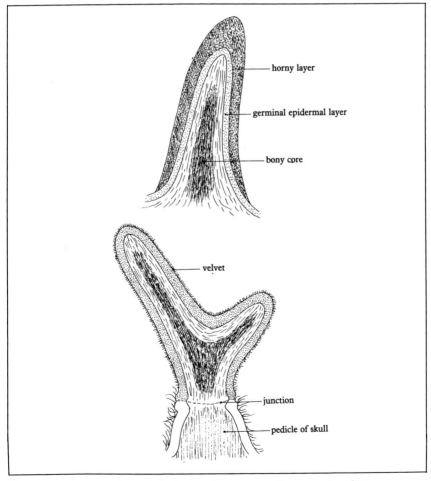

Figure 25. A comparison of the internal structure of horns and antlers.

There are at the moment in excess of half a million deer living wild in Britain and they are expanding, both in population and distribution. The re-establishment of large areas of woodland has been the single most important factor accounting for this increase. The work of the Forestry Commission, which has functioned since 1919, private planting, and government grants to individuals to encourage more trees to be grown has resulted in more than $1\frac{1}{2}$ million hectares ($3\frac{3}{4}$ million acres) being brought under 'leaf', although most of this has been of foreign conifers. Deer tend to be selective browsers rather than systematic grazers and they can do considerable damage to young trees over a wide area. This damage can be increased by the males, which rub their antlers against trees with such force that even well-established trees are vulnerable. Antlers are one of nature's most fascinating 'inventions' and their formation and function are still not completely understood. Most species of deer sport antlers but, with the exception of the reindeer (*Rangifer tarandus*), it is only the males which carry these adornments and, even in this species, the male has the more impressive set.

There is often confusion among naturalists concerning the origins of antlers and horns (see Fig. 25). Antlers are bone-like structures originating from round cylindrical bumps on the skull called *pedicles*. They are solid and are grown afresh each year, which must be a strain upon food supplies which must at times be somewhat limited. Red deer stags have often been observed to eat their own cast antlers in an effort to obtain essential minerals. Horns, on the other hand, are made up of a firm outer skin, growing around a soft inner core. The central portion is richly supplied with blood vessels and, in consequence, is hollow. Horns have been used as drinking vessels and musical instruments for many thousands of years. They are often found on both male and female animals, although those of the male are usually larger, but in either case they are retained throughout the life of the beast.

Despite the annual loss of the antler set, the structures increase in complexity from year to year and this has led to the erroneous assumption that they can be used as an accurate assessment of the age of the animal. It is still often stated that the antlers of red deer gain a point each year and so all that has to be done to calculate the age is to count the points. In fact, the size of the antler and the number of points depends upon a number of factors; age is certainly one, but the quantity and quality of food available, especially its calcium and phosphorus content, are also important. Inheritance is another factor. It has long been known that stags in southern England tend to have larger heads than those from the north of Scotland. Once a deer expert becomes familiar with an area, it may be possible for him to make an accurate estimate of the age of a stag by reference to the antlers, the local habitat and perhaps even recognisable features of his ancestors, but the weather conditions over the previous 12 months must also be taken into account.

The growth, development and eventual shedding of the antlers (Fig. 26)

Figure 26. Antler growth cycle: a) pedicles; b) immature buck with antlers 'in velvet'; c) mature buck with velvet stripping off; d) mature buck with shed antler.

is geared to the reproductive cycle and, in particular, to the levels of male hormone (*testosterone*). After the rut, the hormone level falls and the antlers are cast. The growth of new antlers is initiated by the reduction in hormone level, the fast-developing structures being covered by a soft skin known as *velvet*. Development is delicately balanced at this stage and a blow on the antler while it is in velvet can cause abnormal development. This does not, of course, affect correct antler formation in subsequent years. There is also a proven tendency for injuries to the rest of the body to influence antler development. A broken right leg for example usually leads to the growth of an abnormal antler on the left side and vice versa. This is difficult to explain scientifically, but there are far too many cases of this actually happening for it to be ignored completely. During the spring, the increasing day length

Red deer (*Cervus elephas*)—stag at rest.

OPPOSITE: A buck roe deer (*Capreolus capreolus*).

triggers the release of more hormone and, as this builds up towards the onset of the rut, antler growth stops. The blood supply to the velvet is cut off and it becomes dry and irritating; the animal therefore attempts to rub it off on trees, often causing considerable damage to valuable timber. Eventually the full head of bony antlers is revealed; these eventually fall off and then the whole process begins again. The precise function of antlers has by no means been satisfactorily explained. Are they weapons of defence? It would seem not, since, if this was the case, the females would have more need of them than the males and also there would be no evolutionary value in being without them for 4 months of every year. It therefore seems most likely that they are the male's display mechanism, used for advertisement in the same way as birds use song, plumage or a combination of both.

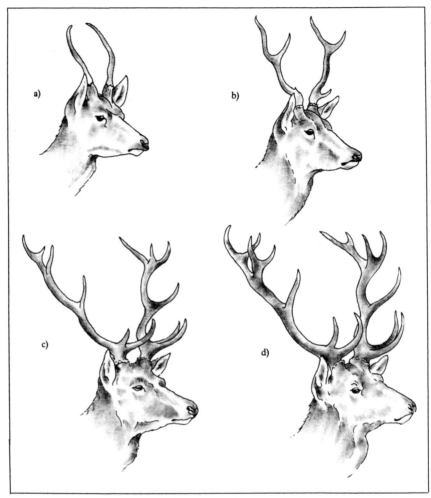

Figure 27. The development of the antlers from stage (a) to stage (d) is dependent not only on age but also on quantity and quality of diet.

In Britain, we have two native species of deer, plus four introductions making six species in all; the relative facts and figures are summarised in Table 17. It is appropriate that the first species to be described is the red deer, our largest living native land animal.

The Red Deer *Cervus elephas*

The red deer is a member of the genus *Cervus*, which is found mainly in the Oriental region, but *Cervus elaphus* is found throughout much of the Palaearctic region and also parts of North America. A second member of the genus, the sika deer (*Cervus nippon*) has been introduced into Britain from Japan and the two species have proved so similar that interbreeding has occurred and has caused some concern, since the genetical integrity of the British subspecies, *Cervus elaphus scoticus*, must obviously be threatened should this hybridisation continue. The close relationship between the

Table 17 COMPARISON OF BRITISH DEER

Common Name	Scientific Name	Average Size of Antlers	Average Height at Shoulder	Average Weight of Male	Average Weight of Female	Average Weight of Young at Birth	Name of Male Female Young	Origins
red deer	*Cervus elaphus*	80 cm (32 in)	120 cm (48 in)	100 kg (220 lb)	70 kg (154 lb)	4.9 kg (11 lb)	Stag Hind Calf	Native
sika deer	*Cervus nippon*	50 cm (20 in)	85 cm (34 in)	60 kg (132 lb)	40 kg (88 lb)	3 kg (6½ lb)	Stag Hind Calf	Japan. Intro-duced in 19th century.
fallow deer	*Dama dama*	Pal-mated. Up to 70 cm (28 in)	100 cm (40 in)	70 kg (154 lb)	45 kg (99 lb)	4.5 kg (10 lb) (Twins occasion-ally)	Buck Doe Fawn	Introduced Roman, pre-Roman times; some Norman addition.
roe deer	*Capreolus capreolus*	Not ex-ceeding 30 cm (12 in)	75 cm (30 in)	26 kg (57 lb)	22 kg (48½ lb)	1.5–2 kg (3–4½ lb) (Twins usual)	Buck Doe Fawn or Kid	Native
muntjac	*Muntiacus reevesi*	Present but short	50 cm (20 in)	14 kg (31 lb)	12 kg (26½ lb)	1 kg (2 lb)	Buck Doe Fawn	China. Introduced to Woburn in 1900. Spreading.
Chinese water deer	*Hydropotes inermis*	None	60 cm (28 in)	13 kg (28½ lb)	10 kg (22 lb)	Less than 1 kg (2 lb). Litter size up to 6.	Buck Doe Fawn	Introduced to Woburn in 1900. Restricted to Bucks and dis-trict.

Cervus deer was well known to Lydekker (1896), who, after pointing out that the red deer was once spread throughout Europe and part of Asia, goes on to say:

Of the allied species, we may mention by name the North American Wapiti (C. canadensis), the nearly similar Thian Shan Stag (C. eustephanus), the Kash-mir Stag (C. cashmirianus), represented by a variety in Yarkand, the Persian Maral (C. maral), the Shou (C. affinis) of the inner eastern Himalaya, and the

The Formosan sika deer (*Cervus nippon*).

OPPOSITE: Fallow deer (*Dama dama*).

Lhasa Stag (C. thoroldi) of the Tibetan plateau; the last-named species agree-
ing with the North African variety of the Red Deer in the absence of the 'bez'-
tine.

All these species, except the wapiti, have not held on to their specific rank
and are now thought to have been variants of the once main species but
Lydekker's account goes on:

As regards their distribution in the British Isles, Red Deer are still to be found
in the wild state in three districts of England, but are elsewhere confined to the
Scottish Highlands and some of the wilder parts of Ireland. In the west of
England there are a considerable number in Devonshire and Somersetshire, the
herd being estimated at about two hundred and fifty head in 1871. Martindale
Fell, in Westmoreland, is likewise one of the last strongholds of the species,
although the number of head now remaining is comparatively small; and as these
Deer are fed in winter they can hardly be considered as absolutely wild.
According to the Hon. G. Lascelles, some fifteen or twenty head still remain in
the New Forest. About a century ago there were wild Red Deer in Cornwall; and
all readers of Gilbert White must be familiar with his description of the Deer in
Wolmer Forest, in Hampshire, which, in the time of Queen Anne, numbered
about five hundred head. Tame Red Deer are now kept in eighty-six English
parks, out of which Batminton has the largest herd. In most of these parks Fallow
Deer are also kept, but in Blenheim (Oxfordshire), Bolton Abbey (Yorkshire),
Barmingham (Yorkshire), and Calcot (Berkshire), Red Deer alone are kept.
In a few English parks, namely, Alnwick, Ashridge, Langley, Welbeck,
Windsor, and Woburn, there is a white or cream-coloured variety of the Red
Deer, in which the nose is flesh-coloured, while the eyes are either pale blue or
straw-coloured. The origin of this breed is quite unknown. It may be remarked
here that formerly there was a prejudice against keeping Red and Fallow Deer in
the same park, as it was thought they would disagree; but this is now ascertained
to be a mistaken idea.
It will be unnecessary to refer to the distribution of the Red Deer in the Scottish
Highlands, but it may be mentioned that even in comparatively recent times the
range of the species extended to the south-west of Scotland. Deer are indigenous to
the island of Mull, though there have been several importations of fresh blood in
order to counteract the ill-effects of in-and-in breeding; and they likewise inhabit
all the Hebrides, but are now unknown in Shetland and Orkney, although there
is evidence of their former existence in the latter.

The old Forest of Martindale, since 1974 part of the new county of
Cumbria, still has its share of the county's red deer, but most now wander
the hills around Thirlmere, where the living can be quite hard, while the
lower Furness Fells support the finest beasts in the area. The majority are
centred around Grizedale and these, although some were emparked at Claife
and Dale Park by the Abbots of Furness, are almost certainly of indigenous
stock. Close to Grizedale, there used to be the deer reserve of Hay Bridge,

which was set up in 1971 by Mrs Helen Fooks as a memorial to her husband who died in 1969. Major Fooks, after a long career in the army and then as a game warden, was appointed as game advisor to the Forestry Commission at Grizedale, which was responsible for the proper control of an expanding red deer population. Unfortunately, the pressures of inflation caused the reserve to close early in 1982. Further south, in the limestone areas around Silverdale, Arnside and Grange-over-Sands, scientists based at nearby Merlewood have been using sophisticated computerised measurements, mostly on skull dimensions, to find out details of possible hybridisations between the red and sika deer; these are coming more and more into contact with each other as the sika expands its range northwards while the red is moving slowly south.

The logical answer to the increased deer populations would be to use them as a source of food and work being done on the Isle of Rhum by Fiona Guinness and the Nature Conservancy Council, and also at the Rowett Research Institute in Aberdeen, would seem to suggest that deer could be farmed quite as well as the more traditional sheep. In an article in *Wildlife Magazine* for April 1973, Russel Kyle considered the past history of the species and looked forward to its possible future as a domestic animal:

The only large animal in Britain which could be better adapted than the conventional domestic species is the red deer in Scotland, which might be farmed instead of sheep. Deer eat the same foods as sheep when there is a free choice— namely grass and young heather shoots—but they can resort to a wider range than sheep in hard times, including older heather, mosses, and browse.

The situation is less productive than the other examples given because the Highland vegetation is not natural. Originally well forested with oak, spruce, pine, and larch, the forests have all been cleared; first of all by the Vikings in an attempt to chase out the hostile natives, and finally by the English landlords who moved in after the defeat of Bonnie Prince Charlie, and whose aim was both to rout the Stewart supporters and to create hunting estates. The heather which has replaced the forests is very coarse, except for the young shoots, and there are few animals adapted to cope with it (though there have been thoughts of trying to introduce other mountain grazers such as the llama). The native red deer is not ideal because the Highlands are really on the limit of its range, which originally spread all over temperate Europe and into North Africa and parts of Asia. It only appears today as an inhabitant of marginal forest and scrub land because it has been forced out of its preferred habitat.

Nevertheless, red deer have some qualities which make them potentially very valuable as meat animals in Scotland. During the brief period of summer plenty they grow faster than even young sheep, a mature deer gaining as much as 3 pounds per day. They lose a large part of this gain during the winter, though not just because of lack of food. Deer which have been kept in yards during the winter with unlimited quantities of high quality feed have still lost weight, simply because their appetite drops.

They also lose some of their summer condition during the rutting season in

September, when the stags rush round in an aggressive frenzy protecting and chivvying their harems of about 15 females; during this period of 4 weeks or so they scarcely pause to eat. The females do not fare much better because they are so constantly chased and molested by the frantic stags that they are never left in peace to graze for very long.

As a result of the rut most animals enter the winter in a condition which is far worse than their prime, and it is not easy to understand why such behaviour evolved. One effect which it must have is to ensure that only the very best animals survive the winter, so that it amounts to a very severe pruning which must improve the health of the species as a whole. This is less surprising when one considers that the normal territory of the red deer is less harsh than the Highlands, and winter feeding further south would be more generous.

A big advantage which red deer have over sheep in the Highlands is that they are more able to fend for themselves in the extremes of winter, largely because they are able to range further in search of shelter and browse; and stags use their antlers to sweep the snow aside to reveal lichen and mosses. But these advantages depend on the animals roaming free in a large area, which means that there would be considerable problems in rounding them up from time to time to select

Red deer (*Cervus elephas*)—stag with harem.

suitable ones for slaughter and for routine veterinary treatment.

The solution would be to develop herds which would gather when required in response to a simple signal, such as the banging of a food bin. Having gathered, they must be amenable enough to accept handling by humans. It has often been shown that red deer will respond admirably in this way if they are bottle-fed from a very young age. But in order to develop herds on a commercial scale, such amenability would have to be passed on from one generation to the next, because it would be completely uneconomic to bottle-rear each generation.

Experiments on this are in progress at the Rowett Research Institute in Aberdeen. Two groups of hinds have been raised by bottle-feeding and are extremely amenable to handling; they even come running to their herdsman from over a mile away when he whistles. The two groups are now pregnant, and when the calves are born one group will be subject to constant human contact for feeding, weighing, and so on, while the other group will have the bare minimum of contact. An attempt will then be made to assess whether one group of calves is more amenable than the other, so indicating whether fear of humans is something innate or must be learned.

There is a parallel experiment on the Island of Rhum, where people and sheep were evacuated in 1957 in order to restore the island to its original deer forest habitat. Two groups of hinds are having calves, but this time it is the hinds rather than the calves which have received different treatment. One group has been hand-reared and is as amenable as those at Aberdeen. The other group has been selected as the least nervous members of a wild population. To make the selection food was placed in an enclosure on successive days, so that the wild deer could come in to eat it. After a number of days the gates were simply shut behind the first dozen deer to enter, and these were assumed to be the least nervous ones.

With long-lived animals, such as the red deer, such experiments will take a considerable time to yield significant results but I think that the long quote given is well-merited for the red deer has, I am sure, a valuable part to play in the future protein supply, just as it has done in the past.

The red deer hunt was governed by the 'Laws of Venerie', dating back to the time of the Normans and the vocabulary of the hunt was precise and no high-bred noble or his servants would dare to make any error. Bell (1837), while admitting that this was taken to a 'most absurd and ludicrous degree', then goes on:

The young of either sex is called a Calf; after a few months the male becomes distinguished by the growth of the bossets, or frontal protuberances, on which the horns are afterwards developed, which during the first year are merely rounded knobs, from whence he takes the name of Knobber. In the second year they are longer and pointed, and are called dags, and the animal has now the name of Brocket. In the third year, the first, or brow antler, has made its appearance, and the Deer becomes a Spayad. In the fourth, the bez-antler is added, and he is then termed a Staggard. He is a Stag in the fifth year, when the third antler, or royal, appears: and in the sixth, the commencement of the surroyal, or crown, is formed; when he takes the name of Hart, *which name he retains through life.* . . . . *The female is a* Calf *in the first year, a* Brocket's sister *in the second, and in the third, and ever afterwards, a* Hind.

The same terminology cannot be applied to the tiny roe deer which, although it is expanding its range, is far too solitary a beast to ever become domesticated and too widely distributed in thick woodland to be a reliable beast of the field.

The Roe Deer *Capreolus capreolus*

Some folk think that the roe is our most attractive deer and I must say I find it hard to disagree, for its alert behaviour, delicate build and lovely pelage make it an attractive beast indeed. It is quite small, only about 600–700 mm (24–28 in) at the shoulder. Both sexes are approximately the same height but the males average about 22.5 kg (55 lb) which is some 4.5 kg (10 lb) heavier than the does. By all accounts, the roe is not the answer to our protein shortage and a humorist once gave this recipe:

Cut the meat from the animal and stand in salt, then rinse off and stand in water for 24 hours. Follow this with 12 hours in vinegar and then smear it with butter and salt. Finally dig a hole 12 feet deep and bury it for good!

There can be no doubt that the roe deer is truly a native of Britain but it has not proved adaptable to moorland habitats. We can tell that its food supply has remained basically the same because fossil antlers are of similar dimensions to those on modern heads. Thus the fortunes of the roe have ebbed and flowed with the fortunes of our native woodlands and, as Forestry Commission plantations increase in number and maturity, the roe is undergoing a population explosion at the moment. In the period following the end of the last Ice Age, the majority of what is now Britain was forest and was affected little, if at all, by the activities of man. The roe deer lived in harmony with its environment, the population being kept in balance by predators such as the wolf (*Canis lupus*) and lynx (*Felix lynx lynx*).

By the twelfth century, the Scots had found hunting pressures and the demand for timber sufficiently noticeable to warrant legislation but, as time went on, trees were felled for industry and the grazing of increasing numbers of sheep allowed little if any regeneration of trees. The loss of woodland throughout Britain meant the extinction of the lynx and wolf but the roe just managed to hang on, although there were periods when it almost went along the same road of no return as that followed by its predators. World War I brought matters to a head and, by 1919, the Forestry Commission had initiated its ambitious planting programme which has resulted in a substantial increase of the tree cover. Life for the roe had seldom been bettered, for here was an expanding habitat, freely available with none of the resident predators which had long since been wiped out by Man. Soon the forester

A hind roe deer.

was forced to declared war against the roe and the lovely beast was destroyed by any and every means at man's desposal.

It was an amateur naturalist, Mr. K. MacArthur, studying the species in southern Scotland, who worked out that great numbers of trees were damaged when many rival males indulged in orgies of tree-bashing. He further pointed out that the stronger the buck, the larger the territory he could command. The answer to the forester's prayer was therefore a *scientific* cull of the weaker males; the stronger individuals left would increase the quality of the species and, because of their larger territories, the damage would be reduced. Further south, in Lakeland's Grizedale Forest, a gentleman called Grant worked out how the Forestry Commission could not only retain the roe, but also make a profit out of it. He suggested the sale of venison abroad (perhaps because of the recipe I mentioned earlier?) and antlers and pelts to tourists. The culls were carried out with high velocity rifles and tree-top hides were constructed for the use of the marksmen. At times these can be hired by naturalists who wish only to observe the lovely animals. Despite their known tendency to damage trees, roe were re-introduced into Dorset (at Milton Abbas) from Perthshire in the year 1800 at the instigation of Lord Dorchester and, together with escapees from Petworth Park in Sussex, have succeeded in colonising the southern counties. Their range is still extending and, despite the fact that they are still a woodland species, there are some signs that they are beginning to colonise moorland areas just above the tree line, although they will never be an animal of the high hills like the red deer.

The roe's social pattern is based not on the herd but on the family group made up of a male (buck), female (doe) and usually twin fawns of the current year. You can occasionally find groups of twelve individuals, but these tend to be winter feeding parties and they soon split up again. Roe bucks, in contrast with other British species, grow their antlers during the winter. Their territories vary in size from 1 hectare ($2\frac{1}{2}$ acres) to 10 hectares (25 acres) or even more, depending, as we have seen, on the character of the dominant buck, but also upon the habitat, in particular the amount of cover and food available within it. All these factors mean that the roe is by no means a suitable parkland animal. This is in complete contrast to the fallow deer, which is able to thrive in a state of almost complete domestication.

The Fallow Deer *Dama dama*

At one time, Britain supported a population of giant fallow deer (*Cervus megaceros*), the remains of which have been found in peat bogs, especially in Ireland. Some of these beasts stood some 2 m ($6\frac{1}{2}$ ft) at the withers and had huge palmated antlers with a span of over 3 m ($9\frac{1}{2}$ ft).

The fallow deer itself has been resident in Britain for so long that it is often regarded as native; indeed fossil remains seem to suggest that a type of fallow deer was found here, became extinct, and was then re-introduced perhaps by the Phoenicians or by the Romans. The Normans also introduced many animals in an effort to increase and improve stock. Fallow deer exhibit a great variety of colour forms, from the very dark types found in the wild to the occasional white form. In parks, the menil variety is frequently

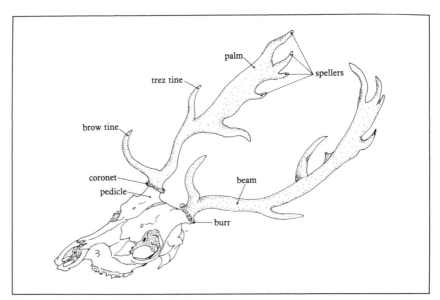

Figure 28. Antlers of a fallow buck.

found and this is lighter and more spotted than the normal type; many landowners have also concentrated on interbreeding to produce their own unique herd. It is unusual for individuals in the wild to differ significantly from the norm because those which stand out against the background are quickly picked off by predators (only Man the poacher these days!) or they may even be physically rejected by their more normal companions. The fallow deer, however, was protected throughout the Middle Ages because of its value as a beast of the hunt and also for the superior flavour of its flesh. Because of these factors, the fallow is still the most widespread deer species and dark herds, indicating wild ancestors of long standing, are found in Cannock Chase (Staffordshire), Epping Forest (Essex), Bringwood (Shropshire), and the New Forest (Hampshire). Dark individuals were imported into Britain by James I in the early years of the seventeenth century and, even earlier than this, in 1465, Baron von Rozmital noted that black, white as well as spotted fallow deer were present in Windsor Park. On his historic and surprisingly well-documented journey through the countryside of Britain, Leland noted a black herd in Lincolnshire in 1535. Levens Hall in Cumbria (and other places) still maintains its dark herd and wild stock is found throughout England and some areas of Scotland and Ireland, usually indicating escapes from collections.

Wild fallow do not seem to cope so well with poor weather as the two native species and, in 1946–47, 1962–63 and 1982, they were hit particularly badly. They struggle to exist in the highland areas and tend to concentrate in the lowlands but, even there, they are often dependent upon supplementary feeding. A few, however, have recently established themselves in Perthshire. There was once a widely held theory that fallow deer did not drink but were able to extract sufficient moisture directly from their food. This may sometimes be the case but results from a study carried out on the Canadian Island of Sidney indicate otherwise. A struggling population suddenly flourished when a reliable freshwater supply was provided. During the hot British summer of 1976, when the natural vegetation was dry and withered, all species of deer were only too glad to drink from those rivers which were still running. On many occasions during that scorching summer, I observed sika deer near my home, close to the Trough of Bowland, lapping at the trickle of water which was all that remained of the usually deep and swift-moving River Ribble.

The Sika *Cervus nippon*

The Japanese sika is the largest of the three Asiatic subspecies, of *Cervus nippon*, the others being the Manchurian and the Formosan. Mature bucks usually have eight points on the antlers, but those of the Formosan and Manchurian are usually longer and, in the latter subspecies, they are also heavier and thicker. There are also colour variations in the antler velvet, that of the Manchurian being a delicate shade of apricot, that of the Formosan being darker while, in the Japanese sika, it is black. Again it is not possible to determine age by specific reference to antler characteristics but some interesting progress has been made from a detailed study of the dentition. Duff, working on sika deer in Dorset, found that, in common with many other deer species, the eruption sequence of the permanent set of teeth could allow distinctions to be made between calves (with only the milk dentition), yearlings (with eruption progressing), and 2-year-olds with new clean teeth showing no sign of wear with use. Beyond this time scale, the age can be determined by the degree of wear on the teeth but this method demands an accurate reference collection of teeth of known age. This means that the research in this area is always likely to be a slow and highly skilled operation.

Although the sika is very closely related to the red deer and, as we have seen, interbreeding can occur, the rutting behaviour in the two differs in several particulars. Compared to the red deer, however, the rut of the sika has received little attention. Stags begin to come out of velvet during August and September, at which time they begin to mark out territories by thrashing away at plants, such as ragwort, dock, nettle or heather, and they seem to do less damage to trees than other species of deer. Some workers have suggested that the males set up territories along the routes taken by the hinds on their journeys between their feeding and resting-up areas. The actual rut can begin as early as September and continue until well into January, but it is not so strenuous as that of the red deer, since the sika male often separates a female from her herd and then chases and buffets her before covering her. He is therefore not required to defend a large harem against all-comers as the red deer stag is forced to do. As the sika deer

The muntjac (*Muntiacus reevesi*).

establishes itself in a new country, its behaviour becomes gradually tailored to meet the demands of the habitat. Should the Chinese water deer and the muntjacs which were introduced round about the same time as the sika, also find a suitable niche, then they too will begin to expand their range and perhaps cause some disruption to the often delicate ecological balance of our woodlands.

The Muntjac *Muntiacus* spp. and Chinese Water Deer
Hydropotes inermis

The muntjac is a small deer distinguished by its comparatively long tail with a hairy end. The hairs can be extended to reveal a white undersurface; this can produce a quite startling effect and is thought to serve the same function as the caudal disc of other deer.

Two species of muntjac have been brought into these islands. The slightly larger Indian muntjac (*Muntiacus muntjac*) does not seem to have survived but the Reeve's, or Chinese, muntjac (*Muntiacus reevesi*) has fared much better. A number of separate introductions have been made this century, particularly to Whipsnade and, as usual, Woburn. Escapes have been regular and the species is well established, although not numerous, in most southern counties and is slowly spreading northwards, having reached at least as far as Lincolnshire. Except in extreme weather conditions, they are not herd animals and small family parties are the usual social groupings. Unlike our other deer species, muntjac breed throughout the year, the doe producing her fawn and mating again within days of giving birth. There is an apparent gestation period of 7 months, which suggests some degree of delayed implanation. This method is in direct contrast to that employed by the Chinese water deer (*Hydropotes inermis*), which retains a regular annual breeding cycle. It can produce as many as six young at the same time,

The Chinese water deer (*Hydropotes inermis*).

although, in Britain, three or four are more usual. The Chinese water deer is longer in the leg and not so heavily built as the muntjac, which is a beast of the undergrowth. *Hydropotes inermis* is the latest species of deer to escape and live wild in our countryside, being originally brought into Woburn Abbey (where else?!) but there were subsequent introductions into Whipsnade, as well as Surrey, Hampshire, Shropshire and Yorkshire. They are unique among British deer in that neither sex has antlers, but the bucks do have long upper canine teeth which look very like tusks. The male muntjac also has this feature but the teeth are much less obvious.

As with the muntjac, the Chinese water deer is found in small social groupings rather than in herds. I remember some years ago listening to a friend express the opinion that this delicate-looking deer would have great difficulty in surviving a severe British winter. In fact, quite the opposite has proved to be the case since the thermal insulation afforded by the coat is so efficient that, when the animal lies down in the snow, very little heat escapes and, when the animal rises, there is no dark stain indicating melting caused by heat losses. The problem seems to come in the summer when the small deer are chased by foxes or dogs and so much heat is generated as they try to escape. Due to the insulating efficiency of the pelt, the heat cannot be dissipated and Chinese water deer can overheat and die.

Here then we have two new species struggling to establish themselves and, from these, it is fitting that the focus is shifted to three animals which, although their lineage can be traced back at least to Neolithic times, are now having problems in remaining part of our native fauna. I speak of our few remaining wild goats, sheep and cattle which are the subject of the next chapter.

13 Artiodactyls: Goats, Sheep and Cattle

Sheep and cattle belong to the family Bovidae. The males are characterised by having horns and, in many species, the females are also horned.

The Wild Goat *Capra hircus*

The distribution of wild goats, to say the least, is patchy and, at present, the species has no legal protection. In these days of high-powered rifles, any population could easily be wiped out were landowners to decide upon this course of action. Protection must therefore be given to the goats before it is too late. They are present in Wales, concentrated mainly on the Snowdon and Cader Idris mountains, as well as in the Kielder Forest area of Northumberland. There are many small groups in Scotland, Ireland, the

The wild goat (*Capra hircus*).

Isle of Man and Anglesey. It would seem that the goat was one of the first animals to be domesticated and may well have been brought into Britain by Neolithic man almost 8000 years ago. They would have been valuable animals at that time and, as such, must have been carefully guarded, but despite this there would have been escapes and goats are such able climbers and scramblers that they would have been difficult to retrieve. Country folk kept goats for thousands of years and both the milk and the flesh would have been valuable, as would the skin. After the Industrial Revolution, there was less need for villagers to keep a goat; this was especially so when the development of the railway network led to improved supplies of alternative foods.

In the wild, goats live in groups of up to fifteen; the males are particularly aggressive during the October and November rut, when they engage in long bouts of head-butting which can be heard over large distances. As a result of mating and after a 150-day gestation period, a single kid (occasionally twins) is born in February or March. A full-grown male can weigh over 50 kg (100 lb) and sport a massive set of lethal-looking horns. The females only average half this weight. The scimitar-shaped horns of goats can be used to estimate age. It has been proved that the horns of a 3-year-old male are about 400 mm (16 in) long while those of a 9- or 10-year-old are double this figure; there are growth ring patterns on the horns which can be used to calculate age.

If a goat and a domesticated sheep are examined, the two look sufficiently different to suggest that they should be placed in separate families. The primitive forms of sheep, however, do look very goat-like. The only place where such a species may be observed in a native setting is the island of St Kilda and it was in a state of high excitement that I set off to look at the Soay sheep.

The Soay Sheep *Ovis aries*

Over 5 hours out from North Uist in the Outer Hebrides, MV St Just bucked and tossed in the swell of the grey Atlantic. Crockery and furniture rattled and rolled in their securing racks as the boat bored on. Over the bow, I could just discern a heavy smudge of mist which seemed to hang suspended between the low cloud and the heaving sea. This was it. My first sight of St Kilda and nothing beyond it save the Americas. To the people of old, here, indeed, was the end of the world.

St Kilda is the collective name for a group of seven rocky islands: Soay, Dun, Levenish, Boreray, Stac Lee, Stac an Armin and the largest, Hirta. Hirta was inhabited until 1930 when the remnant population elected to be evacuated to the mainland. Thus ended a unique association between the villagers and the wildlife which was literally on their doorstep. Their economy was based entirely on the vast seabird populations. Fulmars were harvested for oil, food and feathers and gannets were also slaughtered for food and feathers. The resourcefulness of the people can be judged from the way they made maximum use of the birds they killed. Even the long, dagger-

Soay sheep (*Ovis aries*) on St Kilda.

like bills of the gannets were used as pegs to secure the thatch of the roofs of the cottages. In order to obtain sufficient birds for their needs, the St Kildans became brave and resorceful climbers, a fact vouched for by those pioneers of wildlife photography, the Kearton brothers, Richard and Cherry, who visited the islands in 1897.

At the present time, the army have a missile-tracking station based on Hirta, but the basic geography of the village remains as it was at the time of the evacuation. One tangible connection remains between the old St Kildans and the present ones. The descendants of their sheep are still on the island and are thriving. These animals are not common mainlanders, but a very special breed called Soay sheep and their significance can be realised by reference to a quote from *The Handbook of British Mammals* (Southern, 1977):

No wild sheep have occurred in Britain in post glacial times, but domestic sheep have been present since the Neolithic and only one truly feral herd of sheep deserves mention here, Ovis *(domestic) on the island of St Kilda. They are primitive domestic sheep, but the time of their introduction to St Kilda is not known. They survived only on the Island of Soay, but in 1932 they were introduced to the largest St Kildan island, Hirta.*

As stated in *The Handbook,* there is little direct scientific documentation regarding the origins of Soay sheep, but a peep into the the archaeology books does shed some light on the problem. A search of the middens of prehistoric settlements have unearthed identifiable Soay sheep bones from several continental sites, but a significant record comes from a Roman settlement at Newstead, close to Melrose. There is a suggestion that a certain Viking, by the name of Calum, brought the first Soay sheep to the islands, but some authorities disagree, pointing out that there were sheep in prehistoric Hebridean settlements prior to the Norse invasions. Whatever the truth of the matter, the first documentary evidence is an account written by a man named Boece and dated 1527. He describes the sheep of St Kilda as having a coat that did not resemble that of a sheep nor that of a goat. In the year 1578, Bishop Leslie reiterated Boece's statement but described the species as 'neither sheep nor goat, neither have they wool like a sheep nor hair like a goat, but something between the two'.

Important evidence regarding physical features and population comes from the historian, Martin, writing in 1697. He says that the numbers of Soay sheep did not exceed 2000 on Hirta and that there were 500 on Soay which were hunted by the St Kildans. He mentions that some beasts had white on them, which suggests some interbreeding with a domestic type of sheep. He also says that each ewe had two or three lambs per season, but this does not seem to be supported by subsequent writers.

Later in the history of St Kilda, Macauley gave further and probably more accurate information. He estimated some 500 sheep on Soay, 100 on Hirta, and Boreray supported 400 ewes which had been brought thence from Hirta. This must have been a hazardous operation since the seas between Hirta and Boreray are never easy to cross and, more often than not, literally impossible. The islands at this time only possessed one small boat which must have added to the transport problem. The sheep were kept mostly for their wool or hair. It was Macauley who first mentioned the two distinct colour phases which can easily be discerned in Soay sheep today. The pelt of both types show a similarity to the wild mouflon.

In 1912, Donald Ferguson estimated that there were no less than 300 sheep on Soay (he did not take a census on the other islands) and that 50% were of the light variety and 50% were dark. Estimates made about 1970 showed 25% of the total stock to be pale and 75% to be dark. Another interesting gleaning from the observations of Donald Ferguson is his suggestion that the Soay sheep were gradually becoming smaller. This is acceptable if the earlier writers, who commented upon the large size of the species, are to be believed. In more recent years, scientific investigations, made mainly by Jewell, Milner and Boyd, have shown that, on Hirta, there is quite a marked fluctuation of population from year to year. The highest figure quoted is 1783 and the lowest 610. It seems also that ewes outnumber the rams by a factor of about 4 to 1. Many of the Hirta sheep are marked, usually on the ears, to make identification easier.

During my time on Hirta, I found the Soay sheep to be a strange mixture of timidity and inquisitiveness. A group near the ruined houses in Village Bay played a sort of peek-a-boo around these and the cleits which clothe the steep hills. During heavy rain, which is so much a feature of these islands, the sheep often seek shelter in the cleits, which were originally used to dry both the carcasses of seabirds which the villagers needed for food and the cut turf which in the absence of fossil fuels was used for fires.

One has to wonder if these fluctuations in population are caused by lack of adequate feeding, but a careful investigation of the plants showed Hirta to have a limited but surprisingly lush flora. I identified the following species: sheep's-fescue (*Festuca ovina*) which was in parts dominant and also bell heather (*Erica cinerea*), common heather (*Calluna* spp.), bilberry (*Vaccinium myrtillus*) and, on the upper slopes, dwarf willow (*Salix herbacea*) and even honeysuckle (*Lonicera periclymenum*). I cannot pretend that my list is exhaustive for my time on the island was limited, but in the area being cropped by Soay sheep the following species occurred: butterwort (*Pinguicula vulgaris*), bog asphodel (*Narthecium ossifragum*), milkwort (*Polygala vulgaris*), bird's-foot-trefoil (*Lotus corniculatus*), ragged-robin (*Lychnis flos-cuculi*), scentless mayweed (*Tripleurospermum maritimum*), slender St John's-wort (*Hypericum pulchrum*), thyme (*Thymus praecox*), selfheal (*Prunella vulgaris*), thrift (*Armeria maritima*), bladder campion (*Silene vulgaris*), heath-spotted orchid (*Dactylorhiza maculata*), lousewort (*Pedicularis sylvatica*), tormentil (*Potentilla erecta*), meadow buttercup (*Ranunculus acris*) common chickweed (*Stellaria media*), stinging nettle (*Urtica dioica*), common sorrel (*Rumex acetosa*), eyebright (*Euphrasia* spp.) and heath speedwell (*Veronica officinalis*).

On many occasions while watching the seabird colonies on these, the highest sea cliffs in Britain, I watched the Soay sheep descending almost vertical faces in search of the grass which here, as everywhere else, was greener on the other side of the hill. The dexterity of their descent was only bettered by the ease and speed of their ascent. They never seemed to pause, either due to confusion or because of shortage of breath. It seems that the species show some similarity of behaviour with the red deer. Groups of males tend to associate outside the breeding season and can be identified by their huge curled horns. The females tend to wander less than the males and are usually accompanied by their lambs. Some of the females also possess horns but these are much less ornate than those of the males. The rut occurs in November and the lambs resulting from this are born in April. More often than not, one lamb is produced, but twin births are not unusual.

The more time one spends on St Kilda the less one understands the weather. At 10.30 hours I began watching Soay sheep from the seclusion of a cleit. The sun poured down from a clear July sky. The sea in Village Bay was flat calm. Just after 11.15 hours, a thick mist descended, the temperature fell alarmingly, the sky darkened, the wind rose to a steady force 6 gusting to 7 and rain poured. Time and tide wait for no man and I was obliged to head for my boat or risk being stranded there, maybe for days. Soon MV St Just headed out into a rising sea en route for the comparative safety of North Uist. I left behind a hardy race of sheep as they have been for centuries—successful on the edge of the world.

Before leaving the Bovidae, I should mention Britain's one remaining example of wild cattle—the Chillingham or white cattle.

White Cattle *Bos taurus*

The precise origins of white cattle in Britain are not known but they seem to have been common in the Iron Age. In all probability, they were another Neolithic introduction and a well-documented pure herd is found at Chillingham, Northumberland, where it has been enclosed for over 700 years and is still wild enough to hate the smell of human beings. The bulls are particularly fierce, but even a cow with a calf is best left well alone. I find it difficult to blame 'old Bos' for having a go at unwanted visitors because it has been hunted and killed for centuries, just to provide entertainment. These cruel hunts were described by Thomas Bewick in his *History of Quadrupeds* in 1790:

The mode of killing them was, perhaps the only modern remains of the grandeur of hunting. On notice being given that a wild bull would be killed on a certain day, the inhabitants of the neighbourhood came mounted and armed with guns etc. sometimes to the amount of a hundred horse, and four or five hundred foot

Chillingham white cattle (*Bos taurus*).

who stood upon the walls, or got into trees while the horsemen rode off the Bull from the rest of the herd, until he took to bay when the horsemen dismounted and shot. At some of these huntings twenty or thirty shots have been fired before he was subdued. On such occasions the bleeding victim grew desperately furious, from the smarting of his wounds, and the shouts of savage joy that were echoing from every side. But apart from the number of accidents that happened this dangerous mode has been little practiced of late years, the park-keeper alone generally shooting them with a rifle gun, at one shot.

Other herds occur at Vayno and Dynevor (Carmarthenshire), Cadzow (Lanarkshire) and guess where?—Woburn. At one time, a white herd was kept by Lord Ribblesdale near Gisburn, but all trace of this has been gone for over a century.

This is all that now remains of a once-common inhabitant of our country but, as the final chapter of this book will show, even the white cattle have fared better than the urus or wild ox (*Bos taurus primigenius*), which has been extinct since the Bronze Age. Many other species have disappeared in the last thousand years and it is to these that we turn our attention in the final chapter of this book.

14 Extinct and Mythical Beasts

J ames Edmund Harting, in the year 1880, published his *British Mammals Extinct Within Historic Times with some Account of British Wild Cattle* and, in some respects, this can still be regarded as a standard work for the natural historian.

Although it is not the purpose of this present volume to go into detail of our prehistoric mammals (neither was it Harting's), it should not be forgotten that these islands are surprisingly rich in fossils found in caves, brickearths and river gravels, all dating back to the Miocene epoch (see Table 1). The Tertiary period, so rich in mammalian fossils, is represented by finds from the Hampshire and London basins. During the glaciations of the Pleistocene epoch, all our fauna and flora must have been placed under great

The arctic fox (*Alopex lagopus*).

stress and, for a time, tropical life forms were on the road to extinction in our land (remember we were still in contact with the Continent) and were being gradually—in geological terms—replaced by more northerly forms, better able to cope with low temperatures. Such animals were the glutton (*Gulo gulo*), arctic fox (*Alopex lagopus*), musk ox (*Ovibos moschatus*) and the reindeer (*Rangifer tarandus*), about which I shall have more to say later. All these species indicate a severe arctic climate (whereas the remains of voles, picas and susliks indicate a more steppe-like climate). At times, the climate seems to have been ideal for sabre-toothed tigers, fossils of which have been unearthed from Kent's Cavern near Torquay and were widely distributed during the Pleistocene and Pliocene periods. In addition, many of our cave systems, brick-earths and gravels have yielded fossils of the tiger (*Panthera tigris*), lion (*P. leo*), leopard (*P. pardus*) and lynx (*Felis lynx*). Irish deer, also called giant elks, wandered freely, as did the mammoths and other members of the elephant family, but any reader wishing to know more about these fascinating creatures is referred to the bibliography. Like Harting, I will restrict myself to those mammals extinct in Britain within the period since written records began: this involves an account of the brown bear (*Ursus arctos*), beaver (*Castor fiber*), reindeer (*Rangifer tarandus*) wild boar (*Sus scrofa*) and wolf (*Canis lupus*). Brief mention must also be made of the original wild cattle already referred to in the section on Chillingham white cattle in Chapter 13.

The Brown Bear *Ursus arctos*

There can be little doubt that the bear survived the rigours of the glaciations and is the largest and most formidable of the carnivores to merit inclusion in this written history of Britain's mammals. Harting observes:

The brown bear (*Ursus arctos*).

A nearly perfect skull from the marl below the peat in Manea Fen, Cambridgeshire, and now in the Woodwardian Museum, Cambridge has been described and figured by Professor Owen, who has described portions of another skull from the same locality. In 1868 Dr. Hicks found remains of the Brown Bear in peat at St. Brides Bay; and numerous bones and teeth of this animal have been discovered at various times in Kent's Cavern, Devonshire.

The exploration of the Victoria Cave near Settle revealed the fact that the Brown Bear afforded food to the Neolithic dwellers in the cave, who have left relics of their feasts and a few rude implements at the lowest horizon; the broken bones and jaws of this animal lying mixed up with the remains of the Red-deer, Horse and Celtic Shorthorn.

Nor are we without direct testimony that the Bear was killed by the hand of man during the Roman occupation of Britain. In the collection of bones from the 'refuse heaps' round Colchester made by Dr. Bree, the remains of this animal were found along with those of the Badger, Wolf, Celtic Shorthorn and Goat. Professor Boyd Dawkins has also met with it in a similar 'refuse heap' at Richmond in Yorkshire, which is most probably of Roman origin.

The fact that bears occurred in Britain, and especially in Scotland, was obviously well known to the Romans and many beasts seem to have been imported for use in the imperial arenas.

> *Thus Laureolus, on no ideal cross suspended*
> *Presents his naked body to the Caledonian Bear.*

Camden, the seventeenth-century scholar, follows Plutarch and asserts that 'they transported Bears into Rome and held them in great admiration'—all except poor old Laureolus!

The Celts, too, were aware of the bear and many authorities are of the opinion that the term 'arth' in a place name refers to a bear. I think this is a true derivation but some workers think that 'arth' refers to a shrine dedicated to the goddess Artio, who was worshipped in the form of a she-bear by the Helvetian branch of the Celts. Archbishop Egbert mentions bears in his eighth-century *Penitential* in such a way that it leads one to believe that they were still alive at this time:

If anyone shall hit a deer or other animal with an arrow and it escapes and is found dead three days afterwards, and if a dog, a wolf or a bear or any other wild beast hath begun to feed on it no Christian shall touch it.

There is little evidence, however, that *Ursus arctos* survived much beyond this time, even though, at the time of the *Domesday Book*, the town of Norwich was required to provide the King with one bear each year, along with six dogs to bait it. Norwich, I think, was near enough to the east coast to be able to import the beast from northern Europe. Two further claims to the existence of bears after the arrival of the Normans may also be discounted.

Many references are made to Anglo-Saxon gleemen, who were entertainers of an often crude nature and, included in their varied repertoire, was bear baiting and dancing bears. In the Dark Ages, the animals were doubtlessly obtained in the wild while they were still young and could be trained, but later on they were probably imported. Erasmus, visiting England during the reign of Henry VIII, commented on bears being kept 'in herds for the purpose of baiting'. Likewise, in the reign of that merry monarch Charles II, and in Victorian times, dancing bears were a feature of fairgrounds and doubtless furtive baiting went on down back alleys.

The second claim can likewise be discounted and again I quote Harting's volume of 1880:

The story quoted by Pennant (British Zoology, Vol. 1 p. 91 (ed. 1812) from a history of the Gordon family to the effect that in 1507 a Gordon, in reward for his valour in killing a fierce bear, was directed by the King to carry three boars heads on his banner is altogether a fallacy. Reference to a copy of the original Latin MS from which the translation quoted by Pennant was made (preserved in the Advocate's Library, Edinburgh) shows that the animal killed was a Boar, 'Immanem aprum'. Moreover the arms of the Gordons happen to be Boars not Bears heads. The difference in one letter only in the name might easily account for a mistake which has since been blindly copied by many writers.

It is not my purpose in this book to debate the ethics or the practice of bear baiting and I will content myself by noting that the brown bear has been extinct since Domesday, a fate which also befell the beaver quite soon after this date.

The Beaver *Castor fiber*

Once again the natual historian will find Harting a most valuable source of information and of the beaver he writes:

The earliest notice we find of it is contained in the code of the Welsh laws made by Howel Dha (AD 940), and which, unlike the ancient Saxon codes and the Irish Senchus Mor, contains many quaint laws relating to hunting and fishing. It is there laid down that the King is to have the worth of Beavers, Martens and Ermines, in whatsoever spot they shall be killed, because from them the borders of the Kings garment are made.

The price of a Beaver's skin, termed 'croen llostlydan' at that time was fixed at 120 pence while the skin of a Marten was only 24 pence and that of a Wolf, fox and otter 8 pence. This shows that even at the period the Beaver was a rare animal in Wales.

The superior warmth and comfort which the Beaver's skin afforded, added to the reputation of the medicinal properties of the Castor must have operated as a very powerful incitement to hunt the Beaver in those early times.

The beaver (*Castor fiber*) with its young.

Living as he did in the prudish times (in public life at least) of Victorian England, Harting dared not say that the testicles of the castor (as the Romans called the beaver) were a much sought-after aphrodisiac in the East—actually, it was probably the musk glands of the male, situated behind the testicles, which were of value but these were only accessible once the animal had been castrated.

Some 250 years following the death of Howel Dha, one Giraldus Cambrensis, also called Gerald de Barri, made a journey through Wales (in 1188) accompanied by Baldwin, Archbishop of Canterbury. (The latter accompanied Richard Coeur de Lion on the crusades and fell at the Siege of Acre.) During this journey, Giraldus mentions the presence of beavers on the River Teivi and then, uncluttered by Victorian propriety, provides us with some wonderful folklore concerning the beaver, doubtless liberally sprinkled with poetic licence, but no less fascinating for all that.

When the beaver discovers that he cannot escape from the attentions of the dogs which follow him, he may decide to ransom his body by the sacrifice of the part which by natural instinct he realises they prefer. In the sight of the hunter he castrates himself from which circumstance he has earned the name of Castor. If by chance the dogs should chase an already castrated individual he has the good sense to run to an elevated spot, lift up his leg and shews the hunter that the object of his pursuit has gone. Thus therefore, in order to preserve his pelt which is sought after in the West, and the medicinal part which is coveted in the east, although he cannot save himself entire yet by a wonderful instinct and sagacity he tries to avoid the strategems of his pursuers.

Because the beaver spent so much of its time in water, some medical folk recommended the use of its fat as cures for rheumatism and so, whether it was the activities of the furrier or the apothecary which eventually led to the extinction of the European beaver in Britain is a matter of fruitless debate. Even the gourmet may have played some part! Giraldus mentions the fish-like qualities of the animal's broad tail and, from the 1658 edition of Topsell's *History of Four-Footed Beastes*, we learn that beaver tails:

... are accounted a very delicat dish for being dressed they eat like Barbels ... the manner of dressing is, first roasting and afterwards seething in an open pot, so that the evil vapours may go away, and some in pottage made with saffron, other with ginger and many with wine. It is certain that the tail and forefeet taste very sweet.

Although the beaver has long since gone from our land, a glance at a map will give clear indications of its one-time presence. Among the Yorkshire towns, for example, there is both a Bewerley and the better-known Beverley, which literally means 'the stream of the beavers'. If more evidence is needed, it is provided by the presence of teeth and other bones, which are obviously those of *Castor fiber*, found at Wawne on the River Hull very close to Beverley itself.

So much then for the presence of the animal but is it possible to put an accurate date on its final extinction? Corbet and other workers are of the opinion that the beaver probably disappeared first in England, due to deforestation of lowland river banks in addition to the other important factors already discussed, and they think that it did not survive in Wales for very long after Giraldus paid his visit. In Scotland, however, it may have lasted that bit longer, a situation also true in the case of the reindeer.

The Reindeer *Rangifer tarandus*

Reading the works of Harting and other Victorians, one could be forgiven for believing that the reindeer or caribou thrived in Scotland at least up to, and possibly including, the twelfth century, but the whole fabric of this theory is based upon one account of the Earl of Orkney hunting them in Caithness and confusion with red deer, or even fallow deer especially imported for the hunt, cannot be ruled out. In any event, there is little fossil, evidence to support the presence of 'Father Christmas's sledge-pullers' after the end of the Pleistocene epoch but, every September, a Horn Dance is performed at Abbotts Bromley in Staffordshire. Two musicians, one on melodeon, the other on triangle, play while other members of the group hold a mock fight with reindeer horns. This is said to celebrate reindeer-hunting. It is hardly surprising that such a useful and docile beast found it difficult to survive in the face of hunting pressure imposed by cruel and cunning human societies. The meat is good, whether fresh, frozen or smoked, its hide perfect for clothes and upholstery, while, from its sinews, threads were

The reindeer (*Rangifer tarandus*).

produced which were tough enough to sew boots and even canoes. The fact that the sinews tended to swell when wet meant they were perfect for primitive 'boat' building.

Reindeer are still present in Norway (protected since 1902 by a quota system), Spitzbergen (protected since 1925), Greenland (protected since 1927) and Russia (where hunting reindeer has been limited since 1957). The species has recently been re-introduced into the Cairngorms and, like many people, I envisaged a zoo-type herd (one does, in fact, exist) controlled by a keeper. Imagine my surprise, on a hot day in July 1982, on finding a single beast lying contentedly on a bed of cool crisp snow chewing away. Three thoughts crossed my mind—how easily I could have killed the animal, how simply it could be brought to extinction and thirdly, if this was living wild, then surely *Rangifer tarandus* has as much right on the list of British mammals as the red-necked wallaby. It was also in Scotland that a rather foolish attempt was made to re-introduce the wolf which, by all accounts, was brought to an abrupt and grisly end by the local farmers. This beast and the wild boar are two species which could never, in my view, be sensibly re-introduced into such a heavily populated country as modern-day Britain.

The Wild Boar *Sus scrofa*

The huntsmen cheered on the hounds that first hit the scent, loudly yelling loud words, which brought the other hounds swiftly to the place. These took up the scent, twenty couples at once, raising such a babble and clamour that the rocks rang with it. The hunters encouraged them with horn and voice, and they rushed in close formation between a pond in the wood and the foot of the crag. There was a rocky knoll beside the marsh with a clitter of scree at its foot, and out of this jumble of rocks they pushed their quarry, and the men after them. They surrounded the carr and the knoll for they knew by the voice of the blood hounds that

A wild boar (*Sus scrofa*) with young.

the boar was there. They thrashed the bushes to flush him out, and he rushed with deadly ferocity at the men in his path. He was the most magnificent boar, so old that he had long been solitary ... but for all his age he was formidable still, the biggest boar that ever was seen; the sound of his grunting was terrible. He brought grief to many, for he felled three hounds at his first onslought and he went away at a good pace, unhurt himself. ... All was hurry and clamour to get at the boar. Many times he turns at bay. He maims and wounds some of the hounds so that they howl dolefully. Now men press forward to shoot at him; their bows are drawn full stretch and many arrows find their mark. But the points glanced off his rough sides, and no barb would bite his bristling brow, though the shaven shafts shivered with the shock of impact, and the loose heads ricocheted off. But bruised by the blows and maddened with irritation, he charged the men, wounding them sorely in his assault, scaring some into retreat. But the lord on a swift horse galloped after him, sounding his horn like a trooper on a battlefield he sounded the rally and rode through the briars, pursuing this wild pig till the sun set. So they passed the whole day hunting this one boar. ... The lord galloped across country, after his ill-fated boar which ran up the banks, breaking the backs of the best of his bitches. Every time he stood at bay till the archers forced him into the open despite all he could do, with volleys of arrows, until at last there was no more running in him. With the last of his speed he made for an overhanging bank, above a stream, and put his back into it, scraping the ground with his trotters. The froth foamed at his mouth in the corners, and he whets his white tusks. The men that were after him would have closed to handgrips, but none dared come so near, he had wounded so many up to now. None of them were keen for another taste of his tushes, so fierce and frenzied was he. The knight himself came up, urging on his horse, and saw the boar defying his men. Deftly dismounting he turned the horse loose, drew his bright sword and strode forward, splashing through the ford where the fell beast waited. When the quarry saw the knight standing sword in hand, the heckles rose on him and he snorted so savagely that many were in fear for the swordsman, that he might not come off best. The boar made straight from him in the white foaming water, and together they went down in one heap. But the boar got the worst of it, for when they came together the knight had his eye on the vital spot, aiming for the hollow of the throat with the sword's point. Snarling, he yielded, and was swept downstream swiftly to where the hounds fastened on him with their teeth. The man dragged him to the bank where the dogs did him to death.

This long but fascinating quote, set in the latter years of the fourteenth century, is from *Sir Gawain and the Green Knight*, which some authorities set in the Peak District while others favour the Lancashire Pennines. The actual site of the destruction of England's last boar is reputed to be in Rossendale, the hunt starting off from Swinshaw Hall near the village of Crawshawbooth which lies on the A56 road between Burnley and Manchester, but wherever and however the last boar met its end, we can but guess, although Bell (1837) provides us with a brief summary of its history in Britain:

At the period when Britain was covered with forests, the Wild Boar was found in them as a native, and probably once in some considerable numbers. About the year 940, the laws of Hoel Dha direct that it shall be lawful for the chief of his huntsmen to chase the Boar of the woods from the fifth of the Ides of November (9th) until the Calends of December (1st). . . . In the next century, the numbers had perhaps begun to diminish, since a forest law of William I, established in A.D. 1087, ordained that any who were found guilty of killing the Stag, the Roebuck, or the Wild Boar, should have their eyes put out; and sometimes the penalty appears to have been a painful death. It appears, indeed, that Charles the First turned out some wild swine in the New Forest for the purpose of restoring the breed to that royal hunting-ground; but they were all of them destroyed during the Civil War. A similar attempt has, I believe, been lately made in Bere Wood, in Dorsetshire; but one of the Boars having injured a valuable Horse belonging to the worthy Nimrod who exhibited this specimen of sporting epicurism, he caused them to be destroyed.

The Boar, however, has its name immortalised as an inhabitant of these islands, by having given origin to the name of many places in different parts of

the country, and by its introduction into the armorial bearings of many dis-
tinguished families of every division of the kingdom. My friend Mr. Hogg [sic]
writes thus to me on the former subject:—'The village of Brancepeth, and the
adjoining hill, called Brandon, in this county (Durham), took their names from
a Wild Boar or Brawn, *which is recorded to have been a terrific beast, and the*
dread of the whole neighbourhood; his den *being on* Brandon *(brawn-den) hill,*
and his usual track or path *leading through the woods of* Brancepeth *(Brawn's*
path). Tradition states that one Roger Hodge, or Hoodge, valiantly slew the
monster, and delivered the district from his ravages. The seal of this illustrious
Roger still remains, and represents a Boar passant.*' [*See Surtee's *History of*
Durham, Vol. III, p. 284.]

Harting (1880) points out that the ferocity of the boar was probably
responsible for it being figured on early British coins and in early Celtic
art. The Britons, Romans and Saxons all hunted it. Pennant, during his
travels around eighteenth-century Britain, visited the Roman remains at
Ribchester on the River Ribble and found an engraving of the wild boar.
The site is close to the present author's home and is not far from Swinshaw
Hall, the possible hunting area of the Green Knight. The best known story
involving the boar, however, is centred around Whitby in North Yorkshire,
concerning the ceremony of 'Planting the Penny Hedge'. During October
1159, a group of headstrong 'gentlemen' were hunting the boar across land
belonging to the Abbot of Whitby but without having his permission. They
chased their quarry into a hermitage and, during an altercation which
followed, a monk was injured and died sometime afterwards. Prior to his
death, he forgave his killers on their agreeing, each Ascensiontide, to build a
hedge on the seashore between the tides. The structure was to be constructed of timber cut from the Abbey woods. It seems that the story has
no basis in fact, but the annual hedge construction has certainly stood the
test of time and leaves us with a tangible record of a beast which was very
rare, even in Shakespeare's England, although as usual the Bard of Avon
had some knowledge of it. In his long poem *Venus and Adonis*, he writes:

> *With javelin's point a churlish swine to gore*
> *Whose tushes never sheathed he whetteth still*
> *Like to a mortal butcher bent to kill*
> *His brawny sides, with hairy bristles arm'd*
> *Are better proof than thy spears point can enter*
> *His short, thick neck cannot be easily harm'd.*

In France and Germany, the hunt is still practised and, during the
eighteenth and nineteenth centuries, unsuccessful attempts were made to
re-introduce wild boar into Britain and, long after they were extinct here,
beasts were brought over in cages especially for the hunt. Even though I am
very much an anti-hunting man, I can well understand the adrenalin
flowing as the hunters' undoubted courage was matched by the gameness of

the beast who 'when he strikes his crooked tushes slay'. Perhaps only the wolf could match the challenge presented by such an adversary.

The Wolf *Canis lupus*

This animal generated such fear in the hearts of our ancestors that a whole volume could be written about it. The tale of *Little Red Riding Hood* has been told by one generation to the next and is now a lovely story but, in the time when the woods were full of wolves, it was meant as a grim warning.

In the Pleistocene epoch, wolves were common throughout Great Britain and Ireland and numerous fossil remains have been found in the Norfolk forest bed which has been assigned to the earliest portion of this epoch. Nearly all the caverns and brick-earths in England have yielded some wolf remains, as have the Pentland Hills in Scotland and the Shandon district of Ireland.

When the Romans invaded Britain wolves were still numerous in the thick forests and, in Anglo-Saxon times, although much woodland habitat had been lost, the month of January was devoted to hunting the wolf. During the squabbles of 1066, as the Normans strengthened their hold on the Islands, the bodies of the slain were said to have been eaten by 'worms, wolves, birds and dogs'. Throughout the reigns of the Norman kings, up to

The wolf (*Canis lupus*).

and including Henry III (1216–1272), the wolf is frequently mentioned, but after this date references become fewer and fewer, although reference is made to hunting English wolves as late as 1486 (the last year of the reign of Richard III).

North of the border, however, Scottish wolves still harassed man and his livestock. During the reign of James I (1427), a law was passed to try to combat a plague of wolves, but this was not all that successful and, during the ill-fated reign of Mary Queen of Scots (1560s), the plague had reached such a peak that human corpses were buried on offshore islands, such as Handa, to allow them to rest in peace away from hungry wolves. In the year 1563, five wolves were killed in the Forest of Athol and it is said that the final wolf met its end in 1743.

In England, the date and site of the death of the last wolf is a matter of no little debate. In his book *Lost Beasts of Britain*, Anthony Dent puts forward the claim of Pickering in North Yorkshire as the likely area while I have in my possession a small booklet, compiled by Mary Mercier, which states that the final wolf hunt took place close to the village of Cartmel in Cumbria. Whatever the truth of the matter, it would seem that, by the time Henry VII had secured the English throne for the Tudors by defeating the Plantaganet Richard III on Bosworth field, the most fearsome carnivore had already gone the way of the aurochs, our most terrifying herbivore.

The Aurochs (Urus) *Bos taurus primigenius*

This impressive and awe-inspiring creature was known to the Roman legions involved in the conquest of Gaul, Germany and Austria. The natives they conquered called the beasts 'aur' or 'ur' and this became Latinised as *urus* and was then taken over as the German *aurochs* (ur-ox). The original birth place of the species seems to have been Asia, possibly India, and the sacred cow may well claim an ur-ox as its distant ancestor. From this primitive stock, there is also a link with the bison and the two may well have a common ancestor. No doubt, geographical isolation, long before the advent of Man's written history, led to the evolution of subspecies of aurochs and the northern form reached a splendid peak of development in Germany and Britain, fossil remains in several museums indicating sizes of perhaps twice that of modern prize bulls—formidable beasts indeed. It is small wonder that Caesar's diaries state the bulls in the Black Forest to be the size of elephants. The last British auroch did not long survive the arrival of 'civilised' Man, but may well have been 'domesticated' rather than exterminated. The white cattle described in Chapter 13 may be following the pattern imposed by our ancestors, who would certainly have had the sense to 'fence in' their protein supply, kill the most fierce for food and use the most docile for dairy purposes. Although the last European urus was killed in Poland in 1627, experiments are going on at the moment involving sophisticated breeding programmes in an attempt to 're-create' the extinct ur-ox. I doubt if it will succeed but it is refreshing to conclude this book about the history of our mammals by noting that the human conscience has been pricked and that the desire to restore the ur-ox may prevent us from herding other valuable species along the same road.

It seems that the beasts at large in the countryside were not enough to satisfy man's sense of awe and wonder and the invention of mythical beasts like the pegasus, centaur, cyclops, unicorn and Tolkien's beasts in *The Lord of the Rings* have been a part of our history literally 'since Adam was a lad'. This trend reached a peak in the fifteenth and sixteenth centuries, when many fanciful bestiaries were produced and indeed, were more in demand than works describing actual species. We must remember, however, that the 'average' person in those days would be living closer to and be more knowledgeable about the habits of wildlife than we are today. Bestiaries had their origins in all ancient civilisations and, throughout the Middle Ages were the most popular books after the Bible. While they do nothing factually significant to help the natural historian of the twentieth century, they do show that, deep in our psyche, there is a desire to understand the place of man in the natural world and it is just this drive which motivated me to set down this history of our mammals.

Bibliography

Introduction and Chapter 1

Aflalo, A.F. (1888) *Natural History (Vertebrates) of the British Isles* Blackwood, Edinburgh

Barret-Hamilton, G.E.H.& Hinton, M.A.C. (1910–21) *A History of British Mammals* Gurney & Jackson, London

Bell, T. (1837) *A History of British Quadrupeds* Van Voorst, London

Berridge, W.S. (1934) *Wild Animals of Our Country* Harrap, London

Boyle, C.L. (1981) *The RSPCA Book of British Mammals* Collins, London

Burton, J.A. (1982) *The Guinness Book of Mammals* Guinness Superlatives, Enfield

Burton, M. (1968) *Animals of the British Isles* Warne, London

Burton, R. (1970) *Animal Senses* David & Charles, Newton Abbot

Burton, R. (1976) *The Language of Smell* Routledge & Kegan Paul, London

Corbet, G.B. (1964) *The Identification of British Mammals* British Museum (Natural History), London

Corbet, G.B. (1966) *The Terrestrial Mammals of Western Europe* Foulis, London

Corbet, G.B. (1971) *Distribution Maps of British Mammals* Institute of Terrestrial Ecology, Huntingdon

Freethy, R. (1982) *How Birds Work* Blandford Press, Poole, Dorset

Gotch, A.F. (1979) *Mammals—Their Latin Names Explained* Blandford Press, Poole, Dorset

Harrison Mathews, L. (1962) *British Mammals* Collins, London

Harrison Mathews, L. (1969) *The Life of Mammals* Vols 1 and 2. Weidenfeld & Nicolson, London

Johnston, H. (1903) *British Mammals* Hutchinson, London

Lawrence, M.J. & Brown, R.W. (1973) *Mammals of Britain—Their Tracks, Trails and Signs* Blandford Press, Poole (2nd edition)

Lydekker, R. (1896) *Mammals (Lloyd's Natural History)* London

Millais, J.G. (1904–6) *Mammals of Great Britain and Ireland* Vols 1 to 3 Longmans Green, London

Pitt, F. (1939) *Wild Animals in Britain* Batsford, London

Smythe, R.H. (1975) *Vision in the Animal World* Macmillan, London

Southern, H.W. (ed.) (1964) *The Handbook of British Mammals* Blackwell Scientific Publications, Oxford (2nd edition 1977)

Walls, G.L. (1942) *The Vertebrate Eye and its Adaptive Radiation* Hafner, New York and London

Webb, J.E., Wallwork, J.A. & Elgood, J.H. (1979) *Guide to Living Mammals* Macmillan, London

White, G. (1904) *The Natural History of Selbourne* Henry Frowd, London

Chapter 2   Marsupials: the Red-necked Wallaby

Yalden, B.W. & Hosey, G.R. (1971) 'Feral wallabies in the Peak District' *J. Zool. Lond.* **65**, pp. 513–20

Chapter 3   Insectivores: the Hedgehog, Mole and Shrews

Bell, T. (1837) *A History of British Quadrupeds* Van Voorst, London
Bell, J.P.F. (1904) *Agricultural Gazette*, London. Sept.
Brockie, R.E. (1976) 'Self-anointing by wild hedgehogs in New Zealand' *Anim. Behav.* **24**, pp. 68–71
Brodie, E.D., Jr (1978) *Nature, Lond.* July [Correspondence]
Burton, M. (1957) 'Hedgehog self anointing' *Proc. Zool. Soc. Lond.* **129**, p. 452
Burton, M. (1969) *The Hedgehog* Deutsch, London
Crowcroft, P. (1957) *The Life of the Shrew* Reinhardt, London
Davies, J.L. (1957) 'A hedgehog road mortality index' *Proc. Zool. Soc. Lond.* **128**, pp. 606–8
Evans, A.C. (1948) 'The identity of earthworms stored by moles' *Proc. Zool. Soc. Lond.* **118**, pp. 356–9
Fraser, F.C. & King, J.E. (1954) *Excavations at Star Carr* Cambridge University Press
Godfrey, G.K. & Crowcroft, P. (1960) *The Life of the Mole* Museum Press, London
Harting, J.E. (1880) *British Animals Extinct Within Historic Times* Trubner, London
Harvey, D. (1979) *The Gypsies: Waggon Time and After* Batsford, London
Herter, K. (1965) *Hedgehogs* Phoenix House, London
Jesse, E. (1853) *Scenes and Occupations of Country Life: with Recollections of Natural History* London
Lydekker, R. (1896) *Mammals (Lloyd's Natural History)* London
Pitt, F. (1939) *Wild Animals in Britain* Batsford, London
Sebek, Z. & Rosický, B. (1967) 'The finding of *Pneumocystis* in shrews' *Folia Parasit.* **14**, pp. 263–7
Southern, H.W. (ed.) (1964) *The Handbook of British Mammals* Blackwell Scientific Publications, Oxford (2nd edition 1977)
Topsell, E. (1607) *The Historie of the Foure-footed Beastes* Jaggard, London
White, G. (1789) *The Natural History of Selbourne* London
Worlidge, J. (1697) *Systema Agricultura : the Mystery of Husbandry Discovered* London

Chapter 4   Chiroptera: Bats

Allen, G.M. (1939) *Bats* Harvard University Press
Arnold, H.R. (1978) *The Provisional Atlas of Mammals* Institute of Terrestrial Ecology, Huntingdon

Bell, T. (1837) *A History of British Quadrupeds* Van Voorst, London

Corbet, G.B. (1966) *The Terrestrial Mammals of Western Europe* Foulis, London

Davis, W.H. (1970) 'Hibernation : ecology and physiological ecology' In: Wimsatt, W.A. *Biology of Bats* Vol 1. Academic Press, New York

Griffin, D.R. (1958) *Listening in the Dark* Yale University Press

Griffin, D.R. (1960) *Echoes of Bats and Men* Heinemann, London

Harrison Mathews, L. (1962) *British Mammals* Collins, London

Hooper, J.H.D. (1966) 'The ultrasonic "voices" of bats' *New Scient.* **29**, pp. 496–7

Hooper, J.H.D. & Hooper, W.M. (1967) 'Longevity of rhinolophid bats in Britain' *Nature, Lond.* **216**, pp. 1135–6

Johnston, H. (1903) *British Mammals* Hutchinson, London (2nd edition 1910)

Lavine, S.A. (1969) *Wonders of the Bat World* World's Work, Tadworth

Lydekker, R. (1896) *Mammals (Lloyd's Natural History)* London

Macgillivray, W. (1838) *A History of British Quadrupeds* Lizars, Edinburgh

Macpherson (1884) *The Vertebrate Fauna of Lakeland* David Douglas, Edinburgh

Nature Conservancy Council (1982) *Focus on Bats : Their Conservation and the Law* Shrewsbury

Novick, A. & Leen, N. (1970) *The World of Bats* Rinehart & Winston, New York

Racey, P.A. & Stebbings, R.E. (1972) 'Bats in Britain' *Oryx* **11**, pp. 319–27

Ransome, R.D. (1971) 'The effects of ambient temperature on the arousal frequency of the hibernating greater horseshoe bat, in relation to site selection and the hibernating state' *J. Zool. Lond.* **164**, pp. 353–71

Southern, H.W. (ed.) (1964) *The Handbook of British Mammals* Blackwell Scientific Publications, Oxford (2nd edition 1977)

Stebbings, R.E. (1965) 'Observations during sixteen years on winter roosts of bats in west Suffolk' *Proc. Zool. Soc. Lond.* **144**, pp. 137–43

Stebbings, R.E. (1969) 'Observer influence on bat behaviour' *Lynx* **10**, pp. 93–100

Wimsatt, W.A. (1970) *Biology of Bats* Vols. 1 & 2. Academic Press, New York

Yalden, B.W. & Morris, P.A. (1975) *The Lives of Bats* David & Charles, Newton Abbot

Chapter 5 Lagomorphs: the Rabbit and Hares

Adams, R. (1972) *Watership Down* Rex Collings, London

Bell, T. (1837) *A History of British Quadrupeds* Von Voorst, London

Berridge, W.S. (1934) *Wild Animals of Our Country* Harrap, London

Bishop, I. (1974) *Thorburn's Mammals* Joseph & Ebury

Buckland, J. (1980) *Shooting Times and Country Magazine* May 29

Coward, T.A. (1910) *The Vertebrate Fauna of Cheshire and Liverpool Bay* Witherby, London

Farghar, S.E. (1977) 'The distribution of the brown hare (*Lepus capensis*) and the mountain hare (*Lepus timidus*) in the Isle of Man' *Notes Mammal Soc.* No. 34

Garrad, L.S. (1972) *The Naturalist in the Isle of Man* David & Charles, Newton Abbot

Hewson, R. (1954) 'The mountain hare in Scotland' *Scott. Nat.* **66**, pp. 70–88

Hewson (1958) 'Moults and winter whitening in the mountain hare' *Proc. Zool. Soc. Lond.* **131**, pp. 99–108

Johnston, H. (1903) *British Mammals* Hutchinson, London

Kermode, P.M.C. (1893) 'Contributions to the vertebrate fauna of the Isle of Man' *Zoologist* **17**, 3, pp. 61–70

Kermode, P.M.C. (1917) 'Notes on Manx mammals' *Isle of Man Times* Jan 5

Lockley, R.M. (1964) *The Private Life of the Rabbit* Deutsch, London

Sheail, J. (1971) *Rabbits and Their History* David & Charles, Newton Abbot

Southern, H.W. (ed.) (1964) *The Handbook of British Mammals* Blackwell Scientific Publications, Oxford (2nd edition, 1947)

Thompson, H.V. & Wordern, A.N. (1956) *The Rabbit* Collins, London

Ward, W. (1936) 'Hare versus stoat' *NW Naturalist* **11**, p. 265

Yalden, D.W. (1971) 'The mountain hare (*Lepus timidus*) in the Peak District' *Naturalist* No. 918, pp. 81–92

Yarrell, W. (1820) *Loudon's Magazine of Natural History*, London, 5

Chapter 6   Rodents: Squirrels and Voles

Barret-Hamilton, G.E.H. & Hinton, M.A.C. (1910–21) *A History of British Quadrupeds* Gurney & Jackson, London

Bell, T. (1837) *A History of British Quadrupeds* Van Voorst, London

Bell, T. (1870) *A Hsitory of British Quadrupeds* Van Voorst, London (2nd edition)

Bolwig, N. (1978) *My Friend the Vole* Wayland, Hove

Corbet, G.B. (1961) 'Origin of the British insular races of small mammals and of the Lusitanian fauna' *Nature, Lond.* **191**, pp. 1037–40

Elton, C.S. (1942) *Mice, Voles and Lemmings* Clarendon Press, Oxford

Fraser-Darling, F. (1947) *Natural History in the Highlands and Islands* Collins, London

Harvie-Brown, J.A. & Buckley, T.E. (1887–1911) *The Vertebrate Fauna of Scotland* Vols 1 to 11. David Douglas, Edinburgh

Jeffries, D.J. & French, M.C. (1972) 'Lead concentration in small mammals trapped on roadside verges and field sites' *Environm. Pollut.* 3, pp. 147–56

Laidler, K. (1980) *Squirrels in Britain* David & Charles, Newton Abbot

Lydekker, R. (1896) *Mammals (Lloyd's Natural History)* London

Middleton, A.D. (1931) *The Grey Squirrel* Sidgwick & Jackson, London

Pennant, T. (1761) *British Zoology* Cymrodorion Society, London (1st edition)

Rowe, J.J. (1973) 'Grey squirrel control' *Forestry Commission Leaflet* No. 56, HMSO, London

Ryder, S.R. (1962) *Water Voles* Animals of Britain No. 4, Sunday Times Publications Ltd.

Shorten, M. (1954) *Squirrels* Collins, London

Shorten, M. (1962) *Grey Squirrels* Animals of Britain No.5, Sunday Times Publications Ltd.

Shorten, M. (1962) *Red Squirrels* Animals of Britain No.6, Sunday Times Publications Ltd.

Shorten, M. (1962) 'Squirrels' *MAFF Bull.* No. 184, HMSO, London

Thomas, D.M. (1897) *A Day Book of Wonders* Fisher Unwin, London

Tittensor, A.M. (1975) 'The red squirrel' *Forest Rec.* No. 101, HMSO, London

Wells, A.Q. (1937) 'Tuberculosis in wild voles' *Lancet* **232**, p. 1221

White, G. (1837) *The Natural History of Selbourne* London

Yarrell, W. (1834–5) *British Birds* Vols 1 to 3. Van Voorst, London

Yarrell, W. (1832) *Proc. Zool. Soc. Lond.*

Chapter 7   Rodents: Mice, Rats, Dormice and the Coypu

Barret-Hamilton, G.E.H. & Hinton, M.A.C. (1910–21) *A History of British Mammals* Gurney & Jackson, London

Bell, T. (1837) *A History of British Quadrupeds* Van Voorst, London

Cambrensis, G. (1185–86) *Historical Works* (Revised and edited by T. Wright, 1863) London

Cameron, T.M.W. (1949) 'Diseases carried by house mice' *Pest Control* **17**, 9, pp. 9–11

Chitty, D. & Southern, H.N. (eds) (1962) *Control of Rats and Mice* Clarendon Press, Oxford

Crowcroft, W.P. (1966) *Mice All Over* Foulis, London

Elton, C.S. (1942) *Mice, Voles and Lemmings* Clarendon Press, Oxford

Gosling, L.M. (1974) 'The coypu in East Anglia' *Trans. Norfolk Norwich Nat. Soc.* **23**, pp. 49–59

Hanney, P.W. (1975) *Rodents* David & Charles, Newton Abbot

Hurrel, E. (1962) *Dormice* Animals of Britain No. 10, Sunday Times Publications

Johnston, H. (1903) *British Mammals* Hutchinson, London

Knight, M. (1963) *Harvest Mice* Animals of Britain No. 19, Sunday Times Publications Ltd.

Lydekker, R. (1896) *Mammals (Lloyd's Natural History)* London

Macgillivray, W. (1838) *A History of British Quadrupeds* Lizars, Edinburgh

Millais, J.G. (1904–6) *Mammals of Great Britain and Ireland* Vols 1 to 3. Longmans Green, London

Morris, P.A. (1968) 'Apparent hypothermia in the wood mouse' *J. Zool. Lond.* **155**, pp. 235–36

Norris, J.D. (1967) 'A campaign against feral coypus (*Myocastor coypus*) in Great Britain' *J. Appl. Ecol.* **4**, pp. 191–9

Pennant, T. (1768) *British Zoology* Cymrodorion Society, Chester (2nd edition)

Twigg, G. (1975) *The Brown Rat* David & Charles, Newton Abbot

Vesey-Fitzgerald, B. (1950) *The Vanishing Wildlife of Britain*

White, G. (1789) *The Natural History of Selbourne* London

Chapter 8 Carnivores: the Fox and Cat

Baer, G. (ed.) (1975) *The Natural History of Rabies* Vols 1 & 2. Academic Press, London

Beckford, S. (1810) *Thoughts on Hunting* Albion Press, London

Burrows, R. (1968) *Wild Fox* David & Charles, Newton Abbot

Carr, R. (1976) *English Foxhunting—a History* Weidenfeld & Nicolson, London

Council for Nature (1973) *Predatory Mammals in Britain* Seel House Press, London

Deschambres, E. (1951) 'A propos des évolutions convergentes et parallels' [Convergent and parallel evolution] *Mammalia* **15**, pp. 173–83

Hattingh, I. (1956) 'Measurement of foxes from Scotland and England' *Proc. Zool. Soc. Lond.* **127**, pp. 191–9

Jenkins, D. (1962) 'The present status of the wild cat (*Felis silvestris*) in Scotland' *Scott. Nat.* **70**, pp. 126–38

Kaplan, C. (ed.) (1977) *Rabies—the Facts* Oxford University Press

Lancashire and Cheshire Fauna Committee (1959) 'Scottish wild cat (*Felis silvestris grampia* Miller)' *31st Ann. Rep.* p. 24 [Correspondence]

Lloyd, H.G. (1980) *The Red Fox* Batsford, London

Lydekker, R. (1896) *Mammals (Lloyd's Natural History)* London

MacDonald, D.W. (1980) *Rabies and Wildlife* Oxford University Press

Macpherson, H.A. (1884) *The Vertebrate Fauna of Lakeland* David Douglas, Edinburgh

Mallison, J. (1978) *The Shadow of Extinction* Macmillan, London

Moore, P. (ed.) (1965) *Against Hunting*, Gollancz, London

Ralls, K. (1971) 'Mammalian scent marking' *Science, New York* **171**, pp. 443–9

Robinson, H.W. (1924) 'Wild cats on Lancashire-Westmorland border' *11th Ann. Rep. Lancashire and Cheshire Fauna Committee* pp. 11–13

Roebuck, W.E. & Clarke, W.E. (1881) *A Handbook of the Vertebrate Fauna of Yorkshire* Reeve, London

Topsell, E. (1607) *The Historie of the Foure-footed Beastes* Jaggard, London

York, Duke of (1420) *The Master of Game* (Adapted from Gaston de Foix, 1387)

Chapter 9   Carnivores:
the Marten, Stoat, Weasel, Polecat, Ferret and Badger

Alston, E.R. (1879) *Notes on the Flora and Fauna of the West of Scotland* British Association, Glasgow

Bell, T. (1837) *A History of British Quadrupeds* Van Voorst, London

Berridge, W.S. (1934) *Wild Animals of Our Country* Harrap, London

Burke, N. (1963) *King Todd. The True Story of a Badger* Putnam, London

Burnham, P.M. (1970) 'Kestrel attempting to prey on weasels' *Br. Birds* 63, p. 338

Deansley, R. (1943) 'Delayed implantation in the stoat' *Nature, Lond.* 151, pp. 335–6

Deansley, R. (1944) 'The reproductive cycle of the female weasel' *Proc. Zool. Soc. Lond.*

Drabble, P. (1979) *No Badgers in My Wood* Michael Joseph, London

Drabble, P. (1981) 'Bovine TB—is immunisation possible?' *The Field* Nov. 19

Grice, E. (1980) 'Bovine TB in badgers' *The Sunday Times* Dec. 28, pp. 13–17

Johnston, H. (1903) *British Mammals* Hutchinson, London

Hardy, P. (1975) *A Lifetime of Badgers* David & Charles, Newton Abbot

King, C.M. (1971) *Studies on the Ecology of the Weasel* Ph.D. thesis, Oxford University

Kruuk, H. & Parish, T. (1977) *Behaviour of Badgers* Natural Environmental Research Council. Institute of Terrestrial Ecology, Cambridge

Linn, I. & Day, M.G. (1966) 'Identification of individual weasels (*Mustela nivalis*) using the ventral pelage pattern' *J. Zool.* 148, pp. 583–5

Lydekker, R. (1896) *Mammals (Lloyd's Natural History)* London

Macgillivray, W. (1830) *Naturalist's Library* Lizars, Edinburgh (1st edition)

Macpherson, H.A. (1884) *The Vertebrate Fauna of Lakeland* David Douglas, Edinburgh

Mortimer Batten, H.M. (1923) *The Badger Afield and Underground* Witherby, London

Neal, E. (1948) *The Badger* Collins, London (4th edition 1975)

Neal, E. (1977) *Badgers* Blandford Press, Poole, Dorset

Paget, R.J. & Middleton, A.L.V. (1975) *Badgers of Yorkshire and Humberside* Ebor, York

Pitt, F. (1938) *Wild Animals in Britain* Country Life, Hamlyn, London

Pitt, F. (1946) *Friends in Fur and Feather* Country Life, Hamlyn, London

Ratcliffe, E.J. (1974) *Through the Badger Gate* Bell, London

Rothschild, M. (1944) 'Pelage change in the stoat, *Mustela erminea*' *Nature, Lond.* 154, pp. 180–81

Zuckerman, Lord Solly (1980) *Badgers, Cattle and Tuberculosis* HMSO, London

Chapter 10   Carnivores: the Mink and Otter

Akande, M. (1972) 'The food of the feral mink in Scotland' *J. Zool. Lond.* **167**, pp. 475–79

Bell, T. (1837) *A History of British Quadrupeds* Van Voorst, London

Chanin, P.R.F. (1976) 'Otters' *Conservation Rev.* **13**

Chapman, A. (1982) 'The mink and Cindy' *Sunday Express* June 25, p. 12

Clark, S.P. (1970) 'Field experience of feral mink in Yorkshire and Lancashire' *Mammal Rev.* **12**, pp. 41–7

Delacour, J. (1964) *The Waterfowl of the World* Vols. 1 to 4, Hamlyn, London

Dudley, E. (1976) *The Otter* Muller, London

Harris, C.J. (1968) *Otters* Weidenfeld and Nicolson, London

Hurrel, E. (1963) *Watch for the Otter* Country Life, Hamlyn, London

Laidler, L. (1982) *The Otter in Britain* David & Charles, Newton Abbot

Linn, I. & Chanin, P. (1978) 'Mink versus otter' *New Scientist* March 2

Linn, I. & Day, M.G. (1978) 'The food of mink' *J. Zool. Lond.* **167**, p. 463

Maxwell, G. (1960) *Ring of Bright Water* Longmans Green, London

Neal, E.G. (1963) *Otters* Animals of Britain No. 10, Sunday Times Publications Ltd.

Neville Havins, P.J. (1981) *The Otter In Britain* Hale, London

Serjeant, R. (1966) *Mink on My Shoulder* Hale, London

Stephens, M.N. (1957) *The Natural History of the Otter* Universities Federation of Animal Welfare, Tunbridge Wells, Kent

Stevenson, J.H.F. (1959) *Mink in Britain* Pitts, Exeter (3rd edition)

Thompson, H.V. (1971) 'British wild mink—a challenge to naturalists' *Agriculture* **78**, pp. 421–5

Walton, I. (1653) *The Compleat Angler* London

Wayre, P. (1976) *The River People* Collins, Harvill

Wayre, P. (1979) *The Private Life of the Otter* Batsford, London

Williamson, H. (1927) *Tarka the Otter* Putnam, London

Wisbeski, D. (1964) *An Otter in the House* Methuen, London

Chapter 11   Carnivores: Seals

Backhouse, K.M. (1960) 'The grey seal (*Halichoerus grypus*) outside the breeding season: a preliminary report' *Mammalia* **24**, pp. 307–12

Bonner, W.N. (1976) 'The stocks of grey seals (*Halichoerus grypus*) and common seals (*Phoca vitulina*) in Great Britain' *Natl Environm. Res. Counc. Pub.* Series C, No. 16.

Bonner, W.N. & Hickling, G. (1971) 'The grey seals of the Farne Islands: report for the period October 1969 to July 1971' *Trans. Nat. Hist. Soc. Northumb.* **17**, pp. 33–7

Bonner, W.N. & Wilthames, S.R. (1974) 'Dispersal of common seals (*Phoca vitulina*) tagged in The Wash, East Anglia' *J. Zool. Lond.* **174**, pp. 528–31

Hewer, H.R. (1974) *British Seals* Collins, London

Hickling, G. (1962) *Grey Seals and the Farne Islands* Routledge & Kegan Paul, London

Lockley, R.M. (1966) *Grey Seal, Common Seal* Deutsch, London

Macgillivray, W. (1838) *A History of British Quadrupeds* Lizars, Edinburgh

Wynne-Edwards, V.C. (1954) 'Field identification of the common and grey seals' *Scott. Nat.* **66**, p. 192

Chapter 12   Artiodactyls: Deer

Aitken, R.J. (1974) 'Delayed implantation in roe deer' *J. Reprod. Fertil.* **39**, pp. 225–33

Bell, T. (1837) *A History of British Quadrupeds* Van Voorst, London

Cadman, W.A. (1966) *The Fallow Deer* HMSO, London

Cameron, A.G. (1923) *The Wild Red Deer of Scotland* Blackwood, Edinburgh

Chaplin, R.E. (1977) *Deer* Blandford Press, Poole, Dorset

Chapman, D. & Chapman, N. (1975) *Fallow Deer* Terence Dalton, Sudbury

Chapman, D.I. (1975) 'Antlers—bones of contention' *Mammal Rev.* **5**, pp. 121–72

Clarke, M. (1974) 'Deer distribution survey 1967–72' *Deer* **3**, pp. 279–82

Holmes, F. (1974) *Following the Roe* Bartholomew, Edinburgh

Horwood, M.T. (1971) *Sika Deer Research. 2nd Progress Report* Nature Conservancy Council Report

Hosey, G.R. (1974) *The Food and Feeding Ecology of the Roe Deer* (Capreolus capreolus) Ph.D. thesis, Manchester University

Kyle, R. (1973) 'The possible use of the red deer as a farm animal' *Wildl. Mag.* April

Lydekker, R. (1896) *Mammals* (*Lloyd's Natural History*) London

Lydekker, R. (1898) *The Deer of All Lands* Rowland Ward, Hartfield

MacNally, L. (1970) *Highland Deer Forest* Dent, London

MacNally, L. (1975) *The Year of the Red Deer* Dent, London

Millais, J.G. (1897) *British Deer and Their Horns* Sotheran, London

Perry, R. (1972) *The Watcher and the Red Deer* David & Charles, Newton Abbot

Prior, R.P. (1972) *Living with Deer* Deutsch, London

Prior, R.P. (1968) *The Roe Deer of Cranbourne Chase : an Ecological Survey* Oxford University Press

Ritchie, J. (1920) *The Influence of Man on Animal Life in Scotland* Cambridge University Press

Ross, J. (ed.) (1925) *The Book of the Red Deer* Simpkin, London

Tegner, H.S. (1958) *The Roe Deer* Batchworth, London

Whitlock, R. (1974) *Deer* Priory Press, Hove

Whitehead, G. (1964) *The Deer of Great Britain and Ireland. An Account of Their History, Status and Distribution* Routledge & Kegan Paul, London

Williamson, R. (1973) *Capreol—the Story of a Roebuck* MacDonald & Jane

Chapter 13 Artiodactyls: the Sheep, Goat and Cattle

Bewick, T. (1790) *History of Quadrupeds* Newcastle

Jewell, P.A. Milner, N. & Boyd, J.M. (1974) *Island Survivors: the Ecology of the Soay Sheep of St. Kilda* London

MacAuley, K. (1764) *The History of St. Kilda* London

Martin, M. (1698) *A Late Voyage to St. Kilda* London

Southern, H.N. (ed.) (1964) *The Handbook of British Mammals* Blackwell Scientific Publications, Oxford (2nd edition 1977)

Storer, Rev. J. (ed.) (1879) *The Wild White Cattle of Great Britain* Cassell, London

Tegner, H. (1965) 'Wild goats of Britain' *Scott. Field* Feb., pp. 18–23

Whitehead, G.K. (1953) *The Ancient White Cattle of Britain and Their Descendents* Faber & Faber, London

Whitehead, G.K. (1972) *The Wild Goats of Great Britain and Ireland* David & Charles, Newton Abbot

Zeuner, F.E. (1963) *A History of Domesticated Animals* Hutchinson, London

Chapter 14 Extinct and Mythical Beasts

Bell, T. (1837) *British Quadrupeds* Van Voorst, London

Cambrensis, G. (1185/85) *Historical Works* (Revised and edited by T. Wright, 1863) London

Camden, W. (1637) *Brittannia, 1586* [Translated from the Latin] London

Dent. A. (1974) *Lost Beasts of Britain* Harrap, London

Fiennes, R. (1976) *The Order of Wolves* Hamish Hamilton, London

Fittis, R. (1891) *Sports and Pastimes of Scotland* Paisley

Gilmore, R.M. (1970) 'The identification and value of mammal bones from archaeological excavations' *J. Mammal.* **30**, pp. 163–9

Harting, J.E. (1880) *British Animals Extinct Within Historic Times* Trubner, London

Mercier, J. (1940) *The Last Wolf* Wadsworth, Grange-over-Sands

Strutt, J. (1810) *Sports and Pastimes of the People of England.* London

Summers, M. (1933) *The Werewolf* London

Tolkein, J.R.R. (1973) *Lord of the Rings* Unwin, Surrey

Topsell, E. (1607) *The Historie of the Foure-Footed Beastes* Jaggard, London

Picture Credits

The author and publisher would like to thank the following for providing colour and black and white illustrations.

Colour

Aquila Photographs: pp. 199, 207 (Dr & Mrs J.P. Black); pp. 39, 186 (M. Chesworth); p. 115 (Steve Downer); pp. 119, 139 (E.A. Janes); p. 210 (H. Kinloch); p. 191 (Wayne Lankinen); p. 90—bottom (M. Leach); p. 87—bottom (Duncan I. McEwan); p. 142—top (A.T. Moffett); pp. 138; 143(J. Robinson); pp. 83—bis, 86, 87—top, 91 (W. Walter); p. 126 (M. Wilkes). Alan Beaumont: pp. 131, 135, 142—bottom, 179, 218, 222, 223. Ron Freethy: pp. 47, 183. Jeremy Gunn-Taylor: p. 182. Richard Littleton: p. 55. Wildlife Picture Agency: pp. 35, 46, 54, 59, 178, 198, 211, 219.

Black and White

Aquila Photographics: p. 226 (R.J.C. Blewitt); pp. 159, 203 (Steve Downer); pp. 49, 155, 172, 174 (A. Faulkner Taylor); pp. 101, 147 (E.A. Janes); pp. 201, 232 (M. Leach); p. 42 (R.T. Mills); pp. 209, 229 (W.S. Paton); p. 208 (C.J. Smale); pp. 67, 71, 90—top (W. Walter); p. 140 (P.D. Weaving); pp. 123, 128 (M. Wilkes). Alan Beaumont: pp. 235, 242, 252. Sdeuard C. Bisserôt: pp. 66, 72, 76, 82. M. Chesworth: pp. 160, 187. Ron Freethy: pp. 103, 237. Peter Green: p. 40. Alan W. Heath: pp. 56, 130. Robert Howe: p. 158. Ministry of Defence DPR (RAF): p. 68. Ralph Newton: p. 81. Frank Reeman: p. 45. Nigel Sitwell: p. 246. Wildlife Picture Agency: pp. 111, 145, 248.

Maps

H.R. Arnold/Institute of Terrestrial Ecology: pp. 73, 74, 75.

Index

Numbers in *italics* refer to black and white illustrations. Numbers in **bold** refer to colour illustrations.